BATON ROUGE

Sponsored by the Baton Rouge Area Chamber of Commerce
Windsor Publications, Inc., Woodland Hills, California

River Capital

An Illustrated History of

BATON ROUGE

By Mark T. Carleton
Pictorial research by M. Stone Miller, Jr.

Published 1981
Printed in the United States of America

First Edition

Library of Congress Cataloging in Publication Data

Carleton, Mark T.
   River capital.

   Bibliography: p. 298
   Includes index.
   1. Baton Rouge (La.)—History.   2. Baton Rouge (La.)
—Description.   I. Title.
F379.B33C35   976.3'18   81-65216
ISBN 0-89781-032-5   AACR2

Photographs on pages 78, 145, 148-152, and 217-224 by Dave Gleason

Photographs on pages 4-7, 74-77, 79, and 146-147 by Don Nugent
except where otherwise noted

Below
Adrien Persac painted this gouache of the Hope Estate Plantation, located about four miles south of Baton Rouge, in the late 1850s or early 1860s. The manor house was built by Daniel and Philip Hicky circa 1798. Courtesy, the Anglo-American Art Museum, LSU, Baton Rouge. Gift of Friends of the Museum.

CONTENTS

INTRODUCTION

A few years ago, when I was putting together a book of photographs taken in Baton Rouge during the Civil War, I was surprised to discover that only a handful of the buildings which can be seen in the pictures—I think no more than four or five, including the Pentagon Barracks buildings and the Old State Capitol—were still standing. As a matter of fact, the Capitol, though its external appearance is very nearly the same, is not the building that we see in the Civil War photographs either: that building burned to the walls in 1862, during the Union occupation of the town, and was rebuilt some 20 years later.

The discovery that so little of wartime Baton Rouge remained set me to thinking about buildings I could remember from the 1930s and 1940s—and even as recently as the 1950s and 1960s. For instance, the old City Market, which stood on the site of the Municipal Building and which in the 1940s was used as a USO and still later as the home of the Recreation and Park Commission. And the elegant Garig home, which occupied the whole north end of the block in which the Heidelberg Hotel stood. The view of it that I remember is always the view from the train as the Y&MV's northbound No. 12 was pulling out of the station. There was also the quaint old building at the School for the Deaf that I used to pass as I rode the bus between Stroube's Drug Store at the head of Third Street and the LSU campus. And there was the three-story structure which until fairly recent times stood at the northwest corner of Florida and Fourth, directly across the street from the building where I first came to work for the *Morning Advocate*. I used to drink coffee there with the other reporters those afternoons in the late forties and early fifties, unaware at the time that this had once been the Heroman Building, pride of the city when it was erected in the 1850s.

The simple act of recollection is of course a reminder, if we need one, of just how relentless change is. The Y&MV trains no longer run. The station now houses the Louisiana Arts and Science Center (with a steam locomotive and a few coaches in place on a siding to arouse the curiosity and awe of children who have never heard a train whistle). The Heidelberg, a larger version of it, is now the Capitol House. Third Street is now Riverside Mall, and Stroube's has long since passed into history.

So little of the old remains, in fact, that it is easy to forget that the city has had a long and colorful past, and for that reason we should especially welcome this volume. Here, in words and pictures, is the story of Baton Rouge from its beginnings as an Indian site on the banks of the river to the booming industrial city of the eighties—a city shaped by innumerable twists and turns of history, but perhaps by none more crucial than Standard Oil's decision to build a refinery here

When the Louisiana Institute for the Deaf and Dumb was completed in 1858 in Baton Rouge, it was reputed to be the largest building in Louisiana except for, perhaps, the St. Charles Hotel in New Orleans. Used as a hospital for Federal troops during the Civil War, it later served as the home for Louisiana State University. This opaque watercolor of the institute by Persac is dated 1859. Courtesy, the Anglo-American Art Museum, LSU, Baton Rouge. Gift of Friends of the Museum.

in the early 1900s. There were of course other events that played an important role in determining the city's character—among them the relocation of the Louisiana Seminary of Learning, forerunner of Louisiana State University, and the decision of the state's legislators and political leaders to make Baton Rouge the seat of government (away from, but not too far away from, the pleasures of New Orleans, as Tom Carleton tells us in his history).

The person selected by the publishers to tell the story is, first of all, a Baton Rougean himself, someone who grew up in the community, but, even more important, a professional historian. Tom Carleton brings to his account of Baton Rouge the broader perspective of one who knows, who has in fact taught, Louisiana and U.S. history. The publishers have been equally astute in selecting the person to collect the illustrations for the book and to write the captions. Stone Miller, a professional archivist who heads the Department of Archives and Manuscripts at Louisiana State University, has brought together a rich and varied selection of photographs and other illustrations, and it seems to me the descriptive lines he has written nicely complement, indeed frequently supplement (as captions should), the written history.

The business community deserves a great deal of appreciation, for it was their enthusiastic support, through the purchase of their pages in "Partners in Progress," that made this book feasible in the first place. This is the first time most of the information in the chapter has been published, moreover, and the Baton Rouge historical literature will be richer for it. Their editor, Windsor's Karen Story, deserves special mention for her indefatigable guidance and attention to detail from beginning to end.

Many of the early pictures that appear in the book were taken by A. D. Lytle, who first came to Baton Rouge as an itinerant photographer in the late 1850s. Lytle had settled here permanently by 1860 and was taking pictures of the town and its people into the early 1900s. We may wish for the glass-plate negatives that we have been told his family tossed into a well behind the Lytle home on North Boulevard after his death in 1917, but enough of his work survives— much of it in the LSU Department of Archives and Manuscripts—that we can be grateful.

We can also be grateful for the superb color photography of Don Nugent and Dave Gleason and for the sensitive hand of Windsor's editor, Lissa Sanders, whose Louisiana roots go deep and who made numerous trips between California and Baton Rouge while the book was in preparation.

This, then, is a book for Baton Rougeans of all ages to read, to learn from, to enjoy. It is also a book that one day, like all histories, will have to be updated. Time inexorably moves forward.

Charles East

Guillaume de L'Isle made this early 18th-century map of North America in which the Louisiana Territory and its principal river, the Mississippi, dominate. Courtesy, The Historic New Orleans Collection.

COLONIAL ORIGINS

Baton Rouge, capital of the state of Louisiana, lies on the east bank of the Mississippi River near the southernmost end of a series of bluffs extending northward to Vicksburg, Mississippi. Geologists say that these bluffs comprised part of the natural levee of the river at the termination of the last ice age almost 20,000 years ago.

The climate of Baton Rouge is humid and warm, with an average annual rainfall of 54.4 inches, a mean average summer temperature of 82.7 degrees and a winter temperature of 56.4 degrees. Live oak, pine, pecan, and cypress trees are among the predominant flora while squirrels, raccoons, possums, rabbits, and, in recent years, armadillos, have roamed and inhabited the area. Located in the alluvial plain of the Mississippi, Baton Rouge and its environs have enjoyed the benefits of rich and fertile soil since the first humans moved into the region. With sufficient care and attention, almost any plant can be cultivated successfully in Baton Rouge.

Although successive groups of Mound Builders—three of whose creations survive undisturbed in Baton Rouge—and other Indian tribes may have inhabited the area as early as the time of Julius Caesar, it is reasonably certain that no Europeans visited the site of Baton Rouge until about 1542. In that year followers of the Spanish explorer Hernando de Soto paddled by on the river en route to the Gulf of Mexico and the shores of Spanish Mexico.

De Soto had landed in Spanish Florida some months previously, hoping (in the tradition of avaricious Spanish conquistadores) to discover gold or silver as he marched inland. Soon after his expedition reached the Mississippi River, possibly at the present location of Memphis, Tennessee, De Soto died, either because of illness or in combat with Indians. Since the riches they sought were not to be found, De Soto's companions did not bother to claim the "worthless" Mississippi Valley for Spain, and their Spanish contemporaries did not return to the area. (Two hundred years later, however, Spain received a sizable portion of the area from their defeated French allies and royal cousins.)

During the next century and a half, Europe's three foremost colonial powers, Spain, England, and France, rapidly explored and colonized the New World. The Spanish extended their earlier conquests of Mexico and Central America, vanquished the Incas of present-day Ecuador and Peru, and ultimately seized control of almost all of South America, except for Portuguese Brazil. The English established a colony in the 1580s on the mid-Atlantic coast, but failed to maintain it. After destroying the Spanish Armada in 1588 and initiating the reduction of Spain to a second-class power, however, they returned to Virginia in 1607 and founded Jamestown, the first permanent English settlement in North America. By 1700 other English colonies extended in an unbroken line from Maine to South Carolina. Georgia was founded later, in 1733.

Following the establishment of Quebec in 1608, the French moved southwestward down the St. Lawrence River toward the Great Lakes region. By 1673 Frenchmen had reached the Mississippi River and descended it as far south as the mouth of the Arkansas River. In 1682 René Robert Cavelier, Sieur de La Salle, continued down the "Father of Waters" to its mouth, where he raised the flag of Bourbon France and claimed the entire region drained by the mighty stream and its tributaries as "Louisiana" in honor of his sovereign, Louis XIV, one of the most powerful monarchs of all time. As the result of La Salle's claiming Louisiana, in the vivid words of 19th-century historian Francis Parkman, "the realm of France received on parchment a stupendous accession. The fertile plains of Texas, the vast basin of the Mississippi, from its frozen northern

This stone artifact was found at the Monte Sano Mounds near the Allied Chemical Corporation Plant in Baton Rouge. When Europeans first arrived in the Baton Rouge area, the Houma Indians were the historic group living nearest the bluff. They were later driven from their territory by the Tunicas, who migrated from the north. These first residents left scattered evidence of their presence through flint tools, and later, sherds of crude pottery. Courtesy, Museum of Anthropology, LSU, Baton Rouge.

The earliest evidence that archaeologists have found of Indians occupying the Baton Rouge area dates to about 1500 B.C. Forming part of the Poverty-Point Culture, these Mound Builders were characterized by rudimentary agriculture and crude pottery. A pair of mounds surviving near the mouth of Monte Sano Bayou have been excavated in recent years by archaeologists from Louisiana State University. Here Dr. Carl Kuttruff points to an exposed cross-section of a small crematory platform at the bottom of one of the mounds. The remains appear as a darkened line in the strata. Courtesy, Museum of Anthropology, LSU, Baton Rouge.

springs to the sultry borders of the Gulf; from the woody ridges of the Alleghenies to the peaks of the Rocky Mountains—a region of savannas and forests, sun-cracked deserts, and grassy prairies, watered by a thousand rivers, ranged by a thousand warlike tribes, passed beneath the sceptre of the Sultan of Versailles, and all by virtue of a feeble human voice, inaudible at half a mile."

La Salle immediately recognized the immense strategic value of his claim for France—Louisiana stood as a buffer between French Canada to the north, Spanish Mexico to the southwest, and the aggressive English to the east. The nation controlling the vast interior river system of North America would, in fact, control the continent itself. Returning to France, La Salle persuaded a receptive government to authorize the establishment of a French colony near the mouth of the Mississippi River to serve as

P. LE MOYN
E. S. D'YBERVILLE

Above
In 1682 La Salle claimed for France all the territory through which the Mississippi and its tributaries flowed.

Left
Pierre le Moyne, Sieur d'Iberville, and his party ascended the Mississippi River and reached the locality of Baton Rouge on March 17, 1699. There, in an Indian village on the eastern bank of the river, stood a wooden pole reddened with fish and bear heads. The city that was later founded near this location may have been named Baton Rouge (Red Stick) because of this gruesome discovery. Courtesy, Louisiana State Library.

a base for consolidation of French influence upstream and, it was hoped, as a prosperous French empire in its own right. La Salle himself led an expedition to achieve these objectives, but La Salle's ships, instead of landing near the mouth of the river, proceeded all the way to Texas, where La Salle was murdered in 1687 by his disappointed and fearful subordinates.

War with England and other distractions postponed French attempts to plant a colony near the mouth of the Mississippi, but French determination to do so did not die. Early in 1699 a small group of about 200 French-Canadians, led by naval officer Pierre Le Moyne, Sieur d'Iberville, arrived at Dauphin Island near Mobile Bay. Shortly afterward the expedition moved on to Ship Island off the Mississippi coast. On the mainland, near Biloxi, Iberville erected Fort Maurepus, the first French settlement in "Louisiana."

Iberville, with a few followers, then set out in search of the Mississippi River. Finding one of its mouths, he proceeded laboriously upriver—past the future location of New Orleans, which apparently did not impress him—until on March 17, 1699, he and his comrades beheld on high ground overlooking the east side of the river a vertical pole, red with blood dripping from animal and fish heads attached to it. As has so often been told, they named the spot "Baton Rouge," French for "red stick." Another traditional account affirms that "le Baton Rouge" was not a vertical pole, but an immense cypress tree. Historical consensus has supported the "pole version." (It has been noted in other accounts that the Choctaw Indian expression "itti humma" or "istrouma" meant essentially the same thing.) Rose Meyers, in her authoritative history of early Baton Rouge, has concluded that the pole seen by Iberville was probably located on or near Scott's Bluff, and served both as a boundary marker between the Houma Indians to the north and the Bayagoulas to the south, and as a ceremonial device. Occupying Baton Rouge when the French first arrived in 1699 were the Houma Indians, linguistic members of the Muskhogean culture then inhabiting much of the present southeastern United States. The Houmas were farmers, hunters and fishermen. Although fierce fighters when attacked, the Houmas were naturally peaceful and preferred to be left alone. In 1706 the Tunicas from present-day Mississippi drove the Houmas southward, first to the New Orleans area and subsequently to the coastal parishes of Terrebonne and Lafourche, where their present population approximates 1,000. In time the Tunicas were subdued and dispersed by the French and British. Unlike the warlike and horse-wise Plains Indians, who resisted white incursion into their lands until the 1880s, the Indians of the southeast were "infantrymen," less well organized, and quickly dispossessed. There were no Little Big Horns or Fetterman Massacres in Louisiana between Indians and whites.

While Iberville's party was much impressed by the fertile meadows and profusion of game at Baton Rouge, they only stayed a short time before resuming their explorations upriver, possibly as far north as what is now Natchez. For two decades no Frenchman returned to Baton Rouge, probably because the fledgling Gulf Coast colony of Louisiana was relatively far away and because of French preoccupation, in Europe and elsewhere, with the long and costly War of the Spanish Succession (1701–1713). But in 1718—the same year in which Iberville's younger brother, Bienville, founded New Orleans—a "concession," or land-grant, at Baton Rouge was given to Bernard Diron Dartaguette. Records disclose that also in 1718 two whites and 25 blacks (presumably slaves) resided at the Dartaguette concession. Four years later, on New Year's Day, 1722, what Mrs. Meyers described as "perhaps the first official mass in Baton Rouge" was celebrated by the Jesuit priest, teacher and missionary, Father Pierre Francois-Xavier de Charlevoix. Having traveled all the way from Quebec, up the St. Lawrence, across the Great Lakes and down the Mississippi, the Jesuit had almost reached his destination, New Orleans. The mass he celebrated in Baton Rouge, as the guest of Dartaguette, was solemnized in his host's parlor.

In 1722 low-lying, swampy New Orleans became the capital of French Louisiana and continued to grow and prosper, if somewhat unevenly, as time passed. By 1727, however, the Dartaguette concession at Baton Rouge no longer existed. Why it vanished no one knows. The few settlers could have perished from disease, a natural calamity such as a hurricane or tornado, or possibly—although it is unlikely—in an Indian attack. It is also possible that, after a few crop failures, the settlers might have departed for more prosperous holdings downstream. Adding to the mystery of Baton Rouge's disappearance was the contemporary good fortune of a concession in what is now Pointe Coupee Parish, only a few miles across the Mississippi to the northwest.

Whatever the reason for the original colony's disappearance, there is no record of subsequent attempts to resettle Baton Rouge on any formal basis during the remainder of the French period, which lasted until 1763. Baton Rouge, after all, possessed no strategic value for the French: it was not on or near the coast, and did not border on territory owned by another nation. Thus if no individuals cared to locate there, and seemingly no one did after 1727, the site could be, and was, officially forgotten. "French" Baton Rouge, therefore, is of little historical significance. This is not because so little is known about it, but because, essentially, "French" Baton Rouge never really existed. The origins of Baton Rouge as a continuously settled and increasingly prosperous community do not, in fact, date from the French period at all, but rather from the establishment there in 1763 of a British military outpost following one of the most important wars in European and American history.

This drawing of "An Indian Chief of Louisiana" appeared in Jean Bernard Bossu's Nouveaux Voyages aux Indes Occidentales, *published in 1768. Bossu, who was born in Burgundy in 1720, traveled to French Louisiana in 1751 and 1757. He later made a third voyage when Louisiana had become a Spanish colony.*

For years British colonials had probed beyond the Appalachian Mountains into the French-claimed Ohio River Valley. In 1756, as a result of major confrontations involving French and British forces in that contested area, open warfare broke out between the two nations. This conflict is known as the French and Indian War in British North America, and in Europe as the Seven Years War because of its duration (1756–1763).

Britain's military effort began poorly, but after the vigorous William Pitt (later Earl of Chatham) assumed direction of the government, British performance improved dramatically. By 1762 the French, together with their Spanish allies, had suffered numerous reverses. Facing inevitable defeat, King Louis XV and his ministers resolved to prevent already grave misfortunes from becoming a complete national loss of face.

British and colonial forces had invaded and taken possession of French Quebec and much of the Ohio Valley; consequently France could not realistically hope to regain these possessions after the war ended. To keep western Louisiana—from the Mississippi River to the Rocky Mountains—and New Orleans out of the grasp of its British enemies, France decided to bestow these territories upon Spain.

The Spanish, who had lost their venerable Florida colony to the British during the conflict, could accept western Louisiana and New Orleans as more than adequate compensation because the former French possessions would extend Spain's holdings eastward from Mexico to the Mississippi River and northward to present-day Minnesota. To the French the transfer offered the relief of getting rid of a "white elephant" (as some historians have described the unprofitable French Louisiana colony in its last years) and the deep satisfaction of limiting British expansion in North America. There was the final consolation that western Louisiana and New Orleans would remain "in the family" since the Spanish monarch in 1762 was a Bourbon cousin of Louis XV.

The cession of western Louisiana and New Orleans by France to Spain took place by the secret Treaty of Fontainebleau in the fall of 1762. When the war officially ended in 1763, the British predictably received Canada, in addition to what had been French eastern Louisiana—a vast region between the Appalachians on the east, the Great Lakes to the north, the Mississippi on the west, and the Gulf Coast (between Spanish New Orleans and British Florida) to the south.

France thus lost all its possessions on the North American continent— for the most part, permanently. (Napoleon's three-year ownership of Louisiana in 1800–1803 was a mere interlude.) By 1763 British territory on the east was separated from Spanish lands on the west by the Mississippi River from its source down to Bayou Manchac, which flowed southeastward from the great river into the Amite River and then into Lake Maurepas. South of the bayou was also Spanish Louisiana, down to and including New Orleans. (As one drives today across the bayou from East Baton Rouge Parish into either Iberville or Ascension parish, one is crossing what used to be the international boundary line between the former British colony of West Florida north of the bayou and Spanish Louisiana south of it.)

The territorial adjustments of 1762–1763 had profound consequences on both the immediate and long-range future of Baton Rouge. No longer was the largely forgotten site of Dartaguette's concession an insignificant point in the interior. Located on the east bank of the Mississippi just north of Bayou Manchac, Baton Rouge by 1763 occupied the southwestern corner of British North America, a position of considerable strategic importance.

British authorities moved promptly to organize and provide for the defense of their new possessions. (Spain took over Louisiana at a more leisurely pace: a Spanish governor did not arrive in New Orleans until 1766.) What eventually became the present "Florida" parishes of Louisiana and the Gulf Coast counties of Mississippi and Alabama were constituted by the British as the colony of "West Florida." (Former Spanish Florida, comprising essentially the same area as the present state, became the British colony of "East Florida.")

Two military installations were constructed by the British in the Baton Rouge area. The one on the north bank of Bayou Manchac (facing a comparable Spanish facility on the opposite side) was named Fort Bute, while a more impressive fortification, Fort New Richmond, was raised northward at Baton Rouge itself. Until September of 1779, when the Spanish took both of them, Bute and New Richmond remained precariously remote and vulnerable British military outposts.

A royal proclamation of October 7, 1763, granted West Florida colonists the "rights and benefits of English law" and established a colonial assembly. The colony's first governor was British Navy Captain George Johnstone, who was authorized to award land grants to officers and soldiers who had served in the French and Indian War. According to Mrs. Meyers, "many large estates" in the Baton Rouge area could "trace their grants back to Johnstone and his successors." One of Baton Rouge's earliest and wealthiest British landowners, for instance, was Scotsman Sir William Dunbar, who was granted a plantation near Fort New Richmond in the early 1770s.

Dunbar was a typically energetic young man on the 18th-century American frontier. A Scotsman by birth (1749), Dunbar studied mathematics and astronomy in London before migrating to Philadelphia in 1771 to engage in Indian trading. On a trip into the interior he traveled down the Mississippi River until reaching Baton Rouge, where he decided to settle as a planter and where he lived for almost 20 years. He spent the last years of his life on his plantation near Natchez.

The West Florida colony began to thrive at once, due to rapid settle-

This plat of 300 acres on the Mississippi River near Browne's Cliffs was attached to a vellum deed dated April 2, 1776. The transaction was executed during British control by an attorney for Montford Browne, land speculator and English governor of West Florida for a brief time. The purchase price of 100 pounds sterling was paid by Daniel Hickey (or Hicky). He and his son were long associated with the early history of Baton Rouge. Courtesy, Department of Archives and Manuscripts, LSU, Baton Rouge.

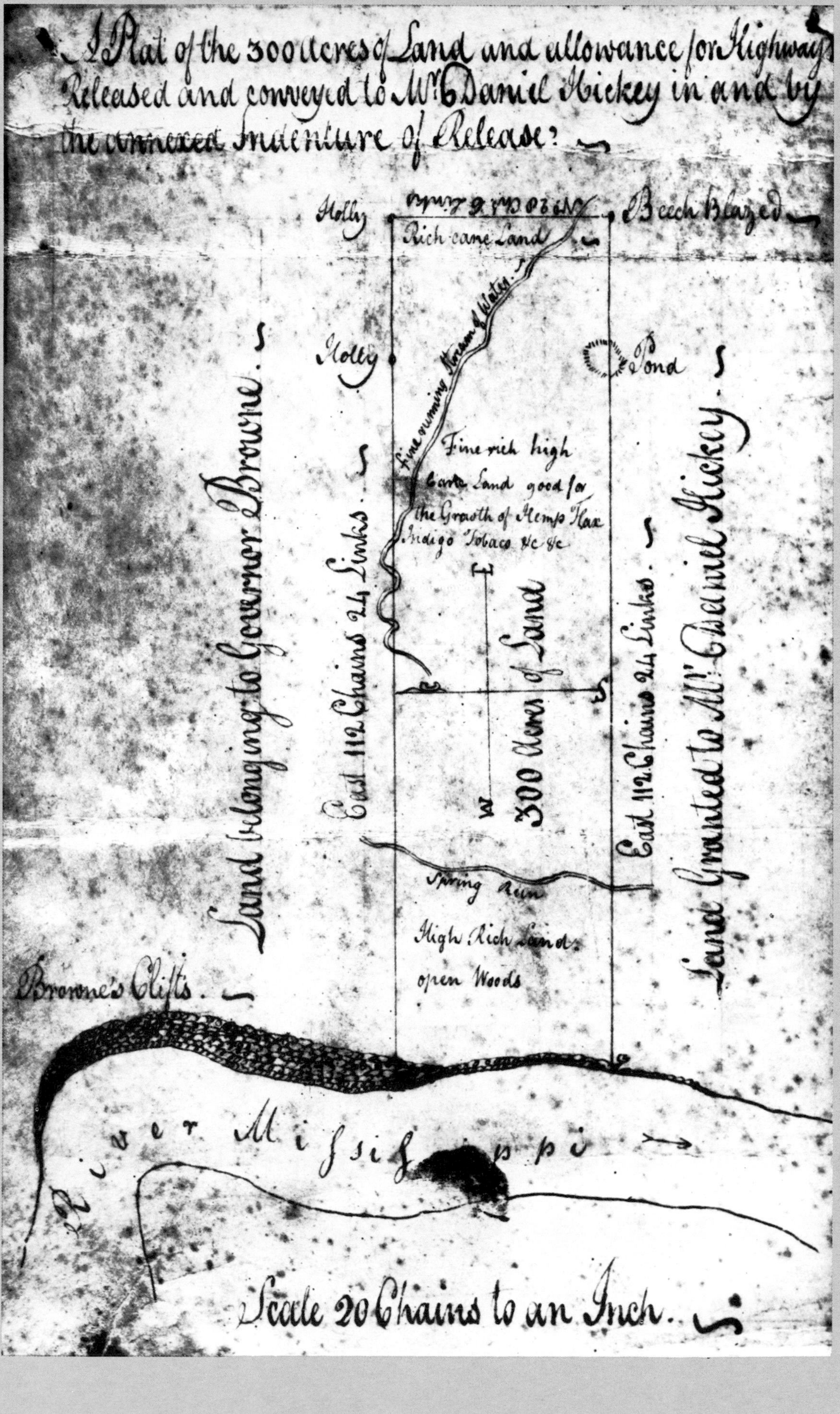

A Plat of the 300 acres of Land and allowance for Highway Released and conveyed to Mr. Daniel Hickey in and by the annexed Indenture of Release.

Holly   West 26 Chains 91 Links   Beech Blazed

Rich cane Land

Holly   Pond

Fine running Stream of Water

Fine rich high Cane Land good for the Growth of Hemp Flax Indigo Tobaco &c &c

Land belonging to Governer Browne.

East 112 Chains 24 Links.

East 112 Chains 24 Links

Land Granted to Mr. Cornel Hickey.

300 Acres of Land

Spring Run

High Rich Lands open Woods

Browne's Clifts.

River Mississippi

Scale 20 Chains to an Inch.

William Dunbar was one of the most remarkable settlers in the Baton Rouge area in the 18th century. Arriving on a crude flatboat, he selected a tract of land near New Richmond (today Baton Rouge) and became a planter and slave owner. His diary from 1776 to 1780 furnishes valuable details on social and economic conditions of that frontier. After 1783 Dunbar moved to American territory south of Natchez. He died in 1810. Courtesy, Mississippi Department of Archives and History, Jackson.

ment and a brisk, if technically illegal, trade with neighboring Spanish Louisiana. By 1776 the area around the fort was sectioned into several prosperous (thanks to slave labor) plantations. Baton Rouge, or more accurately, Fort New Richmond, never really evolved into a town under the British; rather the fort remained the center of an expanding agricultural community of planters and farmers who settled along rivers and streams in present-day East Baton Rouge and East and West Feliciana parishes. Corn, rice, indigo, pumpkins, wooden shipping staves, and livestock were the leading products of the West Florida economy during the brief period of British control. The great cotton and sugar-cane plantations, to the north and south of Baton Rouge, respectively, did not appear until the early 19th century.

Between the end of the French and Indian War in 1763 and the spring of 1775 relations worsened among British subjects in the older Atlantic-seaboard colonies and the home authorities.

Not all British colonies in the New World joined the rebellion that followed. Remaining loyal were Barbados, Jamaica, the Bahamas, Canada, and the two Floridas. Canada and the Floridas had only recently been added to the British Empire and were thus lacking the mature traditions of local self-government so jealously defended by the older colonies. To West Floridians in particular the untrustworthy, less permissive, and potentially hostile Spaniards were only a river and a bayou away. Consequently the decision of most West Florida subjects (who were prosperous and not disaffected) to remain dependent upon and loyal to Britain should not be surprising. (The adherence of West Florida to the Crown is also, incidentally, the reason why most Baton Rougeans who can trace their ancestry to British colonists of West Florida find that they are descended from Tories rather than Patriots!)

For almost three years British West Florida was left alone by participants in the distant conflict. Although Spain remained neutral during the same period, Louisiana's Spanish governor, Don Bernardo de Galvez, gave covert aid to the few rebels in West Florida by furnishing them arms, provisions, and cash. (A wealthy American agent in New Orleans, Oliver Pollock, assisted Galvez in these endeavors.)

But early in 1778 the war finally came to West Florida and especially to Baton Rouge. James Willing, a wealthy and dissipated young Philadelphian, had moved to Natchez to become a storekeeper in the early 1770s. When the War for Independence broke out, Willing abandoned his failing business for professional patriotism. After persuading members of the Continental Congress to back his schemes, Willing (a navy captain by January of 1778) assembled a force of 30 volunteers at Pittsburgh and descended the Ohio River on a vessel named the *Rattletrap*.

Several weeks later Willing arrived in the Natchez district where he raided plantations and took a number of captives. Continuing downstream Willing sold his spoils in Spanish New Orleans, but spent the proceeds, according to a contemporary, "in riotous living and debauchery." Finding himself broke when he sobered up, the convert to democracy and American independence rounded up his cutthroats and proceeded upriver on another raid, this one a more systematic assault upon British plantations in the Baton Rouge area, which Willing had bypassed during his first vandalistic orgy.

Willing's second raid inflicted even more damage. Before they were driven off by militia, Willing's men burned and looted numerous plantations and carried off what was then estimated to be $1.5 million worth of property. Among the despoiled was the affluent Sir William Dunbar.

Willing's raid did nothing to promote the Patriot cause among his victims, but instead resulted in convincing the British to reinforce local garrisons from their larger base at Pensacola.

In February 1778, one month after Willing's raids began, France declared war on Great Britain, recognizing and formally allying itself to the "United States of America." Spain waited for another year and a half to declare war on the British, probably to ensure that its long-standing nemesis had become too thinly stretched and tied down to offer much resistance to the accomplishment of Spanish objectives. French motives for fighting the British stemmed from a desire for revenge; the possibility of recovering their former North American possessions was quite remote. But Spain, while also eager to harass the British, entered the war with expansionist goals as well: to recapture East Florida and acquire West Florida. Added to Spanish Mexico and Louisiana, these thinly populated and marginally defended British colonies would convert the entire Gulf of Mexico into a vast Spanish lake from the Yucatan Peninsula to the Florida Keys. To emphasize the self-interest of its war aims, Spain allied itself to France but not to the United States, whose fraternal differences with the British were of incidental importance to Spain.

Unleashed at last by his nation's declaration of war, Governor Galvez marched northward from New Orleans toward Fort New Richmond on August 27, 1779. He took with him about 1,400 men, most of whom were Franco-Spanish militia. After a minor skirmish on September 7, Fort Bute fell to the Spaniards. Two weeks later Galvez obtained the surrender of Fort New Richmond from Lieutenant Colonel Alexander Dickson after inflicting a three-hour artillery bombardment on the British garrison. This first "battle of Baton Rouge"—two more would follow in 1810 and 1862— was the only military engagement fought in present-day Louisiana during the War for American Independence, and, except for seven American volunteers serving under Galvez, no Patriots fought on either side.

With the fall of Mobile to Galvez in 1780 and of Pensacola in 1781, Spain's Gulf Coast aspirations were realized: the British Floridas were taken and retained (West Florida until 1810 and East Florida until 1819),

After Spain declared war on Great Britain in 1779, Don Bernardo de Galvez, Spanish governor of Louisiana, led a detachment of men to Baton Rouge and bombarded Fort New Richmond, the British fort. In September 1779, Spain assumed control of the region. Galvez, long revered by Louisianians, was the subject of some of the earliest attempts at literary art in the colony, including an epic poem published by Julian Poydras on the Baton Rouge Campaign. Courtesy, The Historic New Orleans Collection.

until each was absorbed by the United States.

British control of Baton Rouge had lasted only 16 years. But, according to historian Meyers, their "influence on its destiny was far out of proportion to the time spent there. Baton Rouge had become an Anglo-Saxon pocket in Latin America, and the Anglo-Saxon love of democracy would linger in the hearts of Baton Rougeans and West Floridians of British ancestry."

While Spain's formal title to the Floridas was not ratified until 1783, the Spanish firmly established their presence in Baton Rouge immediately upon taking it from the British. Don Carlos de Grand Pré became Commandant of the District of Baton Rouge while Don Pedro Jose Favrot was named Commandant of the Post of Baton Rouge, renamed Fort San Carlos. Residents were given six days (from September 25, 1779) to declare their allegiance to Spain's monarch or depart. Those of British descent found this requirement disagreeable, but most complied rather than lose their homes and further disrupt their lives.

Differences between British and Spanish ways of governing soon became apparent. The Spanish permitted no expression of democracy: there was no elected assembly and all officials were appointed by authority of the Crown. While the British had, in practice, permitted West Floridians to trade with anyone, Spain limited trade to Spanish ports and its conduct to Spanish citizens. The result was a diminution in West Floridian commercial prosperity.

There were, however, some compensations. Although invested with autocratic powers, Spanish officials in West Florida generally governed sensibly and tolerantly. These traits were especially evident in Commandant de Grand Pré, who retained his office throughout most of the Spanish period and became a respected figure among the West Floridians. English, French, and Spanish continued to be official languages under Spanish administration. Land was not taxed as it had been by the British, although landowners were required to maintain roads, bridges, levees, and ferries. Baton Rouge finally began to take shape as a town under the Spanish. The district of Baton Rouge, as a modern scholar, Margaret Fisher Dalrymple, has stated, grew "from a tiny collection of miserable huts in 1763" to a "small but flourishing plantation society" by the 1780s. By 1788 Baton Rouge had a population of 682. The city's two oldest subdivisions, "Spanishtown" and "Beauregard Town," had both been laid out by about 1805—the former in the present area of Boyd Avenue near Capitol Lake, and the latter within the rectangle bounded by North, East, and South boulevards and the Mississippi River.

But Spain's rule, however moderate, was never popularly accepted in West Florida. Most older residents of British descent viewed the Spaniards as aliens and enemies. In addition to this burden, irreconcilable tensions quickly developed between Spanish West Florida and her young

Above
Don Carlos Louis Boucher de Grand Pré served under the Spanish as governor of the District of Baton Rouge from 1779 to 1808. He developed part of "Spanish Town," one of the first two subdivisions of the present-day city. This image is taken from a miniature that was painted on ivory prior to Don Carlos' death in 1809. Courtesy, Mr. and Mrs. Samuel J. Lambert, Jr.

Right
Don Pedro Jose Favrot (1749–1824) was appointed the first commandant of the Post of Baton Rouge immediately following the British surrender of Fort New Richmond to the Spanish forces. He held that important position during the crucial period, 1779 to 1781, when the threat of an attack from the English or their Indian allies was always present. After some 42 years in the service of first the French, and later the Spanish, crowns Favrot retired to his plantation. During the War of 1812 he returned to active duty. Don Pedro was buried in Baton Rouge. Courtesy, Mr. and Mrs. Claude Favrot Reynaud, Jr.

Two of the largest land grants given in the District of Baton Rouge during the Spanish period were to Louisiana Governor Manuel Gayoso de Lemos and to Elias Beauregard. Each of these men received a square of land comprising 1,000 arpents. This document signed by William Dunbar in 1797 delineates Gayoso's land holdings as well as those of some of his neighbors. Courtesy, Department of Archives and Manuscripts, LSU, Baton Rouge.

Following the surrender of Fort New Richmond by the British in September 1779, the Spanish troops occupied the post and renamed it Fort San Carlos. The following year the military force stationed there consisted of a captain, three sergeants, and 46 enlisted men. The buildings for their accommodation were very simple wooden structures. This panel drawing, dated 1788, taken from the military archives in Madrid, Spain, shows the soldiers' quarters at the top, the warehouse in the center, and the cosina (kitchen) at the bottom. Courtesy, Jack D.L. Holmes, Portfolio of Louisiana Maps in Spanish Archives, Louisiana Room, LSU Library.

Fort San Carlos, the fortification at Baton Rouge during Spanish rule, was in the shape of a star. This engineer's plan, dated 1798, indicates the location of various buildings at that time. Courtesy, Jack D.L. Holmes, Portfolio of Louisiana Maps in Spanish Archives, Louisiana Room, LSU Library.

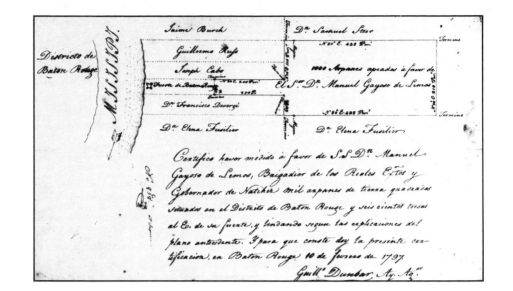

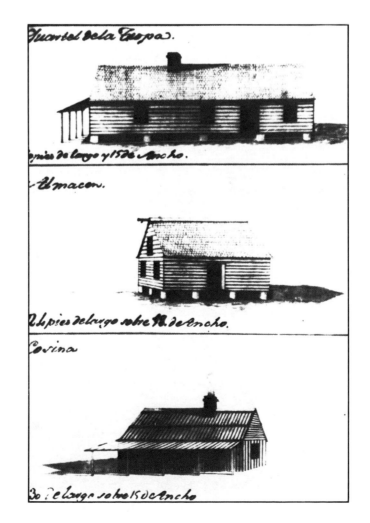

and aggressively expansive neighbor, the United States.

One Spaniard who clearly foresaw the inevitable conflict between his nation and the land-hungry Americans was the Conde de Aranda, Spain's ambassador to France during the 1780s. In a secret memorandum to his royal master, Carlos III, De Aranda expressed some remarkably prophetic insights:

This federal republic is born a pigmy, if I may be allowed to express myself. It has required the support of two such powerful States as France and Spain to obtain its independence. The day will come when she will be a giant, a colossus formidable even to these countries. She will forget the services she has received from the two powers, and will think only of her own aggrandizement. The liberty of conscience, the facility of establishing a new population upon immense territories, together with the advantages of a new government (meaning free, no doubt), will attract the agriculturists and mechanics of all nations, for men ever run after fortune; and, in a few years, we shall see the tyrannical existence of this very colossus of which I speak.

The first step of this nation, after it has become powerful, will be to take possession of the Floridas in order to have the command of the Gulf of Mexico, and, after having rendered difficult our commerce with New Spain [Mexico], she will aspire to the conquest of that vast empire, which it will be impossible for us to defend against a formidable power established on the same continent, and in its immediate neighborhood. These fears are well founded; they must be realized in a few years, if some greater revolution, even more fatal, does not sooner take place in our Americas.

A revolution, in fact, "even more fatal" than what the ambassador envisioned, erupted in Mexico's War for Independence beginning in 1810. In that same year Spain would lose West Florida to the United States; nine years later East Florida was taken by the Americans. In 1836 "Texicans" of American origin successfully revolted against their Mexican overlords and entered the Union as a state in 1845. Finally, after a swift and one-sided war with Mexico, the United States took from her southern neighbor in 1848 the present states of California, Nevada, Arizona, New Mexico, Utah, and portions of Colorado and Wyoming. Only two generations after De Aranda's gloomy memorandum to his king, the diplomat's worst expectations had been completely fulfilled.

The dominant trend in the settlement of the Mississippi Valley between 1783 and 1803, as De Aranda apprehended, was the rapid penetration of the region by land-hungry Americans. British restrictions on settling the interior vanished with independence, and thousands of pioneers soon streamed over the mountains into Kentucky, Tennessee, and Ohio—which became states in 1792, 1796, and 1803, respectively.

This tidal wave of American immigration rolling toward their Louisiana and West Florida possessions evoked mixed reactions from the

One of Baton Rouge's earliest settlers, Don Antonio de Gras, helped to lay out and to develop part of the city. A businessman, he lived north of Fort San Carlos and assisted the rebel cause during the American Revolution. Don Antonio is probably best known for his donation of land on which St. Joseph's Cathedral now stands. It is interesting to note that the very first marriage record in the District of Baton Rouge is that of De Gras and Genevieve Dulat on January 15, 1793, by Father Carlos Burke. That entry is reproduced here. Courtesy, Department of Archives, Diocese of Baton Rouge, Catholic Life Center.

El Dia 15 del Mes de Enero de 1793 en el districto de
Baton Rouge haviendose leidas tres amonestaciones
canonicas sin resultar impedimento alguno yo Dn
Carlos Burke Cura Barocho del dicho districto dispo
= se por palabra de presente segun orden de Nuestra
S. M.a la Iglesia y juntamente Velé Antonio Grass
hijo legitimo de Josef Grass y Antonia Musano
Natural de Mayorca y Genevieuve Dulat Hija
legitima de Luis dulat y catharina Mail. Natural
de de la Parochia de Sn Juan Bautista San Santiago a quienes haviendo
les preguntado tuvé por respuesta su mutuo consen
= timiento fueron Testigos Dn Antonio Estevan y
Dn Nicolas Belanget y padrino Antonio Estevan
y Madrina Catarina Mail Sn Juan Baytysta y lo firme
y valez Bento Bento Carlos Burke

En el districto de Baton Rouge el Dia 15 del mes de
Abril de 1793 Yo Dn Carlos Burke Cura Barocho del
districto de Baton Rouge haviendose leidas tres am
onestaciones canonicas sin resultar impedimento
alguno. deposé y juntamente Velé a Dn Nicolas Kimplin Hijo
legitimo de Juan Kimplin y Maria Hicky Natural Yrlan
dez de Nacion y Anna Williams Hija legitima de Matheo
Williams y Sarah Coyl Natural de la America fueron a qui
enes haviendoles preguntado tuvé por respuesta su mutuo con
sentimiento fueron Testigos Gorge Gairy y Gullermo Colkins
y padrino Migel Williams y Madrina catharina Bouke
y lo firme Carlos Burke

En el Districto de Baton Rouge el dia 16 de Abril de 1793 yo Dn
Carlos Burke Cura del Sobre dicho puesto haviendose leidas tres
amonestaciones Canonicas sin resultar impedimento Ninguno
Casé y juntamente Velé a Dn Pedro Tayler Hijo legitimo de Henrique
Tayler y de Anna Maria Lonon Aleman de Nacion y Catarina
Crevenaugh Hija legitima de Philipe Crevenaugh

The friends & acquaintances of the late Antonio Gras. are req=ueted to attend his funeral at 10 Oclock A. M. to day, at his House

August 1st 1811.

Spanish. On the positive side, hard-working settlers brought increased colonial prosperity. For this reason Spain allowed many Americans to move into Louisiana, and especially into West Florida, where they greatly augmented the number of English-speaking, Protestant, and freedom-loving subjects of his autocratic and Catholic majesty. But Spain came to regard the immigration movement as a whole with growing apprehension. The Spaniards feared the Anglo-Saxon torrent would eventually overrun them, and their Mississippi Valley possessions would be seized. This was, in part, what actually took place, just as Ambassador de Aranda had predicted.

To forestall this calamity Spain in 1785 closed the Mississippi River (the west bank of which it controlled) to American commerce and denied Americans the right of deposit in the port of New Orleans, which at the time was the capital of Spanish Louisiana and entirely surrounded by Spanish territory. This policy was, of course, totally unacceptable to Americans living in the Western territories. Although a "foreign" port, New Orleans was much closer, less expensive to reach, and thus more desirable for Westerners to use than the American ports of Boston, New York, or Philadelphia. Denial of transit down the Mississippi and the suspension of the right of deposit at New Orleans imposed severe handicaps on the Western settlers. Spain hoped that the burden would discourage further American immigration into the West.

Spain miscalculated. The tide of immigration continued while American pressure to repeal the restrictions increased. Ten years later, in 1795, with a new and considerably stronger federal government to back them up, the Americans at last persuaded the Spanish to sign the Treaty of San Lorenzo, which reopened the Mississippi and New Orleans to American commerce for a three-year period, subject to renewal by mutual consent of both parties. The treaty also established the 31st parallel as the north-south boundary between the Mississippi Territory and Spanish West Florida. The Spanish were obliged to give up Natchez, but retained Baton Rouge (Fort San Carlos) as the Spanish post on the Mississippi River closest to American territory. A further result of the treaty was that American immigration into the southwest increased even more. Methodically and inexorably, the United States was closing in on Spanish West Florida.

The Treaty of San Lorenzo between Spain and the United States was followed five years later by a much more significant agreement between Spain and France, of which artillerist Napoleon Bonaparte had recently become virtual dictator. In the Treaty of San Ildefonso, signed in 1800, Bonaparte induced Spain to give western Louisiana and New Orleans back to France, in return for minor territorial compensation in Europe. The Americans would later believe—perhaps because they wanted to— that the Treaty of San Ildefonso had returned West Florida to France as well. The Spanish emphatically denied that it had, while the French merely shrugged. West Florida, in fact, remained under Spanish control until the United States annexed it in 1810. Hence there is no basis for the assumption that the tricolor of republican France ever flew over Baton Rouge, legally or actually. It did not.

By 1800, therefore, a volatile situation had suddenly emerged to affect both the United States and Spanish West Florida. An agreeable Spain was no longer America's neighbor across the Mississippi River—unpredictable Napoleon Bonaparte was. New Orleans, moreover, had also passed under French control. When Spanish officials, who remained on the scene until 1803, again closed the port to American commerce in 1802, President Thomas Jefferson resolved that his country could no longer afford to react passively to the fate of the river and the port. He dispatched emissaries to Bonaparte with instructions to purchase New Orleans *and* West Florida, both of which Jefferson assumed were French.

One year later, in 1803, Bonaparte surprised the Americans by offering to sell them not only New Orleans, but all of western Louisiana as well. The United States agreed to pay approximately $11,250,000 for the territory and assumed another $3,750,000 in French debts to American citizens, bringing the total to about $15 million for the Louisiana Purchase. Napoleon agreed to the sale because he was on the verge of war with the British and needed money. Besides he foresaw that if he did not sell New Orleans and Louisiana to the Americans while he could, the British might take them from him without compensation, or the Americans might eventually take them, with or without compensation. Thus he made the best of a vexing situation.

In 1803, therefore, Spanish West Florida found itself almost entirely surrounded by the United States and its possessions. Whether one looked north across the 31st parallel, west across the Mississippi River, or south across Bayou Manchac, one beheld American territory. More crucially, Baton Rouge (then Fort San Carlos) had become the *only* post on the Mississippi River outside the United States. Spanish tenure in the Baton Rouge area had not only become extremely precarious, it had visibly begun to deteriorate.

Sam and Nathan Kemper—two brothers who had been involved in previous difficulties with Spanish officials—commenced an "invasion" of West Florida from the Mississippi Territory on August 7, 1804. With their band of 30 armed men, they seized a small Spanish outpost near present-day St. Francisville, then proceeded south, intending to capture both Fort San Carlos and the district governor. Foiled by militia resistance, the Kempers retreated back into the magnolia forests of Mississippi. Although a failure, the Kemper affair had been the first, but by no means last, episode of armed opposition by annexation-minded Americans to crumbling Spanish authority in West Florida.

Don Carlos de Hault de Lassus, the last lieutenant governor of Upper Louisiana, succeeded the popular Grand Pré as governor of the District of Baton Rouge under the Spanish. It was during his tenure that the West Florida Rebellion was planned and successfully executed. During the attack on Fort San Carlos De Lassus was imprisoned. He was subsequently released by Fulwar Skipwith, governor of independent West Florida, and died in New Orleans many years later. This portrait of De Lassus was taken from a daguerreotype. From Fortier, History of Louisiana.

Local disaffection markedly increased with the recall to Havana in 1808 of the revered Don Carlos de Grand Pré, who had governed Baton Rouge wisely and well since the beginning of Spanish rule in 1779. An unpopular regime can be made at least tolerable by the virtues of its personal representatives, and De Grand Pré possessed considerable virtues, among them tact, patience, and understanding of the people he governed. Of the many petitions sent by grateful West Floridians for Grand Pré's reinstatement, one sent to the governor himself touchingly expressed local feeling toward the just and tolerant official: "In all the time of your rule, you have exerted yourself to perceive our wants. You have heard our petitions. Every individual always found free access to you and you never refused to listen to the general voice or to individual representations which were for the public good or to remedy some evil." Grand Pré's replacement at a most inopportune time by an unpopular and incompetent successor, Don Carlos de Hault de Lassus, was a costly Spanish public-relations blunder.

By 1810 Spain's position in West Florida was hopeless. American residents had become committed to independence from the petty and corrupt regime of De Lassus, under whom bribery began to flourish. The United States government itself, impatient to absorb the last foreign outpost on the Mississippi River, gave encouragement to the dissidents. On September 22 a convention at St. Francisville deposed De Lassus as governor and ordered the commandant of the militia, Philemon Thomas, to seize Fort San Carlos. One day later the second "battle of Baton Rouge" took place when a file of 75 rebel horsemen crept into the fort before daybreak and took the post. No rebels were lost or injured, but Lieutenant Louis de Grand Pré and one soldier were killed and four other Spanish soldiers wounded. Twenty-one persons, including District Governor De Lassus, were taken prisoner. The victors lowered the Spanish flag and raised in its place a banner containing a single white star in a blue field—the flag of the short-lived "West Florida Republic."

A successful minor skirmish had climaxed weeks of planning and plotting to terminate Spanish authority in West Florida. Among Baton Rouge leaders of the independence movement were Philip Hicky, George Mather, Joseph Sharp, Samuel Fulton, Dr. Andrew Steele, Thomas Lilley, John Davenport, George and William Herries, Philemon Thomas, John Morgan, Edmond Hawes, and Fulwar Skipwith. A former American diplomat, Skipwith would serve as president of the fleeting West Florida Republic.

Events moved quickly thereafter. On September 26 the convention issued a "declaration of independence" from Spanish authority, sending a copy to the American governor of the Mississippi Territory to be forwarded to President James Madison, a not-altogether-casual spectator who must have appreciated the statement within the declaration that

Above
Colonel Philip Hicky (1778–1859), master of Hope Estate Plantation, was a popular figure in the early history of Baton Rouge. He was captain of the guard and militia for the District of Baton Rouge under the Spanish and later colonel of the Louisiana militia in the War of 1812. Elected as a member of the West Florida Convention, he later served on a committee to conduct the government of the Republic. Hicky was always a highly respected member of the community. Courtesy, Department of Archives and Manuscripts, LSU, Baton Rouge.

Left
General Philemon Thomas, statesman and soldier, resided in Baton Rouge and was long associated with its early history. A Revolutionary and War of 1812 veteran, he commanded the troops of the West Florida Rebellion, captured the Spanish fort in Baton Rouge, and held it until the United States assumed control. Thomas served two terms in the U.S. House of Representatives and during his tenure in the state legislature he never tired of trying to get his home town designated as the capital of Louisiana. Courtesy, Louisiana State Museum.

"the present Government and the people of this state" wished to become an "integral and inalienable portion of the United States." On October 27, 1810, Madison issued a proclamation authorizing Governor W.C.C. Claiborne of the Territory of Orleans to "take possession of West Florida as far as the Perdido River." With Claiborne present the American flag went up in St. Francisville on December 7 and in Baton Rouge on December 10. Shortly after the Territory of Orleans became the state of Louisiana, the portion of West Florida between the Mississippi and Pearl rivers on the west and east, and the 31st parallel and Bayou Manchac to the north and south, was attached to the new 18th state. Thus, by August 4, 1812, tiny Baton Rouge could reflect upon a vivid and colorful past under four flags—Bourbon France, Great Britain, Bourbon Spain, and the West Florida Republic. An equally busy future lay ahead under three more flags—the United States, the Confederate States, and the Republic of Louisiana. Many years would pass, however, before the little hamlet of a small fort, 12 frame houses, and 60 cabins began to develop visibly into the present 63rd largest city in the United States.

Construction of the old Louisiana State Capitol, designed and built by architect James H. Dakin, was begun in 1847. The building was first occupied by legislators in 1850. Prior to 1861, its chambers not only accommodated sessions of the legislature, but also were the scenes of many balls and other social gatherings. During Union occupation, the State House was used as quarters for soldiers and Confederate prisoners. The ruins here show the exterior after it was gutted by a fire on December 28, 1862. Courtesy, Department of Archives and Manuscripts, LSU, Baton Rouge.

RIVER PORT AND ANTEBELLUM CAPITAL

After the departure of the Spanish and American annexation of West Florida in 1810, Fort San Carlos permanently reverted to its original French name, Baton Rouge. One year later the little village of 1,463 inhabitants became part of newly created East Baton Rouge Parish. On January 16, 1817, Baton Rouge was incorporated by the four-year-old Louisiana legislature and empowered to elect a town government. There were no "mayors" of Baton Rouge until 1850, when Town Magistrate John R. Dufrocq officially assumed the title. William Williams, the first known town magistrate, was elected in 1818 and served until at least 1820. (The town magistrate appears to have also been ex officio president of the Board of Selectmen, a small council that served as Baton Rouge's municipal government for most of the antebellum period. Since no records survive for the period 1820 to 1832, the men who governed Baton Rouge during those years remain unknown.) For the remainder of the antebellum period Baton Rouge enjoyed the steadily increasing, if uneven, prosperity of a healthy American frontier community and Mississippi River port. Except for one year under Confederate authority and a disastrous battle fought locally—between Yankees and Rebels in August of 1862—Baton Rouge has remained within the United States ever since, its essential peace largely undisturbed.

When incorporated the Baton Rouge city limits extended eastward from the Mississippi River to 22nd Street—although actual settlement for many years did not extend much beyond Fifth Street—and from Garcia's Bayou (later Capitol Lake) down to South Boulevard. The town's principal "subdivision," at least in the dreams of its founder, Captain Elias Beauregard (great-uncle of Confederate General P.G.T. Beauregard) was Beauregard Town, a rectangular area circumscribed by the river and North, East, and South boulevards. Beauregard Town was to have a central square, resembling Jackson Square in New Orleans, reached by a complex of intersecting streets and avenues. Beauregard Town was also supposed to be the most fashionable area in Baton Rouge, comparable to New Orleans' Garden District. Eventually Beauregard Town did become, in part, what the Captain had envisioned, but only after the Civil War, when Baton Rouge's population began to expand in a southeasterly direction, a movement that has continued to the present.

Baton Rouge's other venerable district was Spanish Town, on the northern rim of the community along Spanish Town Road (Boyd Avenue). Here were concentrated Baton Rouge's Spanish and Canary Island residents, although by 1819 several French and Anglo-American families had also moved in. By 1840 several smaller districts had popped up within the bustling settlement: Grass Town, Devall Town, Hickey, Duncan, Mather, and Leonard Town.

Most Baton Rougeans of Anglo-American descent lived in the center of the municipality along North, Main, and Laurel streets while the French resided along Lafayette Street closer to the river. Beyond the southern limits of Baton Rouge lived a hardworking colony of Pennsylvania German farmers, the "Dutch Highlanders," who had settled originally at Manchac during the 1770s but had moved north to higher ground in Spanish West Florida after floods ravaged their lands in 1784. (Early Americans easily confused the German adjective for German—"Deutsche"—with "Dutch" because they sounded similar.) The "Highlanders" established themselves along Highland Road, Bayou Fountain, and Ward's Creek between Ben Hur Road and Seigen Lane. Initially specializing in growing indigo, most Highlanders switched to cotton in the 1790s and added sugarcane cultivation in the early 1830s. Among the more significant Highlander families in Baton Rouge affairs have been

Above
In addition to studying evidence of Indian life in the vicinity of Baton Rouge, then State Archaeologist William G. Haag in 1972 directed excavations of certain historic sites in the area now occupied by the Civic Center. In Beauregard Town he uncovered artifacts from more affluent households that included fine tableware, wine bottles, and other imported articles. An essential item in all homes then was the chamber pot. One of the loveliest found was this deep cobalt blue Staffordshireware piece that probably dates from around 1820. Courtesy, Museum of Anthropology, LSU, Baton Rouge.

Right
This rare 1837 map of Baton Rouge was originally owned by members of the Beauregard family. From North Boulevard to the right, and bounded by South and East boulevards, was Beauregard Town. To the left of North Boulevard were situated the towns of Gras (or later, Grass), Devall, Leonard, Hicky, Wicoff, Duncan, and Mather. Names of other early settlers shown are Tessier, Gardere, Marion, and Lopez. Courtesy, Louisiana Room, LSU Library.

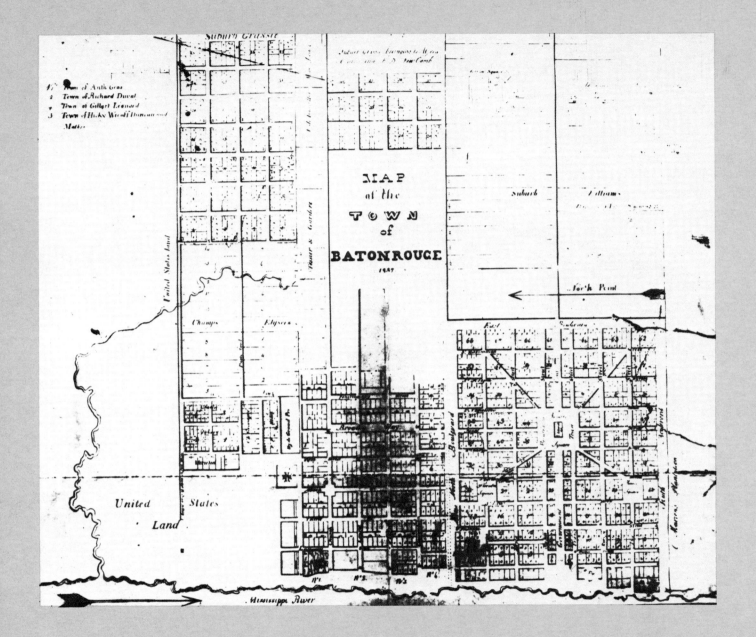

MAP of the TOWN of BATON ROUGE

the Kleinpeters, Garigs, Starings, and Sharps.

The economic vitality of present-day Baton Rouge derives from an immense petrochemical industry; an ever-expanding deep-water facility; and from housing, feeding, and providing recreation and health care for swarms of government workers, students, and university personnel. But none of these sources of wealth, except for river-borne commerce, sustained the small, early-19th-century town. To antebellum Baton Rouge-ans, the Mississippi River, and the farms and plantations surrounding it, furnished the initial basis for economic security and growth. If local plantations such as Mount Hope or Magnolia Mound produced bountiful crops of cotton or sugarcane, and if market demand was strong, then Baton Rouge merchants and suppliers, whose stocks arrived on river boats, also thrived. Conversely bad harvests or glutted markets depressed the entire community. This interdependence of trade, river commerce, and agriculture continued to dominate Baton Rouge's economy throughout the 19th century and was still a significant factor until the third decade of the 20th.

Although Baton Rouge was impressively situated atop the first bluffs to break the monotony of south Louisiana's flat, sea-level landscape as one came upriver from New Orleans, it was hardly a showpiece in the early American period. Baton Rouge, at this time, had unpaved and unlighted streets and scattered, shabbily constructed buildings. But as the town became more prosperous it also matured, and the chief agents of progress were the steamboat and the Mississippi River.

In January of 1812 the infant *New Orleans* puffed optimistically into Baton Rouge. This first visit by a steam-powered craft decisively affected the town's development. Ten years later, in 1822, cargo and passengers came ashore at local wharves from 83 steamboats, 174 barges, and 441 flatboats. As Baton Rouge increased in importance to the growing immediate area, river traffic expanded even more and local prosperity was further enhanced. The steamboat and the river were to Baton Rouge what cattle and railroads would later be to Chicago. Before long Baton Rouge could afford such amenities as improved public services and facilities, schools, churches, and hotels. The first newspapers also were established at this time: the *Gazette,* a bilingual Whig weekly, commenced publication as early as 1817; the *Weekly Advocate,* supporting the Democratic party, first appeared in 1842.

Another geographically important factor in the affairs of early 19th-century Baton Rouge was its continued strategic location. Until 1845 Louisiana remained the southwesternmost state in the Union, successively bordering Spanish Mexico, independent Mexico, and the Republic of Texas. For reasons of national defense, the War Department resolved to establish a large garrison at Baton Rouge. Between 1819 and 1822 it built the Pentagon Barracks, near the site of old Fort San Carlos, to serve

Above
This title page appeared at the beginning of the German Benevolent Society's constitution and bylaws of 1851. During the 1840s and 1850s a great number of foreigners migrated to Baton Rouge. The largest group, the Germans, aside from those on the Highlands, preferred occupations of merchandising and mechanical arts. Courtesy, Department of Archives and Manuscripts, LSU, Baton Rouge.

Left
This stately mansion situated on the northwest corner of Lafayette and Convention was razed around 1927 to make way for the Heidelberg Hotel. According to newspaper accounts, it was built in the first quarter of the 19th century. During its lifetime the building served as the home of some of Baton Rouge's leading families—the Averys, Duncans, Bonnecazes, Bodleys, and Kernans. This photograph pictures the old landmark in its last years of decline. Courtesy, Louisiana Room, LSU Library.

as quarters for an infantry regiment. In the 1830s an arsenal was also erected several hundred yards to the northeast of the barracks, on the grounds of the present state capitol.

Between 1822 and 1823 the officer supervising Pentagon construction was Lieutenant Colonel Zachary Taylor, a professional soldier and native Virginian. Taylor so liked the Baton Rouge area that he made the town his official residence and purchased 380 acres of cotton land in nearby West Feliciana Parish. By 1840 Taylor had advanced to major general in charge of the southwestern army command. From his headquarters in Baton Rouge, "Old Rough and Ready" departed in 1845 to render outstanding service in the Mexican War. Back home in Baton Rouge after the conflict, the national hero became the town's foremost celebrity. Steamboats steered close to the eastern bank so that passengers could view Taylor's home and, perhaps, see his splendid horse grazing in adjacent fields. If the General himself appeared, boat captains blew their whistles in salute. Taylor, as the Whig nominee, was elected President of the United States in 1848, the last Deep South resident to win that office until Jimmy Carter's victory in 1976. Baton Rouge gave the old soldier a rousing send-off when Taylor left for Washington to be inaugurated early in 1849. Unfortunately the General never returned to Baton Rouge—he died in office the following year.

Until shortly after the Mexican War, the Pentagon garrison remained at full strength, and its personnel were welcome additions to the local population. Especially popular with Baton Rouge's young ladies were the garrison's officers, who hosted frequent balls and parties. But as the American frontier moved westward, the Pentagon diminished in importance and its complement of troops became smaller until, as one observer noted, "only a corporal's guard was maintained to raise and lower the flag and to fire the evening gun."

At about the same time that Zachary Taylor decided to settle in Baton Rouge, the town was visited in 1825 by a notable celebrity from the past, the legendary Marquis de Lafayette. The most revered and respected of all foreigners who fought for the Patriot cause during America's War for Independence, Lafayette went on to play important roles in his own nation's revolution as well. Arriving from New Orleans aboard one of many steamers to be named *Natchez*, the Marquis was enthusiastically received at the Laurel Street dock on April 16. The official reason for Lafayette's Baton Rouge visit was his desire to see his old friend and aide-de-camp, Joseph Armand Allard Duplantier, a Baton Rouge resident. (Duplantier died in 1827 and lies buried in Highland Cemetery, in College Town, just south of the LSU campus.)

Immediately after his arrival Lafayette delivered a brief speech in French, then reviewed the Pentagon troops and inspected the garrison. That afternoon a ball and banquet were held in his honor at one of Baton

Above
Zachary Taylor supervised construction of the Pentagon Barracks between 1822 and 1823 and then made Baton Rouge his official residence. After fighting in the Mexican War, Taylor became the celebrity of the town. In 1848 he was elected President of the United States, making him the last resident of the Deep South to serve in that office until Jimmy Carter was elected in 1976. From Cirker, Dictionary of American Portraits, *Dover, 1967. Engraving by Alexander H. Ritchie.*

Right
The United States Army began construction of the Pentagon Barracks and an ordnance depot in Baton Rouge in 1819. By the time that this plan was drawn, 20 years later, the grounds contained the primary installation for ordnance in the southwestern country. Centrally located, troops and supplies could be rapidly dispatched to fortifications on the Mississippi River, the Gulf entrance to Louisiana, or even to the Natchitoches region. Courtesy, Louisiana Room, LSU Library.

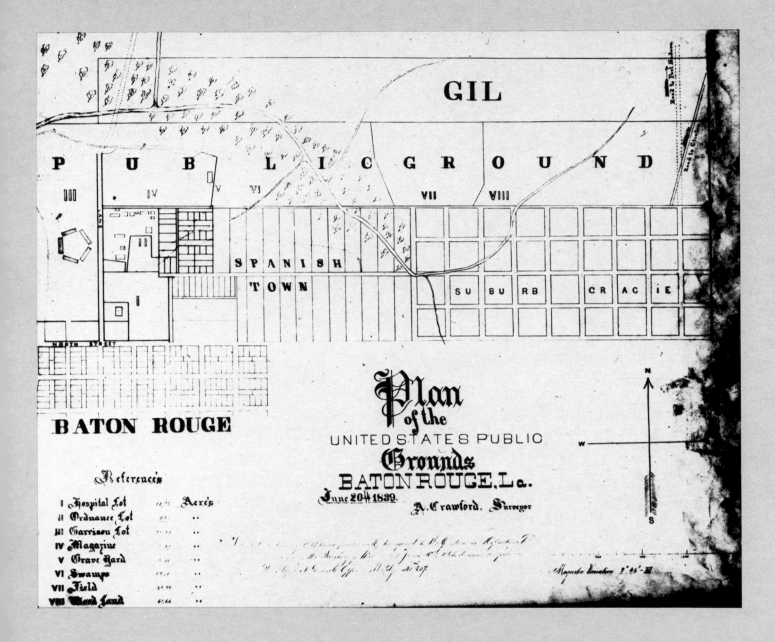

GIL

P U B L I C G R O U N D

III   IV   V   VI   VII   VIII

SPANISH

TOWN   SU BU RB   CR AC iE

NORTH STREET

BATON ROUGE

Plan
of the
UNITED STATES PUBLIC
Grounds
BATON ROUGE, La.
June 20th 1839.
A. Crawford. Surveyor

References

I Hospital Lot	Acres
II Ordnance Lot	
III Garrison Lot	
IV Magazine	
V Grave Yard	
VI Swamps	
VII Field	
VIII Wood Land	

Magnetic Variation

Rouge's earlier inns, Madame Legendre's, a two-story establishment on the corner of Florida and what is now Fourth streets and the town's only building of sufficient size to accommodate all the guests. Introduced to the six-year-old granddaughter of Duplantier, the elderly aristocrat remarked, "Mademoiselle, I am somewhat a lame old duck, but perhaps you would honor me with this dance?" Little Augustine Favrot giggled, "*Merci*, Monsieur, I would be happy to!" To commemorate his visit permanently, the town fathers shortly thereafter renamed Second Street "Lafayette Street," and so it remains.

But all was not cheerful and gay in Baton Rouge as the 1820s came to an end. Yellow fever decimated the Spanish community in 1828, and was followed four years later by an epidemic of Asiatic cholera that killed fully 16 percent of the town's population. Like most other communities at the time, Baton Rouge was generally vulnerable to sickness, especially to diseases like yellow fever and cholera that had their incidence increased by such conditions as poor drainage, inadequate sewage disposal, and the encumbering of public thoroughfares with mounds of garbage and horse manure. Most distressing of all was the primitive and limited level of medical knowledge. Most physicians relied entirely on bleeding, harsh and explosive laxatives, enemas, and the prescription of indescribably foul-tasting nostrums. Having no alternatives to such remedies, many patients may have looked forward to death with stoic resignation.

Between 1810 and 1830 the population of Baton Rouge increased by exactly four individuals—from 1,463 to 1,467. But by 1840 there were 2,269 town residents; by 1850, 3,905; and by 1860, 5,429. As historian Meriel Douglas suggested in 1955: "During the fourth and fifth decades of the antebellum era, Baton Rouge was transformed from a sleepy little river town, depending largely on steamboats for its contact with the outside world, to a more active river port and the state capital of Louisiana, with traders and businessmen and legislators from all parts of the state walking up and down its streets." It was in fact during the last three decades of the antebellum era that Baton Rouge took its first solid steps toward becoming a city—by expanding business and professional services, establishing the frail foundations of a school system, expressing more interest in the cultural and spiritual dimensions of community life, making the town cleaner and safer, and becoming the center of Lousiana's political and institutional development.

In 1833 there were 10 mercantile establishments in Baton Rouge, only three of which were constructed of brick. Most were located near the river along Lafayette or Main streets. Isadore Larguier owned a general store selling almost everything but clothing; George Heroman dealt in books and stationery; O.P. Davis operated a drug store; R.G. Delaroderie was the town's leading jeweler; and George Pike engaged in printing and bookbinding. By 1854 Heroman had expanded his business into a general

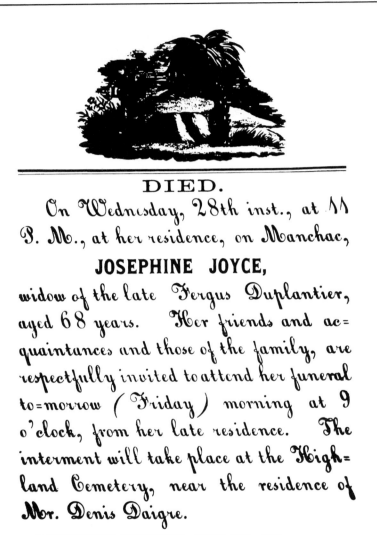

DIED.

On Wednesday, 28th inst., at 11 P. M., at her residence, on Manchac,

JOSEPHINE JOYCE,

widow of the late Fergus Duplantier, aged 68 years. Her friends and acquaintances and those of the family, are respectfully invited to attend her funeral to-morrow (Friday) morning at 9 o'clock, from her late residence. The interment will take place at the Highland Cemetery, near the residence of Mr. Denis Daigre.

BATON ROUGE, THURSDAY, SEPT. 29th, 1859.

☞ Carriages will leave the Stables of H. A. CASTLE, and SAML. B. HARBOUR, at 8 o'clock, Friday morning, to take down persons desirous of attending the funeral.

Prior to the Civil War, the principal business houses in Baton Rouge were located on Main, Lafayette, and Front streets. The latter thoroughfare faced the levee and contained primarily hotels and boarding houses, a bakery, and several grocery establishments and residences. This carte-de-visite view focuses on the buildings looking south from Main Street. Courtesy, Foundation for Historical Louisiana, Inc.

Above
Posting death notices around town was a common 19th-century custom. This one for Josephine Joyce, a member of the prominent Duplantier family and a resident of Manchac, was printed in 1859. Mrs. Duplantier was buried in the Highland Cemetery, which in recent years has been restored. Courtesy, Mr. and Mrs. James H. Huguet.

BATON ROUGE March 31 1860

— N. Gas Light Co

To W. F. Tunnard Dr.

MANUFACTURER OF AND DEALER IN CARRIAGES, HARNESS, WAGGONS, CARTS, PLOUGHS, IRON & C.

CORNER MAIN AND CHURCH STREETS.

1860					
Jan	24	for 5 L rod iron	8	40	
		33 " 2½ x ⅝ "	5	1.65	
		34 " ⅛ round do	6	2.04	4.09
	26	25 " bar iron	5		1 25
	28	328 " 1½ square do	6		19.68
Feb	3	84 " bar do	5		4 20
	6	40 " 2¼ x ½ do	5	2 00	
		1 bar 5/16 rd do		15	2 15
	13	50 3 x ⅜ bolts	10	5 00	
		157 L 2¼ x ⅜ iron	5	7 85	
		11 " 2¼ x ¼ do	7	77	
		11 " hoop do	7	77	14.39
	18	50 3 x ⅜ bolts	10	5 00	
		fitting 2 bits		1 50	6 50
	24	weld'g & piec'g crow bar		2 00	
		32 L ½ in round iron	6½	2 08	4 08
	29	20 " 1¼ x ¼ iron	6		1 20
Mar	2	91 " ¼ in square do	6½	5 91	
		draydge		25	6 16
	3	10 L 1 x ⅛ iron	7		.70
	17	38 bar do	5		1.90
	30	11 1 Light sgl brackets	63	6 93	
		4 1 " dbl "	80	3 20	
		2 1 " " fancy	2 50	5 00	
		2 1 " " #1888	2 50	5 00	
		2 1 " " #1848	2 25	4 50	
		1 2 " pendant #1906		7 50	
		1 4 " " #1662		4 63	
		1 4 " " #126		1 63	38.39
		Amt forwarded			$104.69

Right
Marie Adrien Persac was one of Louisiana's most significant artists during the 19th century. A landscape painter, surveyor, cartographer, architect, and teacher, he is well-remembered for his detailed gouaches of plantations in the state. Persac married in Baton Rouge in 1851 and died at Manchac in 1873. Two of his renderings of Baton Rouge buildings have survived as well as views of the city painted on porcelain and as a lithograph. Courtesy, Department of Archives and Manuscripts, LSU, Baton Rouge.

Left
Located on the corner of Main and Church streets, the three-story factory of W.F. Tunnard manufactured the very finest and most expensive carriages in the region, in addition to common buggies, plantation wagons, carts, harnesses, and iron goods. When the Civil War came, Tunnard closed his doors and went off to war with his sons. For a while the Confederate Government leased his plant to make cannon carriages, knapsacks, tents, harnesses, and blacksmithing products. This bill dated March 31, 1860, lists supplies sold to the Gas Light Company, which furnished the utilities to the town at that time. Courtesy, Department of Archives and Manuscripts, LSU, Baton Rouge.

This rare view of Baton Rouge around the second half of the 19th century was made by J.A. Maurel of the city and lithographed by X. Magny of New Orleans. To the artist, the Mississippi and its traffic seem to be paramount. Courtesy, Southeastern Architectural Archives, Tulane University Library, New Orleans.

store—one of the more prosperous in town—housed in Baton Rouge's newest building, at the intersection of Florida and Fourth streets. Heroman's principal competitors were Colonel A. Matta and A. Rosenfield.

Baton Rouge's banking needs were initially served by branches of several New Orleans institutions—the Carrollton Bank, City Bank of New Orleans, and the Bank of Commerce. The town's first hotels, all opened for business by 1835, were the Baton Rouge, Union, Exchange, and Madame Legendre's. The Harney House, named for Dr. B.F. Harney of the Pentagon garrison, was constructed on Lafayette Street in the late 1840s to accommodate legislators after Baton Rouge had become the state capital. The Harney House survived well into the 20th century as the Louisian Hotel.

As a parish seat Baton Rouge had its share of lawyers from the beginning. But as the town grew, and, especially after it had become Louisiana's capital, local attorneys multiplied almost geometrically with each passing decade. While most earlier practitioners of the law belonged to families long established in the area, the local bar soon became dominated by newcomers, many of them young careerists from the North. (Baton Rouge has continued to import Yankees at an unremitting pace.)

Among the town's first attorneys were I.H. Hatch and David Martin, whose offices were located on the corner of Main and Third streets. (Martin lived until 1856; his last words were, "I die a Christian and a Democrat.") By 1830 F.D. Conrad, Abner N. Ogden, Thomas G. Morgan, Charles Tessier, and H.H. Gurley had put up their shingles. Born in Connecticut in 1788, Gurley represented Baton Rouge in Congress from 1823 to 1831. He died a state district judge in 1833. Among the leading attorneys of the 1840s were H.M. Favrot, J.S. Barrow, Alexander M. Dunn, and J.J. Buck. Dunn and Buck became state auditor and district judge, respectively, in 1847. During the last antebellum decade the Baton Rouge bar included two mayors, John R. Dufrocq (1846–1855) and James Essex Elam (1859–1861); Elam's father, James M. Elam; a Louisiana Secretary of State and longtime prominent politician, Andrew S. Herron; and at least two wealthy planter-lawyers, R.E. McHatton and Joseph Joor.

Attempting, although none too successfully, to save lives from the myriad afflictions of the age were Baton Rouge's antebellum medical men—among them Thomas Beaumont, H.H. Brayton, G.W. Dearing, D.L. McKitrick, F.M. Hereford, and Thomas Rivers.

Most decent schools in early-19th-century America were nonpublic, either church-supported or private. Children who regularly attended school (public, parochial, or private) came primarily from wealthy or otherwise locally prominent families—from the elite, in other words. Thus, in contrast to present conditions and requirements, an overwhelming majority of American school-age children in the early 19th century

Right
Construction of this three-story building situated on the northwest corner of Church and Florida was begun in 1853 by George M. Heroman. For several years after 1879 it was occupied by the Louisiana Institute for the Deaf and Dumb. It then housed several different private schools as well as other offices. Many remember it as the location of the Baton Rouge Business College. It was razed about 1956. Courtesy, Department of Archives and Manuscripts, LSU, Baton Rouge.

BOOK STORE   BOOK STORE

Lytle
Photo
Baton Rouge La.

either attended briefly a second-rate school or never attended school at all. This situation was even more evident on the frontier and almost universally characterized the Southern frontier, where Baton Rouge was located.

In Baton Rouge, as in Hannibal, Memphis, or Natchez, the river provided salvation for the plucky few. There an enterprising youth could join a flatboat crew and escape to New Orleans, hustle on the wharves, or go to work on a steamboat where he might rise through talent and dedication to chief pilot, or even captain.

Young females had a somewhat easier time because their premachine-age mothers required their labor at home. As a result girls learned early to cook, sew, clean, mend, and maintain a home. The fortunate ones married, not uncommonly at 16 or 17, and went off to keep their own households. Others went off to help keep someone else's.

Baton Rouge's earliest schools originated amidst such conditions as the foregoing and had to continue coping with them. As was the case elsewhere, the best schools (while they lasted) were private, public schools were publicly disparaged and neglected, and only a small number of the town's white school-age children ever received a decent education. Most white children and all blacks, whether slave or free, had to learn from—and survive it if they could—the "school of hard knocks."

Baton Rouge, in effect, had no school "system," public or otherwise, prior to 1848. The town in earlier years paid marginally qualified teachers on an irregular basis to instruct "indigents"—white children in trouble with the law, or orphans. As required by the mildly reformist Jacksonian state constitution of 1845, the legislature in 1847 enacted a law making all white children between the ages of six and 16 eligible for state-supported schooling. In Baton Rouge, the best initial results of this statute were three public schools, which were in operation by 1848, two for boys and one for girls. All the schools remained understaffed, financially strapped, and poorly attended.

The reason for this neglect, as historian Douglas found, was that "education in Baton Rouge was dominated by the private school. The only influential schools in the community were called 'academies' or 'seminaries.' In short, emphasis was placed on [preparation for] higher education," to which should be added, for the sons and some of the daughters of the local elite.

Many private academies and seminaries came and went in Baton Rouge between about 1825 and the outbreak of the Civil War. Two of the relatively successful ones were the first St. Mary's, a Roman Catholic girls' school in brief operation during the 1830s, and the College of Baton Rouge, a pretentious semipublic high school whose doors were open from 1838 to 1841, and briefly again in 1844 before financial troubles forced its permanent closure.

The curriculum of such institutions typically included English, French, Spanish, Greek, Latin, algebra, geometry, higher mathematics, natural philosophy, history, geography, music, reading, penmanship, arithmetic and bookkeeping. All these subjects could obviously benefit a lawyer's son or merchant's daughter, but only the last four would have aroused or helped the town's more numerous Huck Finns, who rarely attended school anyway.

Historian Frederick Allen, in his 1936 study of Baton Rouge during the 1850s, fired a devastating critique at the town's limp commitment to public education:

The Free Public Schools were very poorly supported, the citizens preferring to pay the nominal price charged by the private institutions rather than patronize the "free schools." The public school system was poorly managed in all of its phases, and the taxes were not sufficient to support it. The idea of public schools was slow in taking hold in Baton Rouge, probably because of the wide gap between the classes and . . . the old system of private education was so firmly rooted, and had proven profitable to the paying classes for so long that no other was considered of any merit. ... Free public schools meant free education . . . and the word "free" carried with it the stigma of unworthiness. Anything which could be obtained for no extra cost was not considered as of any account, and could be discarded along with the "free pass" to the traveling medicine shows. ... The public school teachers were not ostracized socially, but in the business of education they were of practically no importance, and absolutely no influence.

Perhaps a succession of ephemeral private academies, catering to the prominent and teaching only the status-oriented curriculum of the classics and liberal arts, was better than no schooling at all for any Baton Rouge children. But probably few Southern towns during the antebellum period provided better schooling for their children than Baton Rouge, and a large number most likely did worse.

Unfortunately public education in Baton Rouge received only grudging support from the community for many years afterward. Ravaged and retarded by the Civil War, dislocated socially by emancipation of the slaves (the education of whose children and grandchildren remained deficient for decades), and unwilling to abandon the snobbery of the past, Baton Rouge, along with most of Louisiana, postponed making a genuine commitment to public educaton until the 20th century.

But the passing of nearly a century and a half has by no means settled the ultimate acceptance or success of public education in Baton Rouge. The traditional preference for private schools has drawn recent substantiation and added legitimacy from various afflictions of the public system. Consequently many Baton Rougeans who can afford it, along with some who really cannot, continue to enroll their children in private or parochial schools—and not merely to avoid federally mandated racial desegrega-

Above
The Collegiate Institute was organized in November 1855 by W.H.N. Magruder and was situated on Government Street at the site later occupied by the Louisiana State School for the Blind. After 33 years, its closing exercises on June 30, 1888, marked the end of the old school. Some of the most prominent leaders in the state and city received their education within its hallowed halls.

Right
The College of Baton Rouge, chartered on November 27, 1837, was located on a hill near South Boulevard several hundred yards from the Mississippi River and was later the site for the Deaf and Dumb Asylum. Both courtesy, Department of Archives and Manuscripts, LSU, Baton Rouge.

PROSPECTUS

OF THE

COLLEGE OF BATON-ROUGE.

BATON-ROUGE, August 7, 1841.

THIS INSTITUTION, designed for imparting to the youth of Baton Rouge and its vicinity, a thorough English, French, Mathematical, and Classical education, is now in successful operation : and is so organized as to deserve the patronage, and meet the approbation of all, who consider the morals, the health, and the literary and scientific improvement of youth, as matters of primary importance.

The location of the College, within the suburbs of Baton Rouge, and commanding a beautiful view of the Mississippi, is by far the most delightful, healthy, and convenient of any in Louisiana ; and the constant passing and repassing of steamboats, afford every facility for frequent communication between parents, and their sons coming from New-Orleans, from the various points on the Mississippi, the Red River, and their branches, and also from the Eastern parts of Texas.

The course of instruction pursued, is as extensive as in any other College in the United States, embracing Spelling, Reading, Writing, Arithmetic, Geography, English Grammar, Compositions, Algebra, Geometry, and the higher branches of Mathematics ; the Latin, Greek, and Spanish Languages ; the French and English Languages, Literature and Elocution ; Chemistry, Natural, Moral and Intellectual Philosophy ; Rhetoric, Logic, Political Economy, Book-Keeping, and all other branches taught in the best Colleges of the Union.

The Collegiate year is divided into two Sessions, comprehending forty-four weeks. The first Session, beginning on the 10th of January, ends on the last Friday in July ; and the second, commencing on the first Monday of September, terminates on the third Monday in December.

At the close of the Second Session a commencement will be held, and degrees conferred, securing to the graduates " all the privileges usually conferred by any University in the United States."

No student will be admitted into the College for a less period than one Session ; and all charges for each half Session must be in advance. No deduction will be made for loss of time, except in cases of extreme sickness. Each Student is required to furnish his bed and bedding, one knife and fork, one clothes-brush, one pail, two combs, one tooth-brush, and two napkins, and to dress in a style of neatness suitable to a Collegiate life.

The charge for board and tuition is $200 for a Collegiate year, and at the same rate for a shorter period. For mending and washing $36, will be required for the same time. All extra expense, incurred by sickness, or otherwise, must be borne by the Students incurring it. Necessary books and stationary will be furnished the Students, at the New-Orleans retail prices : Parents will be pleased on entering their sons to give to the President such special directions concerning the education and care of their sons, as may not interfere with the regulations of the College : which directions will, by him, be carefully attended to. All the members of the College will be free, and at perfect liberty to follow any creed, with respect to Christianity, which their parents may desire.

The College of Baton Rouge was established for the promotion of the dearest interests of our country. The patronage of the public is invoked for the accomplishment of this object ; and the hope is confidently cherished by the Trustees, the President and the Faculty, that the South will not suffer herself to be surpassed by the North in sustaining efforts essential to the prosperity and glory of her children.

REV'D. R. H. RANNEY, President of the College.

Hon. LOUIS FAVROT, President of the Board.

Col. P. HICKY,
LEON BONNECAZE,
Dr. A. DOUSSAN,
C. A. CROPPIN, } Trustees.

WM. JOYCE, Secretary of the Board.

N. B. The government and discipline of the College is strictly parental. Spacious and airy rooms, and an excellent nurse, are provided for the Students who may be indisposed : and the President feels himself personally responsible to the Trustees, and also to the parents of the pupils, for the good management of the College, and for the morals, health and comfort of the Students.

nisso del.

BATON ROUGE FEMALE INSTITUTE.

Mrs L.M. Fisher, Principal with three Associates.

This Institution was organized in 1837 and has since that time shared liberally in public patronage.

The Fall Session commences on the 1st of Octb. Vacation on the 15th of August. Great attention is paid to the health of the young Ladies. Only one case of serious illness has occurred among the boarders in nine years. It is intended that boarders shall enjoy all the attentions out of school hours, that could be extended to them in a well regulated home, they will eat at the table with, and be always under the immediate superintendence of the Teachers. Rules necessary for the happiness & welfare of the school are made and all are required to observe them. Annual examinations are held in April, and Friday of each week is devoted to reviews, at which time the Parents are invited to attend.

TERMS PER SESSION OF TWENTY THREE WEEKS.

Elementary Department $12

Higher Department. Primary Class 18

Orthography, Orthoepy and Definitions, Reading Writing Geography with Maps & Globes, Grammar, Arithmetic History, Moral Science Composition.

Higher Classes $20

Natural & Moral Philosophy, Exercises in Parsing & Transposing Descriptive Didactic & Epistolary Composition; Geography & Astronomy with problems on the Globes; Arithmetic, Algebra Geometry, Ancient & Modern History Rhetoric & Chemistry Botany & Analysis of Plants.

Department in Music $35

Vocal and Instrumental under the charge of Dr Grunneburg.

French $16 per Session

Board and Tuition in English $75, Washing $1 per month Furnishing Bed & Bedding $1 per month Plain & ornamental needle work without extra charge The Languages & Ornamental branches will receive as much attention as Parents may desire.

REFEREES:

Rev. P. Woodbridge. Baton Rouge
Hon. Judge Fessier
Capt. A. Gates
J. Scott, Esqr.
J. Phillips, Esqr.
Col. J. Stewart. West Baton Rouge
Rev. W. J. Scott, D.D. New Orleans
Rev. R.J. Stanton
Rev. J. Franklin Ford. Alexandria
Capt. Mumford. St Francisville
Rev. J. Purviance. Natchez Miss.
L.K. Clifton Esqr. Terre Bonne

Rev. J. Vancourt
Capt. R. Whitley U.S.A.
J.B. Scudder Esqr.
J. Reid Esqr.
Gen. J. Bernard
J. Mc Culop Esqr.
Rev. J. Twitchell
J. Waybin Esqr.
Rev. A. Hagaman. Jackson La
J. Iver Esqr.
Rev. Benj. Chase
Rev. D. Rawles. St. Marys

J. Manouvrier & J. Snell Lith. 33 Camp St. N. Orleans

Right

The old St. Louis Street School was an outstanding Baton Rouge building. According to an early resident, it was built around 1814 and was originally the parish courthouse until the 1856–1857 structure was erected. Reconstructed as a high school in April 1860, it was first called Academy Hall and then named St. Louis Street School. In addition to serving as an institution of learning, it was frequently used as an assembly hall for various functions in the city . The school remained in operation until its student body was transferred to the new Beauregard School in 1918. It was torn down to make way for the courthouse built in 1921–1923.

Left

During the antebellum period, only the convent schools in New Orleans were recognized as superior to those educational institutions established in Baton Rouge. According to newspapers of the time, numerous girls' schools operated, some of which survived only a year or two. One, the Baton Rouge Female Institute, also known as the Baton Rouge Academy or Mrs. Fisher's Academy, was founded in 1837 and was well-received locally. Both courtesy, Department of Archives and Manuscripts, LSU, Baton Rouge.

You are requested to attend a " Musical Entertainment, " at St. Mary's Academy, on

MONDAY EVENING, JUNE 1ST., 1857.

☞ Please present this Card at the door.

Much of the social life of Baton Rouge in the antebellum period revolved around invitational balls, thespian productions, visits by circuses, exhibitions and menageries, and the celebration of planned events at holidays. Supplementing these were public examinations of pupils and other school and church activities. The simple invitation reproduced here was to a musical at St. Mary's Academy. In the late 1850s that institution for girls occupied the buildings and grounds of the former Jesuit St. Peter and St. Paul's College on North Street. Courtesy, Miss May Lynn Amiss.

tion. Private and parochial schools are widely perceived to be better administered; better disciplined; unwilling to tolerate use of alcohol and other drugs; immune to the multilayered and unresponsive public bureaucracy; more willing to give good teachers freedom to teach well; inclined to use updated books, materials, and approaches; and thus more likely to produce a better educated student. Whether any or all of these perceptions are accurate is beside the point: there is an established *history* of private education in Baton Rouge that shows no signs of vanishing.

Lukewarm support, at best, for education in antebellum Baton Rouge was somewhat offset by enthusiastic participation in cultural and recreational activities. The performing arts came to town in 1821 with traveling companies of actors, comedians, and minstrels. For the next 40 years these entertainers were supplemented by circuses, state fairs (after 1843), readings, recitations, revivals, and concerts. The first showboat to dock in Baton Rouge arrived in 1833. By 1841 the town had its own amateur theatrical organization, perhaps the earliest forerunner of the modern and respected Baton Rouge Little Theater. "Such amusements deserve encouragement," the *Gazette* wrote concerning the local thespians, "as they tend to dispel *ennui*."

With the expansion in number and variety of performers who came to Baton Rouge, the quality of local criticism became more sophisticated. A mediocre artist inspired this flat comment in 1823: "Dwyer, a comedian of Irish birth, who had arrived in New York in 1810, was a polished gentleman, and had formerly been successful . . . But by 1823 he had grown obese and his present tour was unsuccessful." Almost 30 years later, in 1852, an apparently talentless singer named Anna Bishop received the following nasty review, as quoted in Alban Varnado's account of drama in early Baton Rouge:

She did not please our taste, and we candidly believe that she belongs to that class of bug whose name commences with hum . . . We really believe that there are thousands of young ladies in our State, in every respect her superior; and we think it not at all improbable that we could name half a dozen or more within an hour's walk of our office.

But Baton Rouge had no public auditorium, theater, or meeting facilities; consequently performances had to be staged in saloons, cramped private halls, tents, or the open air. Bemoaning a situation that afflicted Baton Rouge until the 1970s, a local journalist observed in 1855:

It is a remarkable fact, that here at the Capital of the State—the city of Baton Rouge, with a population of very little less than six thousand souls—that there is not a public hall; a theater; a reading room or any other public bulding whereat the people may meet in social reunion for public amusements. There is no reason for the fact, and therefore there is none to offer. . . . There are a hundred men in town who could put up such a building without feeling any pecuniary embarrassment, from the investment.

Early on Baton Rouge's mushrooming private wealth tended to remain in private hands, and no such buildings were erected.

Dancing in Baton Rouge was like marching in Prussia—it was something that everyone did, young, middle-aged and old. Dances were held at the Pentagon garrison, private homes, and rented halls. In 1859 a writer for the *Gazette and Comet* expressed the local Victorian (and British influenced) assessment of dancing:

As dancing has been and will be practiced until time's end, and as it is healthful exercise, harmless and proper, we would like to see all the boys and girls turn out to learn. We mean the temperate kind, not the hugging kind imported from France and Italy. Give us the old Quadrilles and Reels, and so forth. To these the Serious Family can not object.

There have always been plenty of bars and taverns in Baton Rouge, except during Prohibition in the 1920s when thirsty Baton Rougeans, along with other deprived Americans, learned to drink at home. In 1859 the most striking establishment was the Rainbow House Saloon on Third Street, whose interior had been recently done over in purple and gold— possibly the inspiration for LSU's subsequent colors! At the Rainbow "the very best wines, liquors and segars" could be had. The only other memorable opulent bar in antebellum Baton Rouge was located at the race track, which opened near what would become Magnolia Cemetery in 1845 and was renamed the "Magnolia Course" two years later.

Two spectacular events occurred toward the end of the antebellum period. In early March of 1858 a hot-air balloon, with "Professors" Williams and Wells in command, arrived in town. For a modest fee local citizens were allowed to risk their lives in return for a view of Baton Rouge from the lofty altitude of the balloon's gondola. On its last flight, according to a local newspaper account:

. . . The balloon went up at dusk, taking a northerly direction over the city. When it approached the forest it was discovered to be on fire and to be descending rapidly. It fell in the limbs of a dead tree back of the American cemetery, the navigator being hurled from the height of 40 feet to the ground, resulting in a serious sprain of the spine. His wounds are not considered fatal.

Nineteenth-century steamboats, many of them technologically primitive or inadequately manned, often exploded, providing vivid if grim fare for onlookers because such disasters usually resulted in tragic loss of life. On February 27, 1859, the *Princess* blew up just south of Baton Rouge, having departed from a local landing only minutes before. A large crowd of spectators witnessed the horrible aftermath from the levee. Bodies floated or thrashed about in the water. Those still alive, though

Many Baton Rougeans throughout the 19th century were afflicted with "gambling fever." They staged cockfights, raffles, lotteries, and boat races in addition to card playing and other games of chance. One popular diversion was that of horse racing. While several different courses operated during the 1800s, the most famous was the Magnolia Race Track opened in 1847. It contained a two-story building with a club room and bar, a judges' stand, and bleachers for men and women. By the 1850s, purses ranged from $50 to $500. The track was located near where Roseland Terrace was developed, and where the State Fair Grounds once existed. It is thought that this photograph is the historic course or a successor. Courtesy, Department of Archives and Manuscripts, LSU, Baton Rouge.

badly scalded, were quickly rowed ashore to Cottage Plantation on Conrad's Point where, "screaming and shrieking with pain," they were wrapped by slaves in sheets covered with flour, the standard treatment at the time for third-degree burns. Of 250 persons on board, 70 were blown to pieces (including the captain), drowned, or died subsequently. Several of the deceased were prominent local attorneys on their way to New Orleans.

By 1852 there were four church buildings in Baton Rouge, one each of the Roman Catholic, Episcopal, Presbyterian, and Methodist denominations. The Roman Catholic cathedral of St. Joseph's originated in the 1790s, was chartered by the legislature in 1820, and began to construct a new sanctuary in 1830. Prior to 1831 all sermons were delivered in French, but priests spoke in English more frequently afterward, reflecting the ongoing Americanization of the town. In 1852 St. Joseph's sanctuary seated 400 persons and church property was worth $12,000, making it the wealthiest denomination in Baton Rouge.

The Episcopal church of St. James, also chartered in 1820, did not erect a permanent sanctuary until 1847. (Mrs. Zachary Taylor was a member of the congregation.) The Presbyterians formally organized in 1827 and constructed a building two years later. Baton Rouge's Methodists were the last to organize, in 1834, but grew more rapidly than any other denomination: by 1852 their sanctuary was the town's largest with a seating capacity of 450.

In addition to regular religious services the Protestant churches held numerous fairs, box suppers, and pie sales, both for fund-raising purposes and to provide a wholesome social life for their members. St. Joseph's made money by conducting lotteries, a then-legal predecessor of Sunday bingo.

Continued prosperity, additional town revenues, and public insistence produced a cleaner and safer community by 1861. Streets in the central area were improved, a hook-and-ladder company was established to fight fires, the town constructed several modern cisterns to provide water, and the police force cracked down more effectively on public drunkenness, theft, prostitution, and other nuisances. It should be stressed, however, that the police sought not so much to prevent as to contain lawlessness and vice within their acceptable habitat, the river front, leaving the "better" areas of Baton Rouge peaceful and unmolested. Solving individual crimes was not then the basic mission of the police force; rather the constabulary was to keep the criminal classes "in line" and apart from the law-abiding citizenry.

By far the most compelling reason for Baton Rouge to get itself in order was the state legislature's decision in 1846 to make the little river town Louisiana's capital. Except for a mercifully brief year of imprisonment in Donaldsonville (1830–1831), the seat of state government had been in New Orleans since commencement of statehood in 1812. New Orleans—whose fine dining establishments, theaters, opera house, baroque saloons and "quadroon balls" all spelled S-I-N to a growing majority of fundamentalist Protestant Louisianians—had become unacceptable as a place to transact public business. Legislators and other officials could not be expected to resist that wicked municipality's numerous temptations, not all of which were of the flesh. Enemies of the Jacksonian common man—bankers, cotton factors, land speculators, agents of Yankee business, together with their servile and unscrupulous attorneys—also corrupted the Crescent City in the opinion of up-country reformers. Removing the people's representatives from the clutches of that piratical elite became just as necessary to many upstaters as getting them out of bars and whorehouses.

The constitutional convention of 1845, which contained a sizable number of anti-New Orleanians, therefore ordained that Louisiana's capital should thenceforth be "no closer than 60 miles" to nasty New Orleans, but left to the legislature the responsibility of settling upon a precise location.

Above
The original building of the Presbyterian Church in Baton Rouge located on the corner of Main (later Church and then North Fourth) was dedicated in 1829. In 1854 the structure shown here replaced it and was used until 1926, when a new building was built on the northeast corner of North Boulevard and North Seventh Street.

Facing page
Top
This 1843 notice from the Washington Fire Company No. 1 advises members of the scheduled time for the periodic cleaning of the engine. Members of volunteer fire companies of Baton Rouge always exhibited great pride in their respective fire engines. Firemen washed, cleaned, and oiled them regularly and the company foreman reported monthly on the condition of the apparatus. A penalty of 25 cents was imposed on active members who failed to appear for a "washing."

ATTENTION!

WASHINGTON FIRE COMPANY NO 1.

———

Baton Rouge, Aug. 25, 1843.

Mr.

You are hereby notified to attend a washing of the Washington Fire Engine No. 1 to be held at the Engine House on Saturday, the 26th, at o'clock P. M.

By order of the Foreman

Secretary.

Baton Rouge,   186

M C. R. French

To ST. JAMES' CHURCH, Dr.

For Rent of Pew, No. 5 , four quarter , ending

31st. March 186 Cr. By Cash $30. 00

Received Payment   20

Balance $10.00

Treasurer.

Left
Many churches during the 19th century supplemented their regular "income" through charity benefits and other means. One form of certain revenue was from the renting of pews. This receipt for partial payment for the rent of pew No. 5 at St. James Episcopal Church was paid by Dr. Cornelius R. French, a physician and leading civic figure, until his death in 1863. All courtesy, Department of Archives and Manuscripts, LSU, Baton Rouge.

This was a broad constitutional mandate, permitting the legislature to move the capital as far away as Shreveport or Monroe, both hundreds of miles from New Orleans. But many legislators—including those from New Orleans itself, about a third of the total—had grown accustomed to the delights of the Crescent City. Consequently Baton Rouge quickly emerged as the ideal choice—a tolerable location as close to the fleshpots and brokerage houses of New Orleans as could reasonably and constitutionally be attained.

Civic pride largely blotted out the legislature's condescending and insulting considerations. Baton Rouge the new state capital! Some local citizens donated land for a statehouse while East Baton Rouge Parish officially appropriated $5,000 in 1847 for site acquisition. Merchants, hotelmen—and saloonkeepers—rubbed their hands in gleeful expectation of more business. And well they might, because a new "industry" was coming to town, one that would grow to employ thousands of permanent customers and their dependents a century later.

New York architect James Dakin was hired to design a new statehouse, and he came up with a proposal radically different from the prevailing habit of copying the federal capitol in Washington. Dakin conceived a medieval castle, complete with turrets, cupolas, and crenellated parapets, in what has been termed the Neo-Gothic style. The cor-

nerstone was laid on November 3, 1847; construction went on for two years with dedication ceremonies finally scheduled for December 1, 1849. But eight days prior to that happy event, a disaster befell Baton Rouge in the form of a raging fire that wiped out one-fifth of the town. Among other results of the catastrophe were two positive ones—upgrading of the local fire department and the future construction of more brick buildings than wooden ones.

Ten years after its completion, Louisiana's unique statehouse made the pages of *DeBow's Review*, the antebellum South's most prestigious publication: "Grand, gloomy and peculiar, the capitol stands in solitary majesty on the banks of the river. It looks like one of those ancient castles, whose ruins now line the banks of the Rhine." Samuel L. Clemens (Mark Twain), a steamboat pilot in the 1850s, saw the "sham castle" often and did not like it at all, believing it was pretentious, undemocratic, and ugly. Baton Rougeans, on the other hand, felt combatively proud of the building and its interior. After some visitors were beheld expectorating on the premises in 1853, the *Daily Comet* editor erupted:

A man who lays any claim to decency, who will throw his quid (of tobacco) on a beautiful carpet like that was once, in the Hall of the House, or who will set in a corner and squirt his tobacco juice on the mouldings of pannel work, should

be unceremoniously removed, as his counterpart the small cur dog.

The statehouse was not the first, and by no means the last, state building or facility constructed in Baton Rouge. By 1835 a state penitentiary had risen in the center of town. Built of brick with individual cells on its second floor and working areas beneath, the prison turned out cotton garments, leather goods, and tools from the inmates' labor, which caused the facility to become unpopular with Baton Rouge's free artisans who had to compete with cheaper prison products in local markets. Even so, the prison itself was soon a financial burden on the state; this induced officials to lease the inmates' labor to a private contractor in 1844. Two other leases followed until the Civil War disrupted the operation. The warden's house, on the corner of Seventh and Laurel streets, is all that remains of the penitentiary complex and is, moreover, one of the mere handful of antebellum buildings surviving in Baton Rouge.

In 1858 an "Institute for the Mutes and the Blind"—subsequently the State School for the Deaf—was completed at its initial location on the corner of South Boulevard and Saint Ferdinand Street. The parish jail was remodeled at about the same time.

As Frederick Allen perceptively observed, "The growth of Baton Rouge, previous to its selection as the site for state institutions, had been of the mushroom type, ill-planned, hurriedly erected, makeshift as to use, and rapidly deteriorated; there was no thought of the possibility of future usefulness." Although these characteristics were temporarily overcome in the 1850s, Allen (who wrote the above in 1936) might have lingered in town long enough to witness the reappearance of similar difficulties in the post-World War II period.

Probably without realizing the full scope of imminent tragedy, Baton Rougeans in the 1850s were on a collision course with reality. The small but prosperous town was the capital of a slave state at a time when slavery's future in the United States had become seriously threatened.

In 1854 a new political party calling itself "Republican" came into being at Ripon, Wisconsin, from whence it spread eastward across the other free states. Although the Republicans initially sheltered some fringe elements—advocates of free love and prohibition, for example—the party's backbone was antislavery, including some abolitionists who demanded termination of the institution at once, and far more numerous "free-soilers" who tolerated slavery where it existed, in the South, but opposed the expansion of slavery into the territories. Only two years after its birth, the Republican party almost won the presidency in 1856 owing to solid support given its nominee, John C. Frémont, in the populous free states. Looking forward to 1860, Republican leaders knew that victory could be theirs by adding the electoral votes of one or two free states to their 1856 winnings.

The earliest state institution built in Baton Rouge was the Louisiana State Penitentiary, which occupied the entire block between Florida and Laurel and was bounded on the west by St. Anthony (North Seventh). Begun about 1833, it was a brick building forming four sides of a hollow square. Within its walls prisoners manufactured plows and other tools, bagging, bale rope, clothing and other textiles, and molasses barrels. During the Civil War the buildings housed Federal troops. This picture taken during the occupation shows Union tents of the First Artillery in front of the largest building of the prison complex. Courtesy, Department of Archives and Manuscripts, LSU, Baton Rouge.

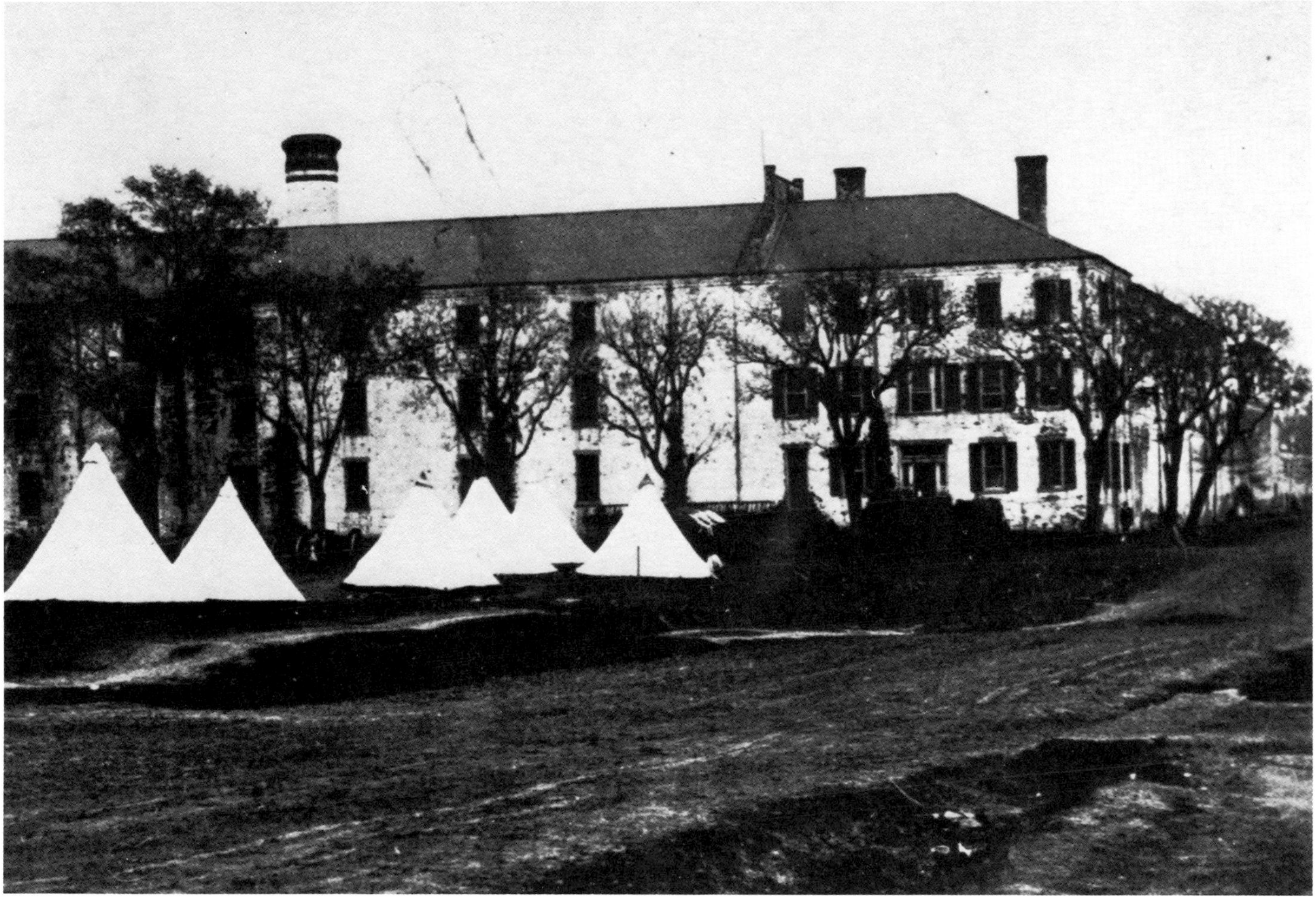

GRAND
VOCAL CONCERT OF SACRED MUSIC,

FOR THE BENEFIT OF THE

FEMALE ORPHAN ASYLUM.

Presbyterian Church, 8 o'clock P. M. July 1st. 1858.

PROGRAMME.

PART FIRST.

1. PSALM 79—" Old Hundred," :   FULL COMPANY.
2. SOLO—" Angels ever bright & Fair," Mrs. HUGUET.
3. CHANT.   -   -   -   -   JUVENILE GLEE CLASS.
4.   Jubilate Deo,   -   -   FULL COMPANY
5. SOLO—"He doeth all things well," Mrs. SLOSSON.
6. QUARTETTE—" Watchman tell us of the Night, "   ——————
7. DUET—" The Old Kirk Yard,"   Mrs. GUION & Mr. WALLER.
8. SOLO—" Ruth and Naomi,"   Miss BARKER.
9.   Gloria Patri,   -   -   FULL COMPANY.

PART SECOND.

10.   Grand Te Deum, -   -   FULL COMPANY.
11. SOLO—"Eve's Lamentation, "   Mrs. GUION.
12. DUET—" Messenger Bird, "   Mrs. DUPLESSIS & Mrs. SLOSSON.
13. HYMN.— -----   -   -   Mrs. GUION'S GLEE CLASS.
14. SOLO—"I know that my Redeemer liveth. " Miss GIBBS.
15.   " Pilgram Fathers, "   FULL COMPANY.
16. DUET—" Eli, "   -   -   -   Mrs. GUION & Miss GIBBS.
17.   " Benedic Anima Mea "   FULL COMPANY.
    CONCLUSION, : : : : : L. M. DOXOLOGY.

The risk of *losing* votes had also to be minimized. Hence, instead of nominating a well-known and probably controversial person in 1860, the Republicans chose an obscure, ex-Whig congressman from Illinois named Abraham Lincoln. Lincoln had gained a measure of renown in 1858 by running against, and losing to, Democratic United States Senator Stephen A. Douglas, a one-time favorite of Southern slaveowners because of concessions he had made to them in Congress. In a series of debates with Douglas, Lincoln had asked the Senator some probing questions about slavery in the territories, which the Senator had not convincingly answered. Consequently Lincoln had acquired stature with fellow Republicans and opponents of slavery while Douglas, though winning re-election to the Senate, had slipped several notches with Northerners and Southerners alike who found him uncomfortably "soft" on slavery expansion.

Stresses within the Democratic Party caused that organization to split into two factions—to the immense delight of Republicans—during the 1860 campaign. The cause of polarization was a decision handed down three years earlier by the United States Supreme Court in the case of *Dred Scott* v. *Sanford.* Put simply, the Court had said that slaves, as property, could be taken by their owners into any of the territories owned in common by the American people. Southerners, naturally, were overjoyed by the decision because it seemed to offer slavery a new lease on life by enabling it to expand. Northern abolitionists and free-soilers, Abraham Lincoln among them, were appalled by the decision for obvious reasons.

When Southern Democrats at the national party convention in Charleston, South Carolina, failed to secure a platform guarantee that slavery would not only be permitted but protected in the territories, some of them walked out. Senator Douglas subsequently received the nomination of "loyal" Democrats, while Vice President John C. Breckinridge of Kentucky was chosen by the defecting Southerners and their sympathizers. A group of worried old Whigs in New England joined with anxious border-staters in an *ad hoc* organization called the Constitutional Union party, which nominated John Bell of Tennessee for President. With Republican nominee Lincoln included, there were thus four presidential candidates in 1860.

Baton Rougeans, together with most other Southerners, could choose between only three of these men—the name of Lincoln, nominee of an antislavery party with no Southern following, was omitted from ballots in the Deep South. A vote for Breckinridge was a vote for slavery expansion, possibly at the risk of war since many Northerners had become unalterably opposed to slavery expansion, the Supreme court notwithstanding. Douglas straddled the issue while Bell ignored it altogether, calling only for "the Constitution, the Union and the laws." Thus a troubled Southerner who placed peace and preservation of national unity first (even though he might also wish to keep his slaves) would have favored Douglas, or more likely, Bell. An ardent supporter of slavery above all would have been a Breckinridge man.

Baton Rouge had become politically aware, involved, and excitable during the era of Andrew Jackson and Henry Clay in the 1830s. The arrival in town of the state government made residents even more politically conscious. In behalf of one candidate or another, local political clubs held rallies, parades and barbecues—customarily enlivened by generous servings of liquor—prior to every state and national election. Members of local "chowder-and-marching" societies managed to keep their behavior within the bounds of decency, for the most part, but the bitterly contested 1860 presidential campaign produced at least one destructive episode, criticized by the *Gazette and Comet* on September 18:

A company of men paraded the streets under the influence of whiskey, committing outrages on persons and property. People fled before them, stores and houses closed their doors and they had possession of the city for a time. Their names or the names of many of them are known, and the editor demands that the city officials get to work and prosecute them.

When ballots were tallied in Baton Rouge after the polls had closed on election day, Bell led with 379 votes, followed by Breckinridge with 274 and Douglas with 98. When Bell and Douglas votes are combined, it is seen that "moderate" candidates outpolled the proslavery extremist, Breckinridge, by almost two to one. This result should not be surprising in a town such as Baton Rouge, whose economy depended crucially upon river traffic, which in turn required continuation of peace and national unity. Bell and Douglas men in Baton Rouge, as elsewhere in the South, might own slaves whom they wished to keep in bondage, but they desired even more fervently to stay in business and remain solvent.

Breckinridge led statewide with 22,681 votes to 20,204 for Bell and 7,675 ballots for Douglas. As the result of his plurality in popular votes, Breckinridge received all of Louisiana's electoral votes, but it must be noted that Bell and Douglas combined received about 5,000 more popular votes throughout Louisiana than Breckinridge did. Along with most voting Baton Rougeans, many other Louisianians might have wished to preserve slavery in 1860, but not at any cost.

Republican Abraham Lincoln won the election with a required majority of electoral votes, even though he received only 39 percent of the national popular vote. Lincoln accomplished this paradoxical feat by narrowly carrying all the heavily populated free states, except for New Jersey, which he divided with Douglas. Breckinridge carried all slave states, except for Kentucky, Tennessee, and Virginia, which supported Bell; and Missouri, which went for Douglas. Although Douglas ran second in the national popular vote, because he ran closely behind Lincoln in all the free states, the Senator finished a poor fourth in electoral votes because he carried only Missouri and a fracton of New Jersey.

Sixty-one percent of those who voted in 1860 had chosen someone other than the winner, which made Lincoln the most dramatic minority president in history. No losing candidate's supporters were angrier or more apprehensive than slave–owning Southerners who had backed Breckinridge. To them a Lincoln administration was unthinkable—had he not denied their rights in the territories, legitimized by no less an agency than the Supreme Court? Almost overnight Breckinridge supporters became secessionists, convinced that further debate and discussion were futile; the slave-owning South must pursue its own destiny, apart from the Northern free states.

On December 20, 1860, South Carolina left the Union, followed quickly by Mississippi, Florida, Georgia, and Alabama. Louisiana Governor Thomas O. Moore, a Rapides Parish cotton planter, issued a call on November 19 for a special session of the legislature to convene in Baton Rouge on December 10. Addressing them on that day, Moore remarked, "I do not think it comports with the honor and respect of Louisiana as a slaveholding state, to live under the government of a Black Republican President." At Moore's insistence, legislators set January 7, 1861, as a day for electing delegates to a state convention that would decide Louisiana's course of action in the ominous gathering crisis.

Those seeking election to the convention presented themselves either as "secessionists" or "cooperationists." The former believed in immediate secession; cooperationists did not rule out secession entirely, but wanted to wait until President-elect Lincoln was inaugurated on March 4, 1861, to see what his Southern policy would be. Should Lincoln, in office, prove unacceptable, then secession might be resorted to. Most Breckinridge men, of course, were secessionists; the moderate partisans of Bell and Douglas took their moderation with them into the cooperationist camp.

Baton Rouge elected men of both persuasions to the convention; E.W. Robertson, Tom Bynum, Bat Haralson, and a "General Carter" served as secessionist delegates, while cooperationism was represented by William S. Pike, Dr. I.A. Williams, Andrew S. Herron, and J.C. Fuqua. Other vocal Baton Rouge cooperationists included Mayor James E. Elam, C.D. Favrot, and three members of the prominent Stuart family—Nolan A., J.D., and Colonel R.A. Stuart.

Secessionist delegates controlled the Louisiana convention, and on January 26, 1861, the delegates adopted an ordinance of secession by a vote of 112 to 17. Most cooperationists chose to vote with the majority in order to reduce discord. After two months' existence as an independent republic, Louisiana ratified the Confederate Constitution, which had been drafted in Montgomery, Alabama, during early February by a group of men from several Deep South slave states, including Louisiana. Louisiana had crossed a Rubicon, taking happy, prosperous, provincial, and somewhat pompous little Baton Rouge with it.

Onrushing events would soon inflict upon Baton Rouge the most devastating and traumatic ordeals that the town and its citizens would ever experience, comparable to an apparently contented and healthy individual being suddenly assaulted physically, losing his job, and suffering a complete nervous breakdown all within a short span of time. The town, its economy, and its character would require decades to recover from what lay ahead.

Jules Lion made this lithographic portrait of William S. Pike in Baton Rouge in 1837. Pike was later a delegate to the Louisiana Secession Convention and noted banker, merchant, and entrepreneur. He migrated to Baton Rouge as a young man and as he accumulated wealth he participated in many projects that helped to develop the city. In the 1860s he moved to New Orleans and lived there until his death in 1875. Courtesy, The Historic New Orleans Collection.

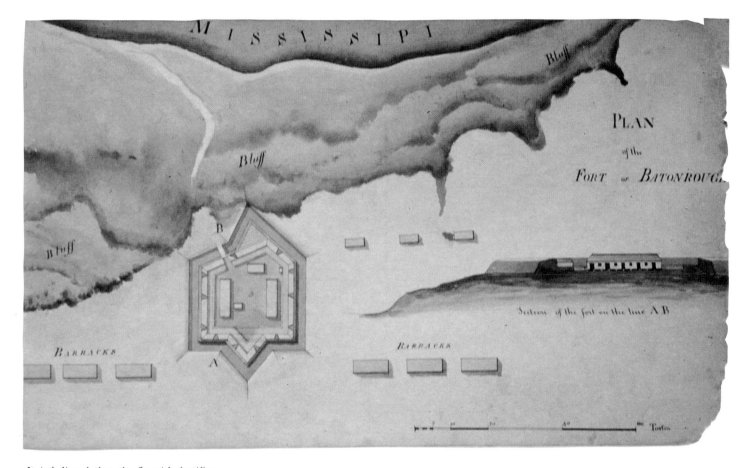

It is believed that the Spanish fortifications at Fort San Carlos were located on the bluff near where the Pentagon Barracks now stand. This handsome map by B. Lafon drawn about 1814, four years after the United States assumed control over the District of Baton Rouge, shows the plan of the fort and a detail of one of its barracks. Courtesy, The Historic New Orleans Collection.

Above
W.T. Kummer of Philadelphia dated his pencil, ink, and watercolor drawing of the Pentagon Barracks at Baton Rouge 1821. At the time, galleries were attached only to the inside of the buildings and there were gun portals on the exterior building on the right. The year the sketch was done, a reservoir was constructed underneath the courtyard. In the foreground of the picture, one can see the overflow spout on the bank. The powder magazine on the left was pulled down in 1826. Courtesy, Magnolia Mound Plantation.

Left
This interior of the Princess by Adrien Persac is dated 1861 and is the earliest known painting of a Mississippi River steamboat. It is probably a memory picture commemorating Persac's wedding trip with his bride, Odile Daigre, following their marriage at St. Joseph's Catholic Church Number 2 at Baton Rouge in 1851. Courtesy, Anglo-American Art Museum, LSU, Baton Rouge. Gift of Mrs. Mamie Persac Lusk.

Many views of American towns published in the 19th century bore little resemblance to their true appearance. This lithograph of Baton Rouge was taken from a sketch made by Henry Lewis (1819–1904) while on a trip from the Falls of St. Anthony to the Gulf of Mexico in the late 1840s and appeared in his Das Illustrirte Missississippithal *(1854–1858) while Lewis resided in Düsseldorf, Germany. It is difficult for one not to be skeptical of this charming panorama of the city. Courtesy, Louisiana State Museum.*

In the early 19th century, painting was often a hobby of ladies of refinement. This delightful folk painting of Baton Rouge was done probably between 1825 and 1835 by Josephine Favrot. To our knowledge, it is the very earliest surviving view of the city done by a native of the area. Miss Favrot died in 1836. Photo courtesy of Anglo-American Art Museum, LSU, Baton Rouge—on loan by the St. Clair Favrot family.

This lithograph entitled Baton Rouge (Capital of Louisiana) *was drawn by Adrien Persac circa 1857. It is entirely a Louisiana piece—depicting a town in the state, by a Franco-Louisianian, lithographed by Pessou and Simon of New Orleans, and published there. Courtesy, Anglo-American Art Museum, LSU, Baton Rouge. Gift of James H. Huguet.*

Following the West Florida Rebellion, United States President James Madison authorized Governor William C.C. Claiborne (residing in New Orleans) to take possession of West Florida as far as the Perdido River. The governor proceeded to Baton Rouge and on December 10, 1810, the short-lived Army of the Republic surrendered and its lone-star flag was lowered for the last time. U.S. troops occupied Fort San Carlos and Claiborne assumed control of the fort, town, and District of Baton Rouge for the United States. Claiborne the officer is the subject of this lovely miniature. Courtesy, The Historic New Orleans Collection.

State of Louisiana   Parish of East
                                      Baton Rouge

To the Rev. Mr. Jas. Purviance. Greeting

You are hereby authorized to join in
marriage John Buhler Esq. of this Parish
to Mrs. Frances S. Coit of the same Parish
there appearing no lawful cause of
impediment to the same
Given under my hand this 25th of
April 1837   Ch. Tessier

Above

The Louisiana Secession Convention convened in Baton Rouge at the State Capitol on Wednesday, January 23, 1861. On the following day an ordinance to "Dissolve the Union between the State of Louisiana and other States . . ." was introduced and two days later, by a vote of 113 to 17, secession became a reality. This unique oil painting by Enoch Wood Perry, Jr., was probably a preliminary sketch prepared as a model for a larger painting which was to be done later. Courtesy, Louisiana State Museum.

Left

Appointed by Governor William C.C. Claiborne after Louisiana became a state, Charles Tessier served as judge of the parish of East Baton Rouge for some 30 years. This delightful 1837 document signed by Tessier authorizes the Reverend James Purviance to unite John Christian Buhler, Jr. and Mrs. Frances S. Coit in marriage. Buhler, a large landowner and early settler, served for 15 years as sheriff of Baton Rouge. Courtesy, Department of Archives and Manuscripts, LSU, Baton Rouge.

Right

The view of Baton Rouge presented on this Bohemian porcelain shaving mug was copied from a lithograph done by M. Adrien Persac around 1857. It is one of three hand-painted views of the city executed on china before the Civil War. To our knowledge, Baton Rouge is the only city in the Mississippi River Valley for which there are hand-painted views prior to the period 1861–1865. Courtesy, Anglo-American Art Museum, LSU, Baton Rouge. Gift of Friends of the Museum.

Looking east (probably from the observatory on the Heroman Building) Andrew Lytle photographed the Union encampment in the sparsely inhabited area between Florida and Convention streets. The large brick building to the far right is the newest Presbyterian Church and the wooden one directly behind is the earlier house of worship. Department of Archives and Manuscripts, LSU, Baton Rouge.

CIVIL WAR AND AFTERMATH

The afterglow of honor, dedication, and bravery that subsequently and fittingly enshrined the "Lost Cause" has enabled later generations to forget that not all Southerners in 1861 were hell-bent to secede and whip "greasy Yankee mechanics" in battle. Available evidence demonstrates that most informed Baton Rougeans would have preferred that Louisiana remain in the Union and that no efforts be spared to prevent the eruption of civil war between Northern and Southern Americans. Whether they owned many slaves, few slaves, or no slaves, other Southerners felt similarly. But Southern peace-seekers had lost the initiative to "fire-eaters" by 1861, with tragic consequences for both sides before the guns became silent and the nation was reunited.

In their early stages wars impose fascinating effects on mass psychology. Animosities and differences of opinion dissolve in emotional displays of unity and patriotism. It is also generally assumed that hostilities will be brief and "our side" will win. When World War I, for example, broke out in early August 1914, Russia's Nicholas II—widely loathed by his subjects beforehand—was greeted when he appeared on a palace balcony by an immense crowd tearfully singing "God Save the Czar." Several hundred miles westward the Czar's cousin (and enemy) Kaiser Wilhelm II assured German troops departing for the front that they would "be home before the leaves fall," a prophecy that applied all too soon only to the dead and wounded.

Kindred attitudes and behavior were expressed in Baton Rouge, and throughout much of the South, during the first weeks and months of the secession crisis. Leading Baton Rouge newspapers initially condemned secession as a rash and potentially dangerous act, but once it was accomplished—and Fort Sumter fired upon—local journalists joined the community at large in giving enthusiastic support to the Confederate cause. (To commemorate the South's first victory in the war, the Rainbow saloon on Third Street became the "Sumter" saloon, and a cannon was imbedded in the sidewalk in front of the establishment. The cannon remains to this day.) As future parish superintendent of schools Robert Aertker revealed in his LSU master's thesis about Baton Rouge during the Civil War, the town was initially proud, optimistic, and confident: "The leave takings of local soldiers were, of course, elaborate affairs. Eating, drinking, speeches, gifts and merrymaking preceded these ceremonies which often commenced many hours before the troops left."

Recalling several departures of local volunteers 60 years later, a Baton Rouge resident provided a nostalgic and gripping description:

The Pelican Rifles were the first to go. It was Sunday and the whole town had turned out to wish them Godspeed. I remember it well; it seems as though it were yesterday. The men and women lined the river bank, cheering, laughing, shouting to friends and relatives who were marching up the gangplanks to the big steamboat. The sun was shining and the girls were dressed in light dresses and wore flowers on their hats . . . nearly every man aboard that boat had a sister, or a wife, or a mother, or a sweetheart in the crowd on shore.

Kissing! I've never seen anything like it! Why, everyone kissed everyone else, whether they were friends or not. Mr. Mouton had a cannon and at intervals it sent its reverberations through the air . . . as long as the boat was in sight, the cheering and waving continued.

The Delta Rifles went a week later. There were 118 men rank and file; it was the kid glove company. This company had been organized at Port Allen. . . . The membership of the Delta Rifles was composed of young men of three parishes; West Baton Rouge and the town of Baton Rouge proper furnished about an equal

During the Civil War an early volunteer military unit was the Baton Rouge Fencibles. After 1865 the group was one of the city's leading military companies. It was in charge of the unveiling of the Confederate Monument in 1890. Here the Fencibles stand with their outstretched banner. Courtesy, Don B. Hearin III.

number of men, and there were some twelve or fifteen from Point Coupee. It was a select organization—composed mostly of boys of wealthy parents—and that was why it was called the kid glove company.

I remember the girls of Slosson's, Castleton's, Readvilla—all schools for young ladies—and the children from other schools turned out in full force to say goodbye to the Delta Rifles. Girls kissed boys they had never seen before. . . . I remember one girl. . . had married the night before. . . her husband never came back.

Well before the young men of Baton Rouge met their supreme test (and often their deaths) at Manassas, Berryville, and Shiloh, the town's first "military" engagement had taken place at home, a farce in which the Federal Pentagon garrison fell to the superior arms of such seasoned "veterans" as the Pelican Rifles, Creole Guards, and Baton Rouge Fencibles. In advance of Louisiana's actual secession, Governor Moore assembled several hastily raised, inexperienced, and amateurishly led militia companies in Baton Rouge to seize the barracks and arsenal. Commanding the 80-man Federal contingent was Major Joseph A. Haskin, a one-armed professional who had fought the Mexicans. A "real" soldier, Haskin viewed with contempt and disdain the militia units camped on North Boulevard; to their demand that he capitulate, the major replied, "I've lost one arm in the defense of my flag and I will lose the other, or even my life if necessary, before I surrender to that lot of ragamuffins on the Boulevard."

But as militia reinforcements continued to arrive, Haskin put aside his initial bravado for the sober realization that he was overwhelmingly outnumbered and could not himself be reinforced. On January 12, 1861 the major gave up, apparently without firing a shot, thus persuading his untrained conquerors that war was fun. But unlike other Southern towns such as Richmond, Raleigh, and Montgomery, which remained under Confederate control for virtually the entire war, Baton Rouge was destined to enjoy only 16 months under the Stars and Bars before the United States government reestablished its authority, if somewhat tentatively, in May of 1862.

While about one in three males from East Baton Rouge Parish served voluntarily either in the Confederate army or in local militia prior to Federal reoccupation of the town, Baton Rouge nonetheless had its share of cowards, slackers, and silent Union sympathizers. Collectively these men were looked down upon by their pro-Confederate neighbors as "Druthers" because "they would 'druther' not fight, or would 'druther' stay at home." Early in the war voluntary enlistments fell off sharply as casualty lists lengthened. Because the conflict was not expected to last long, moreover, the first periods of enlistment had been short, and as they expired the troops returned home, leaving both armies short of men. Conscription—what Americans would later call the draft—was soon the inevitable recourse: in 1862 for the Confederacy and for the Union the following year. But because Baton Rouge slipped out of the Confederate orbit before the Southern conscription law could be fully implemented, few Baton Rougeans were "drafted" into the Rebel army.

Local civilian endeavors to aid the Confederacy remained sincere and consistent for as long as Baton Rouge was a Confederate community. Fund-raising affairs were held, prominent ladies organized the "Campaign Sewing Society" to provide clothing for boys in the field, and other sources of assistance were made available. William Watson, an Englishman residing in Baton Rouge who served in the Confederate army, summarized relief efforts put forth by Baton Rougeans early in the war:

Aged men and women furnished donations in money according to their circumstances. Poor families set to work in preparing shirts, underclothing, stockings, and other necessaries. Wealthy merchants and employers, whose employees and clerks would volunteer for service, made provisions for their families or dependents by continuing their salaries during the time they volunteered for service. . . . Mothers with tears in their eyes came up with their sons of 15 and 16 years of age. . . and requested that they might be accepted as volunteers.

In the spring of 1862 these efforts came to an end. On April 25, the day before New Orleans fell to a Yankee fleet under Admiral David Farragut, Confederate authorities decided to abandon Baton Rouge, moving the state government first to Opelousas and soon after to Shreveport, Louisiana's Confederate capital for the duration of the conflict. Before departing Governor Moore ordered the destruction of cotton in danger of capture by the enemy. "At Baton Rouge on April 26," as Civil War historian John Winters tells us, "Negroes slashed open bales of cotton and set them afire. Along the levee flaming bales were rolled into the water to float downstream. Flatboats piled high with cotton were drenched in alcohol and whisky and ignited with blazing pine knots and set adrift. Neither cotton nor liquor was to be left for the invader." On the morning of May 9, Commander James S. Palmer of the Federal gunboat *Iroquois* landed in Baton Rouge with a small party and took possession of the Pentagon barracks and arsenal. In the same manner that it had withdrawn from the Union a year before, Baton Rouge returned to Federal control—without resistance. Having raised the Stars and Stripes, Palmer warned local officials that any Rebel attempt to reoccupy the town would be met with force; he then departed on the *Iroquois*.

About two weeks later a band of guerrillas attacked a shorebound rowboat bearing an officer from U.S.S. *Hartford* (Farragut's flagship) with a load of dirty laundry he intended to have cleaned in town. The *Hartford*, together with another warship, the *Kennebec*, proceeded to bombard Baton Rouge, causing a local panic, some civilian casualties, and damage to several buildings including St. Joseph's Church and the Harney House

Above
The old Arsenal Complex, located on the northern limits of the city, dated back to the 1820s and 1830s. When the Union troops first occupied Baton Rouge in 1862, they found 11 fine buildings comprising that military installation. This Civil War picture taken by photographer Lytle features the main arsenal building on the right and the stately officer's house on the far left.

Left
In May of 1862, after a band of guerrillas at Baton Rouge attacked a small boat of U.S. sailors, Admiral David G. Farragut ordered his warships to fire on the town. During the shelling Farragut's flagship, the **Hartford**, was one of those vessels inflicting severe damage to the houses near the river and the more substantial buildings farther to the east.

Right
The name of this street was appropriately changed to Church (now North Fourth) Street by the Board of Selectmen in 1857. The building with the steeple is the Methodist Church. Part of the heavy brick facade of old St. Joseph's Catholic Church on Main at Church Street is visible in the background. All courtesy, Department of Archives and Manuscripts, LSU, Baton Rouge.

Hotel. The next day, May 29, 1862, Brigadier General Thomas Williams came ashore with six United States infantry regiments, two artillery batteries, and a cavalry troop. Federal occupation of Baton Rouge had begun.

General Williams, a hard-driving regular army officer and an insensitive martinet, treated his own men much more harshly than he dealt with Rebel Baton Rouge, which he generally left alone so long as the town behaved peaceably and obediently, which it did once the general's disposition became known. While attempting to take Vicksburg some time earlier, Williams had worked troops and black volunteers alike to exhaustion and death, digging canals and preparing other futile projects. Arriving in Baton Rouge just in time for one of the town's unusually hellish summers, the general ordered constant drills and inspections in full equipment. His soldiers, recruited from Wisconsin, Michigan, and Vermont, were unused to such heat and many dropped in their tracks and, in some cases, died. Soon, according to historian Winters, "the military cemeteries of the city had to be enlarged to accommodate the increasing number of dead," while "nearly half of the entire garrison at Baton Rouge was on the sick list."

Before autumn's cooling breezes arrived, this debilitated, demoralized, depleted band of Yankees had to resist a serious Confederate attempt to retake the town in what became the third, and last, battle of Baton Rouge.

After the North's initial attempt to seize Vicksburg failed, in the early summer of 1862, the Confederate high command resolved that the enemy should be further harassed and kept off balance. An immediate objective was the recapture of Baton Rouge, which might permit the Rebels to regain access to the Red River—and with it supplies from northern Louisiana—and even menace Federal control of New Orleans. Accordingly, on July 27, 4,000 Confederate troops left Vicksburg by train for Camp Moore in Tangipahoa Parish, Louisiana, about 50 miles northeast of Baton Rouge. Major General John C. Breckinridge—Vice President of the United States from 1857 to 1861 and the Southern Democratic nominee for President in 1860—commanded the expedition. Breckinridge's artillery would soon crash into the homes and businesses of some of those who had voted for, and against, him two years earlier. The Confederate plan was to squeeze the Federals at Baton Rouge between Breckinridge's troops attacking from the east and the formidable Confederate ram *Arkansas*, which was on its way downriver to neutralize the Federal warships near the town. The role of the *Arkansas* was crucial, because if it did not arrive in time Union naval gunfire would rake Breckinridge's advancing columns.

The campaign did not unfold smoothly for the Confederates. "While waiting for the *Arkansas* to be sent. . . to Baton Rouge," Winters writes, the soldiers under Breckinridge "languished at Camp Moore without

Above
Major general John C. Breckinridge led about 2,600 men in the Battle of Baton Rouge. The battle was a temporary tactical success for the Confederates, but due to the fact that the Confederate ram Arkansas *developed engine trouble and was destroyed by its crew, Breckinridge did not receive necessary support and had to give up the position he held momentarily. He served as Vice President of the United States from 1857 to 1861 and as the Southern Democratic nominee for President in 1860. From Cirker,* Dictionary of American Portraits, *Dover, 1967. Engraved by John C. Buttre from a daguerreotype by Mathew Brady.*

Right
Shortly after the Civil War, in 1867, the Baton Rouge National Cemetery opened. Within two years there were 2,925 interred. Evergreens such as holly, wild peach, and bay were planted along its shell walk and elsewhere. This 1870s photograph was taken by Lytle. Courtesy, Department of Archives and Manuscripts, LSU, Baton Rouge.

shelter from the summer heat and rain, and many of them sickened. In a few days' time the epidemic reduced the ranks to about three thousand effectives." Departing at last, on foot, for Baton Rouge, the Confederates experienced a "nightmare." Only about two-thirds of the Rebels wore shoes, "and the sandy road became almost unbearable to those who were barefoot. Some of the men were bare to the waist; some dressed only in rags. Each man staggered through the blinding heat under the weight of a full pack. There was little water along the route. . . . Thirst-crazed men sighting a stagnant pond pushed aside the thick, green scum and drank greedily. Soldier after soldier, weakened by the heat, bad water, and dysentery, fell out. . . ." By the time Breckinridge reached Baton Rouge he "had only twenty-six hundred men to carry into battle," despite his having acquired additional troops at Camp Moore.

The Civil War Battle of Baton Rouge would thus be fought by an approximately equal number of physical wrecks on each side: men too worn out, hungry, or sick to withstand prolonged exposure to the stresses of combat. Whether Rebels or Yankees, most participants in the engagement should have been in a hospital ward rather than on a battlefield.

Certain that the *Arkansas* would arrive at any moment to support him, Breckinridge commenced his attack at daybreak on August 5. The Confederate line stretched in a semicircle from where Plank Road now branches off from Scenic Highway, on the north, to Clay Cut Road in the vicinity of Webb Park Golf Course, on the south. (In 1862 this entire area lay "out in the country" beyond the eastern periphery of town. Most contact between the combatants occurred around the national cemetery—many Union dead being buried where they fell—near Dufrocq School and as far west as the present Federal Building and Court House (the old post office) on Florida Boulevard.

The battle was a temporary tactical success for the Confederates, whose thirsty and exhausted right wing and center pushed the equally thirsty and exhausted Federals all the way back through town to the protection of Federal gunboats on the river. The Confederate left, however, almost collapsed. There Colonel Henry Watkins Allen, of Allendale Plantation in West Baton Rouge Parish, was severely wounded in the legs, his fall so shocking to the weary troops under his command that they would advance no further. (Allen survived the battle, rose to brigadier general, and rendered outstanding service as Louisiana's last Confederate governor.)

But the *Arkansas* never came. It developed engine trouble four miles above Baton Rouge and was destroyed by its crew. This forced General Breckinridge to withdraw eastward back to the Comite River, out of range of the unmolested Federal gunboats, giving up the town he had momentarily taken and held. Shortly afterward Breckinridge moved to occupy Port Hudson, a stronger position on the Mississippi River just north of Baton Rouge, which held out until July of 1863, the last Confederate stronghold on the river to capitulate.

The battle fought at Baton Rouge in the blazing summer heat of 1862 was not one of the more spectacular in history. Even among Civil War engagements it was relatively minor. Approximately 383 Federals were killed, wounded, captured, or missing in action. (Among the dead was General Williams, who took a hit in the chest and died at once.) Confederate casualties reached a slightly higher total of 456. Federal General U.S. Grant, by contrast, would lose 17,000 men in a few hours at the Battle of Cold Harbor two years later. About 2,500 troops from each army participated in the Battle of Baton Rouge, which was over by ten in the morning, thereby avoiding the worst August heat in Baton Rouge that descends in midafternoon.

For the town itself, however, the battle and its aftermath were dev-

Below
In the 1850s Baton Rouge was the chief trading point for the Florida parishes. One old-timer recollected that wagons for supplies frequently traveled to the city from as far as Liberty, Mississippi, on the north and the Pearl River on the southeast. This rare photograph taken around the time of the Civil War includes the riverfront from Main Street south to North Boulevard and the State Capitol. Courtesy, Department of Archives and Manuscripts, LSU, Baton Rouge.

astating. Hundreds of terrified civilians streamed southward, the only direction possible, along Highland and River roads, to escape the noise, horror, and death of battle. Many of them, maddened by hunger, thirst, and fear, broke into homes, farms, and plantations along the way, gorging themselves with food and drink and plundering their neighbors' property as they went. Gunfire from both sides—especially from the Federal gunboats—badly damaged many buildings. A great many homes and other structures had been razed earlier by Federal troops to provide clearer lines of fire and to make their position more defensible. After Breckinridge and his men retreated in the afternoon, the Federals cut down innumerable trees in order to build barricades in case the Confederates resumed their attack.

Concerned for the security of New Orleans, where he himself was, General Benjamin F. "Beast" Butler, overall Federal commander in Lou-

isiana, ordered the evacuation of Baton Rouge a week after the battle. On August 21, the Federals departed downriver for the Crescent City. Baton Rouge, a "once-beautiful town," according to one account, was left "with its shade trees felled, its streets littered with debris, and over one-third of its houses burned or wrecked by the troops. . . . a shocking sight."

Although the Federal army had abandoned Baton Rouge, the navy did not. The gunboats *Essex* and *No. 7* were detailed to stay offshore and fire on the town should the enemy reappear in force. By then Breckinridge was in Port Hudson and the Confederates sought to inflict no further grief upon Baton Rouge.

With New Orleans in no apparent danger either, the Federals returned to Baton Rouge on December 17, 1862. Brigadier General Cuvier Grover reoccupied the town with 7,000 troops, more than twice the number commanded by the late General Williams. This time the Yankees were in town to stay, not only for the duration of the war, but until the termination of Reconstruction in April of 1877, although by that time the garrison had been reduced considerably in size.

Baton Rouge remained a Yankee town from December of 1862 until the war ended almost two and one-half years later. Although no further major military engagements took place in the immediate locale, Yankee patrols were maintained, and Rebel foragers were occasionally shot at or chased off. The town became a staging area and base of supply for Federal operations upstream. Support of the siege of Port Hudson continued until 1863 and was followed by launching the ill-fated Red River expedition of Federal General Nathaniel P. Banks in 1864.

Present-day "unreconstructed" Rebels will be dismayed to discover that there was no resistance to Yankees in federally occupied Baton Rouge as there would later be to Nazis in occupied France, for example. Yankees, of course, were not Nazis; they were fellow Americans who spoke the same language, shared many of the same customs and values, and longed for the war to end so they could go home. After summarizing the Federal occupation of Baton Rouge, Aertker concluded with a plausible assessment: "It would probably be a rightful assumption that as the occupation continued, feelings of animosity toward the invader dwindled and when a job was well done it received its just plaudits from the people." When one recalls that Baton Rouge was not a den of secessionists to begin with, the town's willing acceptance of Federal authority, when that acceptance became inevitable, should not be surprising. Even the presence, for a while, of black troops in Baton Rouge does not appear to have caused unusual difficulties. (Many of the city's white citizens, however, did not wait out the occupation, choosing instead to leave their homes, not to return until 1865.)

What did prove to be naggingly difficult was recovery from the dam-

Above
Perhaps no photograph by Lytle during the Civil War expresses more vividly the tragic plight of citizens than this one taken circa 1863. In August 1865, a "Rambler" toured the city and elaborated on the startling changes since the war. Spanish Town was for the most part divested of its original buildings except for an occasional Negro cabin or modest dwelling of the poor. In fact, virtually all improvements north of North Street from the river to Dougherty's Square, except for John Hill's house which had served as headquarters, were burned and a total waste.

Right
Three Federal soldiers stationed at Baton Rouge entertain a civilian at camp circa 1863. Frequently, officers took pride in their quarters and wrote letters home detailing the steps they had taken to make life more comfortable. Many acquired loot from homes in the city and surrounding country. One cannot help but question how the furniture seen here was obtained. Both courtesy, Department of Archives and Manuscripts, LSU, Baton Rouge.

NOTICE!

PROVOST MARSHAL'S OFFICE,
Baton Rouge, La., January 10, 1863.

On and after Saturday next, (January 17th) no contrabands to be allowed about the streets of the ci.y, without a pass, signed by those in charge of them, or some officer of the "Provost Guard."

No contrabands to be allowed to occupy houses, other than those assigned to them by the "Quartermaster"—under the approval of the "Provost Marshal," except by an order from the "Provost Marshal," or one of his "Deputies."

No colored persons (contraband or otherwise) allowed about the streets of the city after 9 o'clock P. M.

No enlisted man allowed about the streets of the city, without a pass from the General Commanding Post, Brigade Commanders, or Surgeons in charge of Hospitals. Passes for men belonging to unbrigaded commands, must be procured from the General Commanding Post.

No soldier or soldiers belonging to the "Provost Guard," are allowed to enter houses (public or private) for the purpose of search, without a written order from the General Commanding Post, the "Provost Marshal," or the "Deputy" commanding the District in which said search is to be made.

No person or persons allowed to sell intoxicating liquors, without an order from the "Provost Marshal."

No meetings or gatherings (of any character whatever) for amusement or other purposes—to be held or permitted—without permission from the "Provost Marshal."

By order of

C. GROVER,

Brig. Gen. Comd'g. Post.

W. H. SEAMANS,
Captain and Provost Marshal.

Above

Major Samuel M. Hart helped to promote the welfare and growth of Baton Rouge through much of his lifetime. He was credited with being one of the first to adopt brick instead of the customary wood for store buildings. Recognized as one of the wealthiest in the city at the time of the Civil War, he lost a fortune but in the postbellum period engaged in various business ventures including a bank, wagon factory, and foundry. Elected by his peers, he was the very first fire chief of the city. His son, Mayor Robert A. Hart, later continued his father's efforts to build up the city. Courtesy, Mrs. John T. Anderson.

Left

After temporary abandonment of the city as an outpost, Federal troops returned in December 1862 under Brigadier General Cuvier Grover and remained there until the end of Reconstruction. This 1863 broadside was posted around Baton Rouge in January and laid down the rules both for civilians and Federal soldiers. Notice the regulations concerning contrabands who were posing quite a problem then. Courtesy, Department of Archives and Manuscripts, LSU, Baton Rouge.

age and chaos of war. Soon after hostilities ceased, a local newspaper expressed in statistical terms what the community had lost since 1861:

88,000 freed slaves	$8,000,000
100 buildings burned	300,000
cattle and crops destroyed	100,000
15,000 cotton bales burned	1,500,000
5,000 cotton bales stolen	500,000
property carried off or destroyed	50,000
horses and mules lost	150,000
	$10,600,000

Although the number of freed slaves far exceeded the number in Baton Rouge alone and must have included losses in several surrounding plantation parishes, the newspaper gave no more than a conservative estimate, since it would have been impossible to account for all property stolen or destroyed during the conflict. Even so, if one can imagine a disaster resulting in a $2–2.5 *billion* property loss to present-day Baton Rouge, one can begin to perceive the comparable damage inflicted on the community by the Civil War. Added to, and at the same time resulting from, war losses, came a sharp decline in assessed value of property parish-wide—from $10,259,000 in 1861 to $3,458,000 in 1865.

Not included in the newspaper assessment were "ripple effect" damages: losses not realized or foreseen at the time but all the more harmful in the long run because most of the defeated South would suffer from them. These included the drying up of local investment capital, prolonged dislocation of transportation facilities, disrupted and diminished markets, loss of morale and initiative, emergence of a vulnerable one-crop agricultural economy, and an unsatisfactory labor situation. Most of these problems had been resolved in the Baton Rouge area by the 1920s, but two of them—inadequate capital and labor—still afflicted Baton Rouge when the author was a little boy, and that was not too long ago.

The only redeeming result of the war was emancipation of the slaves, a moral imperative long overdue. (But emancipation spawned its own serious dilemmas, as will soon be noted.) In other respects participation in the Civil War did more harm to the South and to Baton Rouge than is possible to express concisely. Like Germany after the Thirty Years' War, the South showed the destructive social, economic, and moral ravages of the Civil War for decades afterward.

But life does go on for those who survive. As the veterans returned, Baton Rouge endeavored to clean itself up, start rebuilding, and resume as normal an existence as possible. Fraternal organizations, churches,

Right
A Turkish bazaar, described in adver-
tisements as the "8th Wonder of the
World," drew a large crowd in front of the
old Harney House Hotel. Eight hundred
dollars in silver, gold, and greenbacks
were given away daily. The man with the
derby a little to the left of center presided
over the event and an orchestra stationed
on the roof of the veranda furnished mu-
sic. Acting upon a petition from citizens,
the mayor shut down the bazaar in 1875.
Courtesy, Department of Archives and
Manuscripts, LSU, Baton Rouge.

Below Right
For several decades immediately follow-
ing the Civil War, ex-Confederate soldiers
established and actively supported vet-
erans associations while their womenfolk
honored the "Lost Cause" and its partici-
pants through similar organizations. The
first annual reunion of the Baton Rouge
Confederate Veterans Association was
celebrated on May 20, 1879. Members
formed a procession at Pike's Row on
Florida Street and proceeded to Pike's
Hall on Third Street for a morning of busi-
ness and refreshments. In the evening
every seat was filled for dramatic presen-
tations and dancing. This program lists
officers of the Association and those giving
responses to the concluding toasts of the
day. Courtesy, Miss May Lynn Amiss.

Far right
Even during the Civil War there was regu-
lar theatrical activity in the town. After
Union occupation the Baton Rouge Vari-
eties Company resumed performances
and in 1864 the troupe, then managed by
Miss E. Forrest, presented its season at
Academy Hall, the public school. In con-
temporary newspapers the building was
popularly called the "Union Theater."
This unique playbill for May 18–19, 1864,
lists plays offered and shows the admis-
sion for adults to be 50 cents. Courtesy,
Department of Archives and Man-
uscripts, LSU, Baton Rouge.

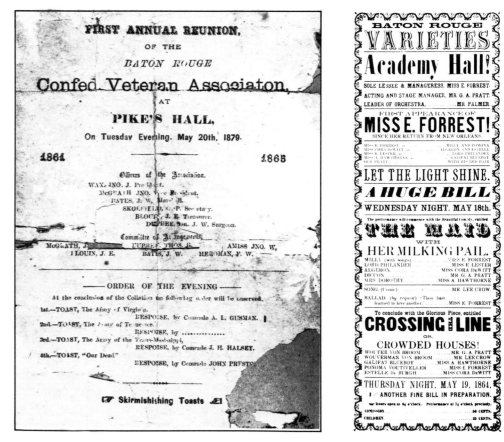

Above

Built around 1861 by William S. Pike, Pike's Hall was located on the east side of Third Street between Convention and Florida. In the early days of the Civil War, ladies of Baton Rouge assembled there to make clothing for the Confederate army. Later the Hall was used as a hospital for the sick and wounded and as quarters for soldiers during the battles of Baton Rouge and Port Hudson. *Courtesy, Department of Archives and Manuscripts, LSU, Baton Rouge.*

Right

The historic old building in this 1900 photograph, Pike's Hall, Pike's Opera House, or Third Street Theater, was Baton Rouge's only real theater until the spring of 1900. Although the building was originally constructed around 1861, its interior was not completed until after 1866. Only small and local companies performed there until railroad service was instituted in the 1880s, and then larger troupes bringing special scenery and effects were booked. Moreover, many political conventions were held there including ones nominating Kellogg for governor in 1872, Moncure in 1874, Wiltz in 1880, and S.D. McEnery in 1892. *Courtesy, Baton Rouge Room, East Baton Rouge Parish Library.*

and business groups once again sponsored balls, fairs, benefits, and similar entertainments. Pike's Hall, Baton Rouge's sole theatrical structure until 1900, went up in 1861 in the second block of Third Street. In that spacious, though privately owned, facility, Baton Rougeans regularly enjoyed dramas, comedies, and musicals. The town even raised a baseball team, the first "Red Sticks," who were inept enough to have made the early New York Mets seem champions by comparison. In two games played in 1867 the locals were stomped 54 to 24 in seven innings by the local occupation troops and utterly wiped out (100 to 0!) in nine innings by an outfit called the "Southerns." A new race course opened on Highland Road the same year and evoked the following newspaper description of how the "sport of kings" was carried on in rough-and-tumble post-bellum Baton Rouge:

The judges will settle no squabbles between private parties. The fastest horse will win the race. Colored people will be removed from the track if they do not behave like white people. No fighting will be allowed until after the race and then not within six hundred yards of the track. No liquor to be brought on the ground, "outside" of the person carrying it.

As the quote suggests, crime and violence were common in Baton Rouge during the late 1860s, with fights, robberies, murders, drunkenness, and prostitution heading the list of convictions. Both free blacks and whites were among the culprits, but whites were much more alarmed by black crime than by offenses committed by members of their own race.

Four years after the war Baton Rouge had made little tangible progress toward recovery; in 1869 a visitor described the town as being "at a dead standstill." Although a number of new businesses had opened, the volume of trade was sluggish and Baton Rouge was not prosperous. Had the seat of state government returned to town in 1865, the local economy would have received at least a modest boost. But the Federals made New Orleans the state capital, and the Crescent City retained that distinction—and the business that went with it—until 1882 when state officials again moved upriver, permanently, to Baton Rouge.

In 1870 only five men in the entire parish could be described as wealthy in terms of their own standards: John A. Dougherty, the most affluent, owned property worth $161,000; next was Charles A. McHatton, who was worth $150,00; followed by F.M. Hereford ($116,500), R.H. Phelps ($109,575), and Nathan K. Knox ($59,250). Dougherty and McHatton were planters, Hereford a physician, Phelps a civil engineer, and Knox a "money-lender." As would be true also of many wealthy Baton Rougeans in the post-World-War-II era, not one of these gentlemen was a native of Baton Rouge or of Louisiana.

Among Baton Rouge churches only St. Joseph's had incurred damage

Above
For about 60 years, Baton Rouge photographer Andrew D. Lytle preserved his city's history through the camera. He came to Louisiana's state capital around 1857 and remained there until his death in 1917. During the Civil War Lytle served as an agent for the Confederate Secret Service and recorded practically every aspect of the war experience—civilian hardships, camp scenes, and military installations, officers from both the Union and Confederate armies, and gunboats on the Mississippi. After 1865 he continued to capture the times through his photography. Without Lytle many of the subjects preserved in this book would have been lost to future generations. Courtesy, Louisiana Arts and Science Center, Baton Rouge.

Facing page
Top
This valuable photograph, taken about 1866 near Lytle's studio on Main Street, shows the intersection of Main and Third under Capdevielle's sign. Farther to the east can be seen the roof of St. Joseph's Catholic Church set back from the street. The two-story white frame building on the left is Mrs. J.N. Piper's furniture store. Brooks' Drug Store was situated next to Lytle's building. Courtesy, Don B. Hearin III.

Left
This two-story building situated on the south side of Main Street between Lafayette and Third, housed Lytle's studio for many years. On the ground level to the left may be seen Lytle's shingle and framed examples of his portraiture. Photographers frequently placed invitations in the newspaper to come by and view their work. When this photograph was taken prior to 1890, the Fougerrouse shoemaking business was also there. Courtesy, Louisiana Arts and Science Center, Baton Rouge.

Above
The simple frame building in the center was the original St. James Episcopal Church completed in 1846 and consecrated on May 23, 1847, by Bishop Leonidas Polk. It was later moved from the present church site to Convention Street where it is pictured here with a group of parishioners. Courtesy, Louisiana Arts and Science Center, Baton Rouge.

Above left
This photo of the interior of Lytle's home at 720 North Boulevard in Baton Rouge was probably taken between 1885 and 1890. A curious blend of architectural styles and furnishings is apparant. A framed Audubon print, an Elizabethan chair, and mill work from the antebellum period exist next to wallpaper and a dining room suite of the 1870s and a lamp and leather library chairs from the late 1880s. Wicker, rattan, and palms were used in an attempt to "lighten" the heavy appearance of the room. Courtesy, Louisiana Room, LSU Library, Baton Rouge.

Right
This former Brothers' School on the corner of North Fifth and Laurel streets became the synagogue of the Hebrew Congregation of Baton Rouge in 1877. The city's first Jewish group was organized in 1859 and changed its name to Congregation B'Nai Israel (Children of Israel) sometime prior to 1882. The synagogue, which appears here before an annex was built, was torn down in 1954. Courtesy, Department of Archives and Manuscripts, LSU, Baton Rouge.

Far left
The Baptist Church of Baton Rouge was organized on September 30, 1874, with 15 women and three men. Its first pastor was Walter E. Tynes, an independent missionary from the state of Mississippi. This little brick building, constructed about 1882, was located on the south side of Florida Boulevard between North Third and Church (later North Fourth). It remained the house of worship until a new sanctuary was occupied in 1920. Courtesy, Department of Archives and Manuscripts, LSU, Baton Rouge.

Left
The Very Reverend Cyril Delacroix was pastor of St. Joseph's Catholic Church during the turbulent years of 1865 to 1893. It was during his tenure there that the sanctuary and "Grotto of Lourdes" were built. This rare photograph of the interior shows St. Joseph's prior to 1924. Courtesy, Mr. and Mrs. A.M. Hochenedel.

during the war. All church buildings fell into disrepair, however, owing to wartime privation, and services were held erratically until 1865. Even though membership in all denominations increased dramatically afterward—especially among the black congregations—pastors were poorly compensated, repairs were makeshift, and services remained barely adequate for years.

All schools in Baton Rouge, both public and private, essentially closed down in 1862 when the Federals arrived. Despite repeated efforts by a handful of dedicated citizens, public education went nowhere in the immediate postbellum period. By 1871, according to Aertker, of 17 public schools in the parish, only two were in Baton Rouge itself. Both were elementary schools attended by a mere 127 pupils. The town's five public schoolteachers were paid $65 per month. On the other hand 10 private schools in Baton Rouge served 450 pupils. Emancipation had added another dimension to the town's traditional preference for private schooling—racial segregation. Because postbellum public schools were initially open to both whites and blacks, a majority of white parents enrolled their children in private or parochial schools to keep them away from black children.

After the buildings of the Louisiana Seminary of Learning at Pineville burned down in 1869, the institution moved to Baton Rouge where it briefly occupied the facilities of the State School for the Deaf. The following year, by legislative act—the first of many of its kind in Louisiana—the seminary became Louisiana State University. In 1877 the institution absorbed the State Agricultural and Mechanical College, previously located in New Orleans. Heading the university during the turbulent 1870s was David French Boyd, a charter member of the original 1860 faculty and a former Confederate officer. A lifelong servant of LSU—as was his younger brother and eventual successor, Thomas Duckett Boyd—David Boyd helped the institution grow and develop in many ways. But he almost caused LSU to disappear, because of his determination that LSU should remain for whites only. When presented with an essential ultimatum by the Reconstruction government that he either accept black cadets or forfeit state financial support, Boyd chose the latter. If a change in administrations had not occurred in 1877, LSU might not have survived.

With hardly more than a squad of cadets by that time, the insolvent little military academy gave no indication of becoming the vast "city-within-a-city," provider of leaders, athletic colossus, source of most local culture, and major Baton Rouge employer of a century later.

Economic hard times notwithstanding, Baton Rougeans, like most other Americans in the pretelevision era, remained avid newspaper readers, and the town's press evolved into recognizable journals during the postbellum period. The old *Gazette*, having merged with the *Comet* in

Above
In February 1879, William T. Sherman, commanding general of the United States Army, visited LSU and reviewed the corps of cadets. Sherman had been the institution's first superintendent in 1860. Though the general served "on the other side" in the Civil War, he continued to cherish his association with the University and to support it in various ways. From Cirker, **Dictionary of American Portraits**, Dover, 1967. Courtesy, New York Historical Society.

Left
Torn down in 1965, this fine old building on the east side of Church Street (North Fourth) was originally the home of Major Samuel M. Hart in the 1850s. It was once the residence of LSU President David F. Boyd and later that of politician, community leader and utility-company owner John D. Fisher. Prior to its becoming the Parish House for St. James Episcopal Church, it was used by the Knights of Pythias. Courtesy, Department of Archives and Manuscripts, LSU, Baton Rouge.

Above
Born in Baton Rouge in 1834, Douglass C. Montan was prominent in the city for many years. He was a successful merchant, editor of the **Advocate**, president of the Grosse Tete Railroad, state senator, city councilman, and parish treasurer. Montan is, however, best remembered for his book **Red Stick; or, Scenes in the South**, published under the pen name B.R. Montesano in 1856. Although the book was labeled as fiction, the close resemblance to actual people in the city caused speculation as to whether it was indeed solely an invention of the mind. Courtesy, Department of Archives and Manuscripts, LSU, Baton Rouge.

Above
David French Boyd, a member of the original faculty of the Louisiana State Seminary of Learning in 1860, returned from the Civil War to become its superintendent. For the next 15 years, largely through his sacrifices and efforts, Boyd kept the institution, renamed Louisiana State University in 1870, from utter failure. Removed in 1880 by an unfriendly board of supervisors, he later returned for a brief period as president before resigning. Up to his death in 1899, Boyd felt unappreciated; nevertheless his successors today recognize his numerous contributions to the university in its formative years. Courtesy, Department of Archives and Manuscripts, LSU, Baton Rouge.

1850, did not long survive the war, perishing in 1868. Its rival, the *Democratic Advocate* (1842–1853)/*Daily Advocate* (1853–1857) continued as the *Tri-Weekly Advocate* until it became a daily again in 1874. In 1882 the *Advocate* absorbed the *Capitolian* to become the *Daily Capitolian Advocate*. Between 1888 and 1904 it became, once more, the *Daily Advocate* until purchased in the latter year by a Shreveport publisher who renamed it the *Times*. When it combined with the *State* in 1909, the paper assumed its final and familiar name, the *State-Times*.

The multifaceted dilemmas created by emancipation of the slaves cut across and massively disrupted all aspects of Southern life after 1865, and conditions in Baton Rouge conformed to the regional pattern. White attitudes toward blacks rapidly hardened during the postwar years and by 1882, when Baton Rouge again became Louisiana's capital, its leading white citizens were convinced and outspoken racists. What the leaders preached, the white public readily accepted, and postbellum Baton Rouge's determination to segregate blacks in a subordinate status from whites has bequeathed its divisive, inequitable, and irrational residue to the present.

Black slavery originated in Baton Rouge, as it did elsewhere in Louisiana, during the 18th century, but the institution did not become locally significant until the early American period. In 1820, as historian William L. Richter found, there were 266 slaves in the community. That number had multiplied fivefold to 1,247 chattels by 1860. After 1840, approximately one adult white in three owned slaves in Baton Rouge, with the number of slaves possessed by each owner averaging five. How the percentage of mulattoes among Baton Rouge slaves increased from 20 in 1850 to 29 in 1860 has not been explicitly accounted for, at least not by local residents. The increase could have resulted from miscegenation between white males and female slaves, a frequent practice in the antebellum South, or from importation of mulatto slaves into the Baton Rouge area.

Male slaves in Baton Rouge were foundry and sawmill workers, apprenticed to carpenters, bricklayers, and other craftsmen, or were "hired out" by their owners (of whom white females comprised a sizable number) to perform whatever tasks the employer directed. Urban dwellers working at urban occupations, Baton Rouge slaves were, however, surrounded by armies of other slaves who labored at the more widespread tasks of cultivating cotton and sugarcane in the adjoining rural parishes. The town's female slaves did the same kind of work they would have done on farms and plantations, except for field work—serving as cooks, maids, nurses, and laundresses.

Antebellum Baton Rouge, along with other Southern communities, provided no formal schooling for black children, slave or free; thus the black who could read and write by 1865 was a rarity. In their off hours

According to this bill of sale, a Negro woman, Julia, was sold for $400 in 1844. Witnessing the transaction was one of Baton Rouge's most influential men, Judge Daniel D. Avery. Although New Orleans was the major slave-trading center in the Lower South, local transfers of blacks were commonplace. Courtesy, Department of Archives and Manuscripts, LSU, Baton Rouge.

Rochefort:

Baton Rouge April 29th 1844 – Whereas
Messs Philips Hoffeland of the State of
Missouri has bargained & agreed to sell to
Dr C. K. French of this place for the sum
of Three hundred dollars, a negro woman
named Julia; now I do by these presents
hereby warrant & defend the titles to the
Slave aforesaid; and do guarantee the
same in favor of the said Dr C. K. French
And against all loses & trouble arising from
the titles to said Slave – And agree to become
a party to the act of Sale to be passed
for the same as guarantor of title –

Test David Avery   Charles Pipes

Above
This Lytle photograph shows dandy Scott Gordon, who was married in the city on October 10, 1876. We know little about him other than in 1890 he resided at No. 23 North Street and was employed at the Baton Rouge Water Works. Courtesy, Department of Archives and Manuscripts, LSU, Baton Rouge.

Left
This camp of contrabands located on the grounds of a former female seminary in Baton Rouge was photographed around 1863. A Northern soldier described a similar congregation at the old Magruder's Seminary, also in the town. He related that around its buildings, then used as a school and church for the blacks, were "about a hundred and fifty of all ages." Courtesy, Department of Archives and Manuscripts, LSU, Baton Rouge.

Baton Rouge slaves amused themselves in much the same way that whites in town did—by dancing, gambling, fighting, and drinking. White supervision and control were always present, however, and Sunday church attendance, while genuinely popular among the slaves, was also encouraged by the masters as a device for inculcating docility and obedience among their chattels.

White attitudes in Baton Rouge regarding slaves, according to Richter, were "typical of the South." Baton Rougeans "thought their chattels to be child-like, inherently inferior, incapable of living as free men, irresponsible, and in need of discipline." As was also the case throughout the South, developments following emancipation served to reinforce these assumptions rather than to dispel them.

Probably the factor most aggravating to whites was the mass migration of blacks into Southern cities and towns when slavery came to an end. No longer held as chattels on farms or plantations, thousands upon thousands of propertyless and illiterate ex-slaves "went to town" after 1865 in search of other work, to be cared for by the army or the Freedmen's Bureau, or just to loaf around in the enjoyment of the freedom they had never before possessed. Although most blacks soon returned to the countryside as tenants or sharecroppers, others stayed to become large components, often majorities, in Southern urban populations.

Such was the case in Baton Rouge. On the eve of the Civil War in 1860, blacks comprised 32 percent of the town's population. All but a handful were slaves. Five years later, however, a nervous white resident observed that Baton Rouge was already a "Negro Village." "Take the Army out and four-fifths of the Town would be Negroes," he continued. "They tare down Houses and build for themselves upon Confiscated Ground. The Whole flat Down in Catfish [in south Baton Rouge along the river] is covered with Little Negro Shantyes and the [public] Schools are very full of Negroes." By 1870 Baton Rouge was 52 percent black, the partial result of a decline in the white population since 1865. In 1880 the town was 59 percent black. Not until 1920, in fact, did Baton Rouge again have a majority of white residents. By then the percentage of blacks in Baton Rouge had fallen off to 39 percent of the total, only slightly higher than it had been 60 years previously in the twilight of slavery.

Along with other Southern communities, white Baton Rouge was ill-equipped and psychologically unprepared for the sudden postbellum influx of blacks. Where and how blacks lived, how they supported themselves, and white reaction to their numbers, close proximity, and behavior remained tense and vexing problems for decades. And invariably it was the blacks who came out on the short end—pushed by segregation into the lowest, most poorly drained and unhealthy sections of town, securing only the lowest paying menial jobs, denied a decent education, ultimately deprived of the vote, and constantly badgered and shaken down by the police. Living standards and amenities for the majority of black Baton Rougeans did not even begin to improve until the 1920s; even today, despite the tremendous impact of the "Civil Rights Revolution," the general level of black life in Baton Rouge is still considerably below what most whites have long taken for granted. These conditions are by no means limited to Baton Rouge, Louisiana, or even the South, but continue to trouble the nation itself. Their prevalence, however, does not permit their historical origins locally to be neglected.

Race relations in the entire region after 1865 were further shaken by Radical Republican insistence that blacks should enjoy the same rights of citizenship as whites, including the right to vote and to hold public office. The Radicals were morally correct, of course, but the problem was that almost no Southern whites agreed. The latter believed it not only foolish but dangerous to bestow "equality before the law" upon a recently servile and irresponsible segment of the population, which, moreover, outnumbered the whites in many areas of the South. Intermarriage, violence, and other highly "undesirable" consequences would inevitably follow, whites believed.

As a Northern observer commented in 1866, Southerners felt that "blacks at large still belonged to the whites at large," which meant that Southern whites regarded emancipation as a mere legal abstraction that should in no way undermine the basic social and political mastery that whites had always held and should always maintain over blacks.

Initially prevented from setting Reconstruction policy by Presidents Lincoln and Andrew Johnson, the Radical Republicans acquired a "veto-proof" Congress in the 1866 elections and enacted *their* program for "reconstructing" the South the following year. The history of Radical Reconstruction in the South is detailed and complex. Its voluminous literature cannot possibly be summarized here, not even the Louisiana experience, possibly the most corrupt and Byzantine of all Southern states during the period. Suffice it to say that Southern states, as prerequisites for readmission to the Union under the Radical plan, had to ratify the proposed 14th Amendment to the federal constitution and embody adult male suffrage in their state constitutions. The first requirement was designed to make citizens of the ex-slaves, which the 13th Amendment failed to do. (Ratified in 1865, that measure had only abolished slavery, leaving blacks in a limbo between property and citizenship.) The second requirement would allow adult male blacks to vote, and was reinforced in 1870 by the 15th Amendment to the federal constitution. By 1868 most former Confederate states, including Louisiana, had complied with the Radical program, if somewhat grudgingly in some cases, and were readmitted to the Union. Most Southern states, again including Louisiana, also had biracial Radical Republican state administrations that rested largely upon a newly enfranchised and extensive black electorate. For

Louis Francois, along with Victor Lange, represented East Baton Rouge Parish at the 1868 Louisiana State Constitutional Convention. Francois, pictured here, was an educated free man of Afro-French ancestry and a veteran of the Louisiana Infantry Native Guard from the Civil War. Although residents of East Baton Rouge Parish sought to intimidate blacks during Reconstruction, several served in the Louisiana legislature from 1868 to 1876: Robert and Victor M. Lange, J. Henri Burch, Joshua Wilson, and Augustus Williams. Courtesy, Department of Archives and Manuscripts, LSU, Baton Rouge.

varying lengths of time, these administrations remained in power, but for no longer than nine years, as in South Carolina—and Louisiana.

As Louisiana's capital during the entirety of Radical Reconstruction, New Orleans was the abode of the governor, the legislature, the supreme court, and the largest federal military garrison in the state. But the further from New Orleans one went, the weaker the authority or even the influence of Radical Reconstruction over the rest of Louisiana. This situation consistently existed even in a community as relatively close to New Orleans as Baton Rouge, where, as historian Terry Seip found, the impact of Radical laws, policies, personnel—and commitment to blacks—was almost nonexistent. As Seip himself put it:

Despite occasional power disputes, Baton Rouge remained in the hands of traditional (i.e., Democratic) white leadership, and the course of municipal government was marked by stability and continuity in both personnel and function during reconstruction. While white Baton Rougeans might detest the personnel and actions of the state or national government during the period, they were scarcely touched by Radical reconstruction and they could feel some sense of security and satisfaction that things were going well at home.

In 1866 the *Advocate* had stated with obvious pride that "there is not a town in the South containing as large a negro population as ours that can boast of as quiet and as orderly a set of darkies." Thirteen years later Democratic Mayor Leon Jastremski, also editor of the *Capitolian*, observed in his column that "the Darkies in this section are very well satisfied." Aside from capitalizing "Darkies"—his only concession to progress—Jastremski's view differed not at all from the earlier prognosis and revealed, as Seip concluded, that in Baton Rouge "the dominant white attitude toward the Negro would be paternalism—that recurring attitude in Southern race relations which, by its very nature, implies white over black."

Three years after publication of Mayor Jastremski's analysis of local race relations, Baton Rouge again became the state capital. Much the same argument that had persuaded the constitutional convention of 1845 to move the state capital from New Orleans to Baton Rouge resurfaced a generation later and convinced the 1879 gathering to reach the same decision. Accordingly, the delegates provided for rebuilding the Gothic statehouse, which had been gutted during Union occupation in December of 1862, and for transfer of the legislature and executive offices to Baton Rouge after repairs had been completed. All necessary preparations having been effected three years later, Governor Samuel Douglas McEnery, his then miniscule executive establishment, and the legislature all returned to Baton Rouge in 1882, to the rejoicing of merchants, hotelmen, and saloonkeepers. The state government has remained in town ever since, generating ever more local prosperity and affording Baton Rouge-

Above

In 1874 local groups of the White League were formed in Louisiana to combat radicals and black leadership in government. A White League Convention met in Baton Rouge in August to unite various political groups against Governor William P. Kellogg and his men, who were running in the upcoming legislative and congressional elections. Urging all whites to return only Caucasians to office, the convention nominated candidates for the national house of representatives. This "White People's Ticket" from Baton Rouge not only lists those local candidates endorsed, but also contenders for district and state positions.

Leon Jastremski was one of the leading political figures of Baton Rouge for nearly 40 years. A Confederate veteran, he served as mayor from 1876 to 1882 and was best remembered for his role in obtaining the restoration of the state capital to Baton Rouge. Jastremski was brigadier general of the state militia and chairman of the Democratic Committee in Louisiana. He ran twice for governor but was unsuccessful. As a newspaper man, he established and edited several papers including the Baton Rouge Capitolian and its successor, the Capitolian-Advocate. In the 1890s Jastremski was consul to Peru. He died in 1907. Both courtesy, Department of Archives and Manuscripts, LSU, Baton Rouge.

ans ringside seats for one of the greatest continuous shows on earth, Louisiana politics, about which more will be said in Chapter IV.

By 1882 the town had cleared away the rubble, if not the memories, of war, had been a virtual spectator to the most bitter and violent Reconstruction regime in the South, and was inching slowly upward toward its prewar level of bustle and prosperity. With a population in 1880 of only 7,197, however, Baton Rouge was still a very small town. It had not pushed substantially beyond its boundaries of 60 years earlier; the town simply "filled in" available space between the Mississippi River, Garcia's Bayou (Capitol Lake), South Boulevard, and Fifth Street—anything east of which still remained "out in the suburbs," according to later memories of a longtime resident. Streets reverted to muck or dust depending on the weather. Some attractive Victorian residential construction graced Beauregard Town and Spanish Town in the postbellum era, but municipal services and structures languished because of lingering indebtedness and reduced revenues from the upheaval of the Civil War.

Baton Rouge was, in addition, a racially divided and somewhat cynical and defensive community. Unfortunately the arrival of the most reactionary clique of state officials in the history of modern Louisiana did little to soften the prejudice or broaden the horizons of its citizenry. The last two decades of the 19th century would prove to be the most unbecoming in the entirety of Baton Rouge's existence as an incorporated municipality. For this period and two decades of the 20th century, Baton Rouge would be a truly enjoyable place to live only if one were white, possessed a degree of prominence or wealth, and professed loyalty to the Democratic Party.

In February 1934, Huey P. Long, then United States Senator, launched the Share-Our-Wealth Movement. Within the first year, its membership rolls totaled over 3 million and in 1935, the growth was even more spectacular. This interesting photograph of a Share-Our-Wealth rally at the new State Capitol has as its focal point the enormous portrait of Long. Courtesy, Louisiana State Library.

POLITICS, PROGRESS, AND PROSPERITY

As the former Confederate States of America struggled to overcome the devastation of the Civil War, their state and local governments were fiscally restrained, and rife with corruption and repression. Louisiana by no means escaped these sorry conditions. The men who assumed the reins of Louisiana's government after disposition of the "carpetbaggers" and "scalawags" were Democrats who, for the most part, were middle-aged and middle-class, had served in the Confederate army, loathed the Republican party for its part in Reconstruction, and worked to eliminate its influence in state and local affairs entirely. Because they were several notches above the mass of poorer whites in wealth, education, and position, the ruling Democrats had little difficulty in obscuring potentially divisive class conflicts by preaching the unifying doctrine of white supremacy and by eulogizing the Confederacy and its unsung heroes, always compelling topics in the postbellum South.

If poor whites strayed from the prescribed path by voting for candidates other than Democrats, and if black voters became similarly troublesome, the Democrats fell back on violence, intimidation, and electoral fraud—the same devices employed to eject Reconstruction—to remain in power. Democrats in this period were often called "Bourbons" because, like the French royal family of that name, they were reactionaries, unable to forget the past or learn from it. As the capital of a Bourbon state, Baton Rouge became a thoroughly Bourbon community in the 1880s, though not as intensely as Shreveport, Louisiana's Bourbon Vatican during the last part of the 19th century.

Baton Rouge's Bourbon spokesman during several of these years, both as mayor and as editor of the official state journal, the *Daily Advocate*, was Leon Jastremski. Jastremski consistently supported the familiar Bourbon dogmas of Democratic solidarity, white supremacy, and suspicion of Yankees (unless they came to town with money to spend or invest). The terms "darky" and "nigger" often appeared in the *Daily Advocate* to describe blacks during the period when Jastremski and his immediate successors edited the paper.

In such a climate, Baton Rouge race relations continued to be tense, sometimes exploding into violence. Black legislators accustomed to service in the integrated Crescent City found themselves unable to patronize rigidly segregated establishments in Baton Rouge after the seat of state government returned to town. In 1890 local whites imposed what historian William I. Hair called a "reign of terror" upon "industrious, reliable" blacks in the area by shooting, whipping, and otherwise molesting those who refused to sell their property.

The arch-Bourbonism of the Jastremski persuasion did not, however, afflict Baton Rouge for long. With changing administrations and circumstances, virulent racism abated in Baton Rouge; harsh attitudes regarding Yankees were also steadily muted as increasing numbers of Northerners, with their money, came to town.

As residents of Louisiana's capital, Baton Rougeans frequently witnessed and sometimes participated in some wild political shenanigans, especially between 1890 and 1896 and again during the heyday of Huey P. Long and his associates from 1928 to 1940. The interval between 1896 and 1928 was a relatively quiet period in normally noisy Louisiana, but this unusually subdued and generally conservative era in state politics complemented Baton Rouge's own upper-middle-class, management-oriented mentality.

One of the most sordid episodes to disgrace the old Gothic statehouse occurred during the legislative session of 1890. The mighty, corrupt, and corrupting Louisiana State Lottery Company applied in that year for an

Above
Following the return of the seat of government to Baton Rouge in 1882, a statewide movement was begun to transfer the remains of Louisiana Confederate Governor Henry Watkins Allen to the capital city. Without opposition, a state law appropriating money to ship the coffin and monument from New Orleans was passed. Allen's remains were carried by train and on July 4, 1885, at an elaborate program, they were received by one of the largest crowds ever assembled up to that time. Pictured here is his monument made of Missouri granite, originally erected in New Orleans in 1872 and subsequently placed at his final grave on the north side of the Old State Capitol. Courtesy, Department of Archives and Manuscripts, LSU, Baton Rouge.

Above
Beverly V. Baranco, Sr., was a highly respected Baton Rouge businessman and leader of the black community for over 40 years. Quite active in the Black and Tan faction in the Republican Party in Louisiana, he led it for over a decade in seeking participation in party politics for those of his race. Baranco served as delegate-at-large to the Republican national convention in 1920 as well as later ones. Courtesy, Dr. B.V. Baranco, Jr.

Left
Civil War veterans pose in front of the Confederate Monument on North Boulevard at Third Street (now Riverside Mall). A Confederate Monument Association organized in the 1870s worked toward the erection of this monument commemorating the Confederate dead from East and West Baton Rouge parishes. The cornerstone was laid in 1886 and on August 5, 1890, the monument was unveiled. Courtesy, Department of Archives and Manuscripts, LSU, Baton Rouge.

extension of its state charter, generating more immediate and heated controversy than any previous proposal in state history, including the decision to take Louisiana out of the Union 30 years before.

Chartered in 1868 by the first Reconstruction legislature, the company received a monopoly on the conduct of lotteries in Louisiana until 1894, for which it had to pay the state $40,000 annually. Because it was widely known that the company took in millions of dollars a year from sale of tickets all over the country and beyond, many Louisianians came to believe that the state deserved a larger slice of the pie. Others opposed the lottery altogether because it resulted in bribes to legislators, other public officials, and journalists to obtain favorable treatment. (Governor McEnery, an intimate of lottery higher-ups, was snidely dubbed Governor "McLottery" by his many enemies.) Democratic "purists" feared the company because it divided their party and created the dire possibility that black and white Republicans might jump into the breach and seize control of Louisiana's government.

In the 1879 legislative session, lottery opponents had enacted a measure to repeal the 1868 charter, only to behold a New Orleans federal district court set their repeal aside because it sought to abrogate a contract. Moving quickly to blunt future legislative assaults, the company persuaded the 1879 convention to write the charter into the constitution where it would be secure from tampering or repeal. During the next 11 years the company grew richer, more powerful, and increasingly arrogant. When lottery president John A. Morris introduced his proposal in 1890 to renew the charter for another 25 years—to 1919—he polarized the entire state.

Having been written into the constitution of 1879, the lottery charter could be altered only by constitutional amendment, a process requiring initial approval by two-thirds of the elected members of each legislative house and subsequent ratification by a majority of voters at the next state election. Securing a two-thirds' vote from a legislature containing many enemies would not be easy; consequently Morris endeavored to make his proposal as attractive to as many special interests as possible.

What emerged was a sweeping attempt at public bribery. Morris offered to pay the state the colossal sum of $1.25 million per year, to be divided between public education, Confederate pensions, charitable institutions, levee construction, New Orleans drainage—and the general fund! Lottery supporters praised the generosity and public-mindedness of the much-maligned company. Opponents condemned the lottery for its crass hypocrisy and cynicism. Charges and countercharges of insincerity and bad faith were hurled back and forth—in the legislative chambers, in newspaper editorials, and on the streets of the capital. Emotions in Baton Rouge, and throughout most of the state, could hardly have been more highly charged.

Facing page

With the return of the seat of government to Baton Rouge in 1882, life again revolved around the Gothic State House and its occupants. This photograph taken about 1900 shows the western view of the Capitol after its two-year restoration, which was begun in 1880 by William Freret of New Orleans. The most conspicuous changes in the structure are the addition of cast-iron turrets to the top and the color of the exterior from its original white to dark. The marble shaft to the left of the building is the Henry Watkins Allen Monument. Courtesy, Louisiana State Library.

The measure finally passed both houses—narrowly—only to be vetoed by Governor Francis T. Nicholls who, in point of fact, did not actually have the authority to do so because a proposed constitutional amendment is immune to gubernatorial review. A visceral lottery enemy owing to rough treatment at the company's hands during his previous (1877–1880) administration, the one-armed governor and former Confederate general observed in his academic veto message that he would rather lose his remaining hand than use it to sign the odious lottery proposal.

All the commotion, as it turned out, proved to be moot. An 1892 decision of the United States Supreme Court affirming a prior act of Congress prohibiting all lotteries from using the mails doomed the lottery in Louisiana. Several weeks before the 1892 election, Morris withdrew his proposal. It remained, meaninglessly, on the ballot and the voters rejected it. When the company's original charter finally expired in 1894, the lottery moved to Honduras to conduct its operations for a few more years. But the "great lottery struggle" was remembered in Baton Rouge for a generation afterward, while the unsavory legacy of the company's operations inspired specific prohibitions of future lotteries in all Louisiana constitutions down to 1974.

Six years later another political crisis reached its climax in Baton Rouge. By 1896 the Bourbons were in deep trouble with most black and many white voters, whose patience with the corrupt, overly frugal, and insensitive Democrats was exhausted. Economic hard times caused by a severe national depression compounded voter outrage at the country's worst public school system, poor roads, inadequate public institutions, and official indifference to popular demands for reform. In 1891 a branch of the People's Party, or Populists, had organized in the hill parishes of north Louisiana, attracting thousands of white farmers away from the Democrats and spreading to other areas of the state. In 1895 wealthy Republican sugar planters in south Louisiana joined with their own numerous black rank and files and with the Populists to offer truly formidable opposition to the incumbent Democrats. As the contest of 1896 approached, the Bourbons became more seriously concerned about being ejected from power than at any time since 1877.

The result was the most fraudulent election in Louisiana history. Fabricated Democratic returns from north Louisiana cotton parishes, where Populists and Republicans had no poll watchers, retained the Bourbon administration and legislature in office. Although Baton Rouge was a Bourbon town, the parish as a whole supported the Populist-Republican "Fusion" ticket by 4,859 votes to 1,470 for the Democrats because, as historian Hair concluded, "East Baton Rouge Parish was heavily Negro, and factional fights among the Democrats allowed black men to vote freely in 1896."

But "Fusionists" were enraged at the bogus "official" returns statewide, which gave Democratic Governor Murphy J. Foster 116,116 votes to his opponent's 87,698. For a while angry and determined Populists considered resisting the verdict with force and marching on Baton Rouge to pressure the legislature into investigating the returns and calling for a new election. As Hair described the reaction:

Nine thousand populists from North Louisiana's hills were said to be preparing to march upon the state capitol; and what the Daily Advocate *described as a "boat load of sugar-teats" from downstate, equipped with munitions of war "sufficient to accomplish the successful bombardment and siege of Baton Rouge" lay at anchor in the Mississippi. Democratic stalwarts in the capital city and the Florida Parishes organized into paramilitary units and made plans to defend the Foster government.*

The governor, however, controlled the administration, the militia, and the legislature. When the legislature refused to investigate the returns, opposition melted away. The armed Populists failed to appear, the "boat load of sugar-teats" headed downstream, and "only a fistfight or two in the streets of Baton Rouge marred the restoration of quiet to the city."

Two years later, in 1898, to prevent similar difficulties in the future, a Democrat-dominated convention in New Orleans wrote property-ownership and literacy requirements for voter registration into the state constitution, the effects of which prohibited or discouraged poor-white voter registration for a couple of decades, and eliminated, for all practical purposes, meaningful black political participation in Louisiana until passage of the federal Voting Rights Act in 1965. Louisiana governors and legislators remained committed segregationists for many years after 1898, but did not have to harp on the subject because disfranchisement and legal segregation had "solved" the "Negro problem."

With blacks off the registration rolls and white opponents discouraged or demoralized, Louisiana's conservative Democratic elite ruled rather serenely and without interruption—squabbling occasionally only among themselves—until Huey P. Long scattered their heirs to the winds in 1928. In Baton Rouge, state politics assumed a quiet, businesslike, and dignified tone. Baton Rougeans liked the change because it put their own business and civic leaders in tune with each other. Baton Rouge, in fact, had become a corporate town, its values those of the emerging urban-industrial middle-class: moderate taxation wisely spent and honestly accounted for, responsible and scientific management of government, observance of proper governmental forms and procedures, and, above all, decorous behavior on the part of public officials.

During the 1880s Baton Rouge gradually awakened to its potential as a modern, well-serviced, and forward-looking community, responsible, as is any individual, for most of its own destiny. Driven by an aggressive

Above
In late 1897 a quarantine camp, "Fort Vigilant," manned by volunteers and members of two local military companies, was established to guard roads leading to and from Baton Rouge during an outbreak of yellow fever. This photograph of the camp on North Street shows horseman Irenee Pujol on the right. Seated directly in front of the tent are General John McGrath and John J. Wax. During the last half of the 19th century there were deaths recorded from at least five different outbreaks of yellow fever in the city. Courtesy, Department of Archives and Manuscripts, LSU, Baton Rouge.

Right
Governor-elect Murphy J. Foster receives the oath of office on the Old Capitol grounds, probably in 1892. When this picture was taken, much of the social life in Baton Rouge centered around the presence of the legislators and other state officials. The inauguration of a new governor was always an event celebrated with much enthusiasm and the whole community turned out to participate in the activities of the day. Courtesy, Department of Archives and Manuscripts, LSU, Baton Rouge.

and purposeful spirit of civic-mindedness, and further aided by outrageous good fortune, the town steadily matured, expanded, and prospered.

The year 1883 was a major milestone in the history of the city: railroad connections were established between Baton Rouge and New Orleans via the New Orleans & Mississippi Valley Railroad, whose first train from the Crescent City arrived in the capital on December 15. Tracks between the two cities, as well as other railroad lines in Louisiana, were constructed by convict labor under the direction of the state's notoriously brutal postbellum convict lessee, Major Samuel L. James, who at his death in 1894 was possibly the wealthiest man in Louisiana. In October of 1884 the NO & MV completed its line northward to Memphis, Tennessee, via Vicksburg, Mississippi. In the same year the company became the Louisville, New Orleans & Texas Railroad, which in 1893 underwent another name change to the Yazoo & Mississippi Valley Railroad. (Later, in the present century, the company was absorbed by the Illinois Central, now the Illinois Central Gulf.)

Baton Rouge did not have direct rail connections with any other city prior to 1883. Almost 50 years earlier, the "Baton Rouge & Clinton Railroad Company" was chartered by the legislature, but it was never constructed. In 1857, however, the Baton Rouge, Grosse Tete & Opelousas Railroad began service between present-day Port Allen and Grosse Tete. The line failed to reach Opelousas, and Baton Rougeans had to cross the

Mississippi by ferry to reach the company's eastern terminus at Port Allen. This tiny railroad did not long survive the Civil War. Subsequently purchased by the Southern Pacific, the Baton Rouge, Grosse Tete & Opelousas was destroyed by its new owner, its rails and rolling stock taken for use elsewhere.

Reconstruction, a prolonged national recession in the 1870s, and a Congressional scandal involving construction contracts postponed further railroad building on a large scale until the 1880s. But when the road gangs went back to work, the South shared in the great expansion of all railroad systems. By 1940 Baton Rouge was connected additionally with Kansas City via Shreveport and Alexandria on the Louisiana–Arkansas, subsequently absorbed by the Kansas City Southern, and with the main line of the Illinois Central between Chicago and New Orleans via a branch line eastward to Hammond. Connections existed at Port Allen with the Missouri Pacific and the Texas & Pacific as well.

Although steamboats, barges and, eventually, ocean-going vessels continued to serve Baton Rouge and to enhance its economy, the coming of railroads made travel and commerce possible between Louisiana's capital and the entire nation—all portions of which were not located on navigable or accessible waterways.

Railroad travel notwithstanding, life in Baton Rouge did not change radically until after 1900. In the meantime the town grew at its tradi-

In late 1887 the city council signed a contract authorizing the company of Smedley and Wood to build, maintain, and operate a waterworks for the city of Baton Rouge, including the construction of six miles of cast-iron mains, a water tower, and 75 fire hydrants. Although the river was originally used, artesian wells soon replaced it for the source of water. This photograph taken by Lytle shows the first building and the 75-foot brick chimney. Behind it looms the renovated Capitol with its cast-iron turrets. Courtesy, Department of Archives and Manuscripts, LSU, Baton Rouge.

The wooden-hull steamboat, City of Baton Rouge, was truly a lovely vessel. Built in 1881 at Jeffersonville, Indiana, it belonged to the Anchor Line and ran from St. Louis to New Orleans. Nicknamed the "Bat an' Ball" by the roustabouts, it sank at Hermitage, Louisiana, at 3:00 P.M. on December 12, 1890. Two deck passengers drowned. Here, the boat is moored at the levee of its namesake. Courtesy, Department of Archives and Manuscripts, LSU, Baton Rouge.

The Baton Rouge, Grosse Tete, and Opelousas Railroad was officially opened on July 4, 1857, with a big barbecue and dance at Rosedale. Funds for its construction were obtained through private subscriptions and from a $50,000 bonus paid by the city of Baton Rouge. After the Civil War the old railroad was partially resuscitated, but in view of the wide destruction of sugar lands and mills and damage to other agricultural enterprises, it failed. This stock certificate for 52 shares in the company at $25 a share is dated 1867. Courtesy, Department of Archives and Manuscripts, LSU, Baton Rouge.

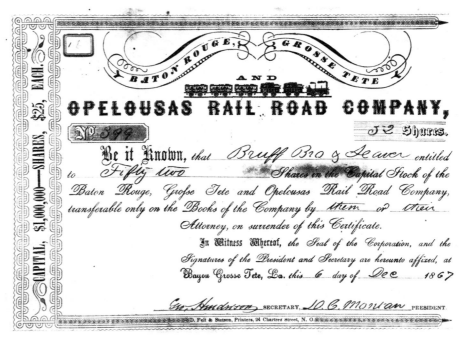

tionally tranquil pace, a secure and familiar sense of "home-townness" prevailed, and most citizens seemed to know each other personally. Interviewed in 1952, Dr. E.V. Whitaker recalled that, during his boyhood in the 1890s, "I knew everybody who lived in Baton Rouge, and I remember well the day that my father remarked, 'I saw at least six or eight people up town today whom I do not know.' " The unfamiliar faces probably belonged to legislators from distant parishes who had just alighted from a train.

By 1893 a municipal streetcar line encircled the town, running westward on Main Street, thence south on Lafayette and St. Louis, east on Government Street, north on Dufrocq, and west on Main again. According to Whitaker Baton Rouge's young men liked to impress their girl friends by taking them for rides around the "belt" at five cents per trip on Sunday evenings. Whitaker also remembered the coffee stand within the Old City Market on North Boulevard—torn down in the 1950s to make room for the Municipal Building. "Here over the coffee cups, many local elections were won or lost, here many candidates for local office were made or broken." (Such powwows today take place over martinis at the City Club, the Baton Rouge Country Club, and other oases where local movers and shakers gather.)

In 1898 Baton Rougeans elected as mayor a wealthy property owner and real-estate developer named Robert A. Hart, whose four years in office constitute a major transition in the city's history. Clear-eyed, and with striking features behind a well-trimmed moustache, Hart was not only one of Baton Rouge's handsomest chief executives, but he was also the mayor with the vision and leadership required to lift the town out of the mud and launch it toward a better future of its own making. It was during the Hart administration and its successors that Baton Rouge at last acquired the means with which to grow up, and decided to invest hefty slices of the new prosperity in civic improvements leading to a better town in which to live.

In 1915 a local journalist confessed that "Baton Rouge as a city owned nothing to speak of and had made no improvements worth noting" prior to Hart's administration. But in 1899 the mayor, together with a "small band of progressive citizens," persuaded local property owners to approve a series of bond issues for "improvement purposes." The first issue, for $200,000, paid for a new city hall, the Convention Street school, and the paving of Third and Main streets plus North Boulevard. Successive issues of $100,000 (1905), $75,000 (1913) and $225,000 (1914) were spent for paving additional streets in the center of town, constructing the Florida Street High School, making sewerage and drainage improvements, providing a black public school and a city abbatoir, as well as purchasing a hospital site and additional property, mostly from the state, which sold the remaining penitentiary buildings to the city in 1918.

Robert A. Hart, a Baton Rouge native, first entered public life in 1892. Serving a term as mayor in 1898, he inaugurated a new era of city improvements in schools, streets and roads, sewage, and other areas. During his long tenure on the school board and as chairman of the finance committee of the Police Jury, Hart shaped much of the policy for both groups. At the time of his death in 1939, he was reputed to be the wealthiest man in the community. Courtesy, Mrs. John T. Anderson.

Facing page
Top
The physical appearance of Third Street changed relatively little for several decades prior to 1900. This view taken at Third and Main in the 1890s shows the Verandah Hotel and Saloon on the left. On the far right is the Reymond Store and, farther down, Wong Bing's Chinese Laundry. Courtesy, Department of Archives and Manuscripts, LSU, Baton Rouge.

Left
The annual firemen's parade was the grandest holiday in Baton Rouge for almost three decades. It was held on February 22 each year to commemorate the birthday of George Washington and the establishment of the city's first fire-fighting group. Each engine or hose carriage was decorated with paper flowers and other ornaments lovingly made and arranged by wives and daughters of the firemen. These floats, with entries from social and fraternal organizations, were judged and awarded monetary prizes. In 1900, this third-place winner was made by Washington Fire Company No. 3 and stands on Convention Street near St. Joseph's Academy. Courtesy, Department of Archives and Manuscripts, LSU, Baton Rouge.

Top

Outgrowing their former quarters, the Sisters of St. Joseph moved to a new building on the corner of Church (North Fourth) and Florida streets in 1890. There, in addition to their orphanage and academy, they ran a commercial laundry for the first 20 years to support their orphans. Around 1940, the Sisters vacated the Academy buildings and moved to a new modern facility on Broussard Street. In this picture of St. Joseph's Academy or Convent, dated 1890, the front is primarily hidden by trees. However, the view down Church Street is excellent. In addition to the Reddy-Morgan, Knox, and Queyrouze homes, there is the Methodist Church, Washington Fire Company No. 1 Hall, and St. Joseph's Cathedral. Courtesy, St. Joseph's Academy, Baton Rouge.

Right
While there were no breaks in levees below Red River Landing in Louisiana in 1897, the flood of that year was nonetheless a serious one within the state. In this picture, high water in Baton Rouge inundates part of the first block of Main Street, yet life still seems to go on undisturbed—a young boy fishes from the railing and other people stop to pass the time of day. The two-story brick building on the right with the iron railing was the White Elephant Saloon; the tall white structure next to it housed the office of the **Advocate**. *Courtesy, Department of Archives and Manuscripts, LSU, Baton Rouge.*

Left
The old City Market, constructed in 1859, was located between St. Louis and St. Ferdinand streets, directly north of the 1921–1923 courthouse. The center of town life for many years, its bell rang to announce fires and the opening and closing of the market. In addition to providing fresh vegetables and meat, the market had a coffee stand that was the congregating point for men of the town and the distributing point for gossip and other news. Abandoned as a market sometime after World War I, the building was used as a police garage and after 1941 as a recreational center for enlisted men stationed in the vicinity of Baton Rouge and for others. It was razed after 1954 to make room for the municipal building fronting North Boulevard. *Courtesy, Charles East.*

Below right
Situated on a square bounded by North Boulevard, Convention, Ninth, and Tenth streets, this building was originally called Public School. Later the name was changed to Convention Street School. All grades were taught here from about 1902 until 1913, when the high school on Florida Boulevard was opened. In 1957 the historic building was razed to make room for the expressway. *Courtesy, Miss May Lynn Amiss.*

While the sums of money provided by these bond issues may appear trivial by present standards, at the time they were sizable, all together the equivalent of at least $10 to $12 million in today's inflated currency and worth a great deal more. Hart's leadership in obtaining financing for improvements is further commendable because Louisianians in general, and Baton Rougeans in particular, were tighter with their money in those days, much more conservative and far less inclined to tax themselves than they are today.

By 1899, therefore, Baton Rouge not only badly needed to clean itself up, but could finally afford to do so. The local economy was on a steady upswing from the national depression that had commenced in 1893. Cotton and sugar prices began to rise, enabling farmers and planters to buy more equipment and supplies and to purchase additional land. Money poured into Baton Rouge wholesale supply houses from customers as far away as southern Mississippi. Holmes & Barnes, Ltd., a wholesale grocery firm established in 1902, prospered at the outset and did $1 million worth of business by 1908. Perhaps the surest sign of Baton Rouge's "getting with the times" was the arrival in town in 1896 of the Coca-Cola Bottling Company, a branch of the Southern firm (Atlanta) whose beverage soon became internationally synonymous with "refreshment."

Another "cleanup"—this one of a literal nature—was undertaken in this period, also, but the source for this one was not local. It came in the form of Dr. Oscar Dowling, president of the Louisiana State Board of Health who, in 1910, decided to launch a massive campaign against Louisiana's penchant for dirty living. He told Louisianians that "other states think of Louisiana as the home of swamps, and malaria, and mosquitoes, and fever, and general unhealthiness," but that the unhealthiness—which was all too real—was due simply to "plain dirt . . . that's all that's the matter with us." There was little or no regulation of food or water or the conditions under which they were transported and sold; and to make matters worse, few people seemed to care, shrugging off a high illness and death rate as unavoidable. Dr. Dowling changed all that with his 7,000-mile inspection and lecture tour of the state, and helped Baton Rougeans to eventually take clean food, water, and medicine for granted.

The increased enjoyment of everyday living in Baton Rouge around the turn of the century was a delightful by-product of the community's (and state's) growth, increasing prosperity, and continued civic progress. A happy life must also include leisure, and Baton Rougeans found more time for play as the 19th century came to a close. They went to the theater, as before, and after 1900 they went to the movies. The area had always teemed with fish and wildlife and Baton Rougeans began to hunt and fish more often—for enjoyment rather than from necessity, as in former years—and they also took up golf and tennis. Those who could afford

The country story was an institution in the South for much of the 19th and early 20th century. In 1899 there were no less than 58 retail grocers in Baton Rouge. Most of these establishments handled practically everything needed for the home, from staple groceries, dry goods, crockery, liquors, and tobacco to plantation supplies. The T.E. Doiron's Fancy Grocery on Government pictured here is typical for the time. Courtesy, Louisiana Room, LSU Library.

Above
At the turn of the century, Main Street remained one of the most important thoroughfares in the city. On the left, the clock marks S.P. Schuessler's jewelry establishment and next door is Mendelsohn's Fancy Grocery. H.L. Stoutz's bicycle manufactory was across the street at No. 217. The men working next to the tracks are breaking ground for the sewage line laid in 1901. Courtesy, Department of Archives and Manuscripts, LSU, Baton Rouge.

Right
For many decades the cotton industry remained an important element in the economy of Baton Rouge. Fields surrounded the city and gins were in constant operation at harvest time. When the Ronaldson and Puckett Dixie Ginnery on Florida Street opened on July 1, 1890, it was equipped with the Munger Improved Cotton Machine, described by its proprietors as being the "most complete" in Louisiana. In addition to cleaning, ginning, and baling, the Ginnery provided a hauling service as well. This photograph was taken at the height of the ginning season. Courtesy, Louisiana Room, LSU Library.

CERTIFICATE OF HEALTH.
OFFICE OF BOARD OF HEALTH.

BATON ROUGE, LA., *Aug 2 1905*

To Whom it May Concern:

THIS IS TO CERTIFY, That the bearer *J. W. Menget*
of *Baton Rouge* is in good health and has given satisfactory
evidence at this office that *he* has not been in contact with *Yellow fever*
or any contagious disease, or been in any place infected with said disease for a period
of _____ days.

Description: Race *White*, age *38*, height *5* feet *11* inches,
weight *190* pounds, color of hair *Dark*, color of eyes *Gray*

C. F. Duchein , M. D.,
Health Officer.

Facing page

Top

Sugar production was always important to the capital city in the 19th century. Around 1900, of 68 cane growers and sugar manufacturers in the parish, some 44 gave their mailing address as Baton Rouge proper. Pictured here in 1899 is the Baton Rouge Sugar Company Refinery, located on the Yazoo and Mississippi Valley Railroad about one mile north of the city and a little northwest of where the old Lady of the Lake Hospital stood. Around 1908, the refinery went into receivership. Courtesy, Department of Archives and Manuscripts, LSU, Baton Rouge.

Bottom

The last major threat of yellow fever in Baton Rouge occurred in 1905. To safeguard the city, a parish board of health was appointed, a quarantine was enacted, and a health certificate was required for the first time as proof that an individual wishing to enter the city had not been in any infected area of the country for ten days. This certificate of health for a member of the prominent Monget family of Baton Rouge is signed by Dr. C.F. Duchein, a physician and leader in the community for many years. Courtesy, Old Arsenal Museum, Louisiana Office of State Parks, Department of Culture, Recreation and Tourism.

it began to travel widely and frequently. Most notably, however, and in steadily increasing numbers after 1893, Baton Rougeans went on Saturdays to watch LSU students run, throw, and kick a ball down a field.

Baton Rouge's theatrical fare had improved noticeably as early as the 1870s and became even better after the town could be reached by railroad in 1883—the larger and more seasoned companies, with their elaborate sets and extensive wardrobes, could travel more easily on trains than by steamboat. As the quality of shows improved, so did the sensitivity of local criticism, as this 1887 assessment of actress "Madame" Janish attests:

. . . Her success in this play was well earned. At the commencement of the play the audience were disposed to view her acting with a feeling of disappointment, which no doubt she observed with the quick intuition of one who knows how to read human faces, but she seemed in no hurry to win applause, continuing to work her way carefully through the first parts of the play to that part where she could make some display of her talent and power as an actress. . . . Janish made the most of the occasion and before the curtain fell she had firmly established herself in the good opinion of the audience. Her acting is of a quiet, unobtrusive sort. Her pathetic scenes were especially well acted. At all times brimful of womanly gentleness, she was continually permitting the audience to catch glimpses of an under current of intense passion, boding and baleful.

But not all performances were so highly praised. The Pike's Hall management was frequently condemned for fleecing their audiences by charging "a dollar admission for a two-bit show." One of the many "two-bitters" that came to town was an "opera" entitled "The Turkish Bath," which the *Daily Advocate* scalded on November 25, 1898:

Without making any individual distinction we declare all the actors to be absolutely rotten. . . . To charge the price of 75 cents to see such a gigantic fraud was obtaining money under false pretenses, and the sooner the managers of the theater here cancel all engagements with such breezy comedies the better it will be. . . . Readers through the country, stay clear of "The Turkish Bath" if you don't want to be cheated.

As they had done since antebellum days, Baton Rouge journalists continued to bemoan the lack of a public auditorium in town. But promotional efforts in the 1890s were no more successful than earlier appeals. After a few attempts to raise sufficient capital from "gentlemen of means" had failed, interest in the project evaporated and did not revive for some time.

Pike's Hall, demolished at last in April of 1900, was replaced by another private facility, the Elks' Theater, whose cornerstone was laid at Third and Florida streets on May 26 of the same year. Motion pictures appeared in town soon after, and as occurred nationwide, the cinema rapidly displaced live stage performances as the standard fare of public

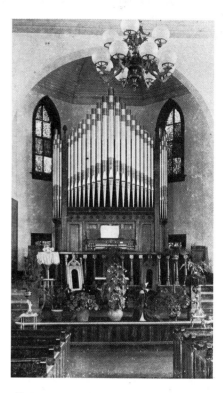

Above
In small country towns many years ago, the arrival of even a family troupe of entertainers could be a big event. Social historians are indebted to local photographer Alvin E. Rabenhorst, Sr., for his picture of a trapeze "artiste" around 1900. Courtesy, Messrs. A.P. and Philip Rabenhorst.

Above
In 1891, the old Presbyterian Church on the southeast corner of Church (North Fourth) and Florida streets was remodeled. The following year, its congregation purchased a handsome pipe organ made by John Brown. Upon installation in 1892, a Grand Organ Recital was given by Professor W.B. Clark, a blind musician who was an integral part of the city's musical life for many years. While there was not an admission fee, a newspaper announcement of the forthcoming recital indicated that an offering would be taken afterwards to be applied on the cost of the organ and it was hoped that contributions would be "liberal." This early photograph of the interior shows the church after its renovation. Courtesy, Department of Archives and Manuscripts, LSU, Baton Rouge.

Above

Since the early 1840s, various local organizations of thespians have come and gone in the city. In the 1920s, some of the most serious acting locally up to that time was presented by the Little Theater Guild, a predecessor to the present Baton Rouge Little Theater. The cast and set in this photograph are from the concluding production of the Guild's first season in 1921–1922: Hubert E. Davies' Cousin Kate. It was also the first three-act play offered by the Guild and was presented in the Woman's Clubhouse. *Courtesy, Louisiana Room, LSU Library.*

Right

When a 1909 city ordinance declared it unlawful for any person to engage in "any manner of sparring match, glove contest or any other such contest generally known as boxing," those who participated in the sport retreated from the city limits on occasion to box. *Courtesy, Messrs. A.P. and Philip Rabenhorst.*

entertainment in Baton Rouge. Paramount Theater, along with a couple of lesser downtown houses, provided most of the town's cinematic entertainment until the 1930s when suburban theaters began to appear. In 1980 the Paramount shared the fate of many other older buildings in the downtown area—it disappeared, to be replaced by a parking lot.

American college football commenced in 1869 with a savage contest between Princeton and Rutgers. By the 1890s most Eastern schools had taken up the game which Yale's Walter Camp, who conceived the All-America teams, had considerably refined and debrutalized. LSU chemistry professor Charles E. Coates, a former player for Johns Hopkins in Baltimore, organized the first "Fighting Tigers" with himself as coach in 1893. LSU's charter squad played only one game that year, with Tulane, and lost 34-0. But young Ruffin G. Pleasant, the team captain, did not remain a loser. After graduating he became a lawyer and subsequently state attorney general; in 1916 he was elected governor of Louisiana. While all recent Louisiana chief executives have been avid LSU football fans, Pleasant is the only governor ever to have actually played the sport for the "Old War Skule."

LSU football got much better very quickly. The years 1907–1909, in fact, were fantastic. Sparked by two Pennsylvanians named John Seip and the incomparable George Ellwood "Doc" Fenton, the Tigers during those three seasons compiled a record of 23 wins, 5 losses, and no ties, scoring 896 points to 100 for their opponents. (The great 1908 team alone won all 10 of its games and outscored their opponents 442 points to 11!) Not until a half-century later, when LSU won its first official national championship in 1958 under Head Coach Paul Dietzel, would the Bayou Bengals perform as magnificently on the gridiron. Local rooters were ecstatic over "Fenton & Company," and LSU football—with competition from political kibitzing and partying—has remained the focus of Baton Rouge popular culture ever since.

Higher education in Baton Rouge remained not only modest, but marginal, until at least the third decade of the 20th century. Prior to 1898 the state constitution limited LSU's annual legislative appropriation to the appallingly deficient sum of $10,000, and until 1904 the limit was only $15,000. Even though a dollar stretched much farther back then, it should require no elaboration to conclude that academic programs and instruction at Louisiana's leading educational institution must have been of questionable value so long as such a tight rein was maintained on public funding.

The state's commitment to black higher education—LSU enrolled only whites until the 1950s—existed in name only. Southern University was authorized by the constitution of 1879, but as historian Hair points out:

The legislature appropriated a small fund but failed to provide for one detail—

Above
This impressive hall erected by the Benevolent and Protective Order of the Elks about 1906 was a familiar landmark on the eastern side of Third Street between Florida and Laurel for many years. During the Depression, the building was remodeled with the front extended nearer to the sidewalk. It remained the lodge until 1974, when members moved to their new quarters. At various times the Hall contained a reading room and parlor, billiard room, gymnasium, bowling alley, and restaurant. Courtesy, Department of Archives and Manuscripts, LSU, Baton Rouge.

Right
The Benevolent and Protective Order of the Elks No. 490 was organized in Baton Rouge in May 1899. Subsequently, the organization began plans for their own meeting hall which eventually resulted in the Elks' Theater. The building initially served a triple purpose: a theater, an office building, and a home for the Order. This photograph of the group was taken in 1900. Eugene Cazedessus, the Grand Exalted Ruler, sits in the center of the back row. Courtesy, Eugene R. Cazedessus, Sr., Family.

Text continues on page 153

Above
This group of women called the "Comus Edic" was the first musical organization for women students at Louisiana State University. Shortly after Henry Wallace Stopher became director of the department of music at the university in 1915, the music program was expanded tremendously. Courtesy, Department of Archives and Manuscripts, LSU, Baton Rouge.

Right
The Battle of Baton Rouge began at dawn on August 5, 1862, and while short in duration, it was costly for both sides. Union casualties numbered about 383 (84 killed, 266 wounded and 33 captured or missing) and Confederate losses were estimated at around 456 (84 killed, 315 wounded and 57 missing). This map of the battlefield by Joseph Gorlinski shows the fighting concentrated in an area bounded on the north by North Street, on the south by Government, and on the east by the State Penitentiary. From atlas to Official Records of Rebellion, U.S. War Department.

TOPOGRAPHICAL PLAN
OF THE CITY
AND
BATTLE-FIELD
OF
BATON ROUGE, LA.

Fought on the 5th of August
1862
drawn by
JOSEPH GORLINSKI, Civil Eng.

Scale of feet.

0   300   600   900   1200   1500   1800   2100   2400

—— Union
—— Confeder[ate]

The burning of the State House of Louisiana on December 28, 1862, is preserved in Frank (Francis) H. Schell's gouache drawing of the fire. The sketch was submitted to Frank Leslie's Illustrated Weekly Newspaper *and reproduced there in wood-block form. Courtesy, Anglo-American Art Museum, LSU, Baton Rouge. Gift of the Friends of the Museum.*

Frank H. Schell, war correspondent for
Frank Leslie's Illustrated Weekly
Newspaper *of New York, completed this*
gouache drawing of Union troops crossing
Monte Cino (Sano) Bayou north of Baton
Rouge on March 13, 1863. This event
marked their advance on Port Hudson.
Courtesy, Anglo-American Art Museum,
LSU, Baton Rouge. Gift of Friends of the
Museum and Dr. Edward M. Boagni III.

DR. MENDENHALL'S AGUE CURE,
No Cure! No Pay'—Sold by
R. R. JONES.   BATON ROUGE, LA.

Above
In late 1861, Baton Rouge joined other towns and businesses in the state in printing its own paper money. By December of that year, there was about $105,000 in circulation. Denominations ranged from five cents to three dollars and served as the primary medium of exchange. This issue for one dollar is dated November 4, 1861, and is counter-signed by Mayor J.E. Elam.

Left
In a day when printed color pictures were not abundant, trade cards like this one frequently were mounted in scrapbooks and enjoyed for many years. This card given out by druggist R.R. Jones of Baton Rouge advertises Dr. Mendenhall's Ague Cure. On the back, the manufacturer promises that if taken three times a day, the tonic will cure all types of chills and fevers, regulate the stomach and bowels, restore lost appetite, and prevent the development of malaria and other diseases. The price per bottle was 50 cents.

Right
The Pelican Hook and Ladder Company No. 1, organized in 1874, had as its motto, "We Raise to Save." The third organization of firemen formed in the city, its membership contained some of the most influential men of Baton Rouge. This invitation is to the second anniversary ball of the company at Pike's Hall on March 29, 1875. All courtesy, Department of Archives and Manuscripts, LSU, Baton Rouge.

PELICAN HOOK & LADDER CO.
No. 1,

Request the pleasure of your company
AT THEIR

Second Anniversary Ball

TO BE GIVEN AT

PIKE'S HALL,
Monday Evening, March 29, 1875.

Invitations (Not Transferable) will positively be required at the door.

GRAND MARCH AT EIGHT O'CLOCK.

DEDICATED TO THE PANSY CIRCLE OF BATON ROUGE, LA.

HEART'S EASE

Reverie

BY

Selina Kugler

PUBLISHED
BY
JUNIUS HART.
NEW ORLEANS.

5

BATON ROUGE. La.   Louisiana Institute for the Blind.   F.W. Heroman, Pub.

Left
Around the turn of the century, music was one of the most popular pastimes both in the home and in the community. In 1899, there were no less than six bands or orchestras in Baton Rouge. Local musicians frequently tried their hand at music publishing and often dedicated the composition to an organization or "deserving" individual. "Heart's Ease" by Selina Kugler was published by the New Orleans music firm of Julius Hart in 1887 and is dedicated to the Pansy Circle of Baton Rouge. Courtesy, Department of Archives and Manuscripts, LSU, Baton Rouge.

Above
From 1904 to 1914, the collecting of picture postcards became one of the most popular hobbies in the world. In many cases, the only surviving images of historic structures or events are found on souvenir cards lovingly placed in albums then. In the early 1900s F.W. Heroman published many Baton Rouge scenes in beautiful colors. This early view of the old School for the Blind was produced by Heroman and printed in Saxony. Courtesy, Mr. and Mrs. A.M. Hochenedel.

Baton Rouge

Politics, Progress, and Prosperity

153

Left

By the 1920s, Baton Rouge had begun to spread rapidly in all three directions from the river. In this promotional booklet published in 1928 by Perry Brown and Company, Inc., it states that "Big Cities Grow North and Upstream." To contribute to that trend, the company advertised the sale of 1,000 lots in the Fortune Addition, which was on the Plank Road northeast of Monte Sano Avenue and south of Hooper Road. The auction held on the site under a big tent was a gala affair with prizes, entertainments, and fireworks, a bonfire, barbecue, and band concert. Courtesy, Dr. and Mrs. Henry W. Jolly, Jr.

construction. Subsequently, the board of trustees managed to pay for a single building [in New Orleans] by reducing faculty salaries and by putting up future salaries as collateral for a loan. The faculties' money was still being used in 1902 to pay off this mortgage. Neglected, the university did not turn out a single graduate until 1887, and as late as 1898 it had only ten students taking college-level courses. The [New Orleans] Daily Picayune *fittingly described it [in 1881] as "Southern University, a Colored High School With Grammar School Characteristics."*

Southern University was relocated from New Orleans to Scotlandville, just north of Baton Rouge, in 1914. But many years would pass before the separate-and-glaringly-*un*equal institution, together with black public education generally, received support and encouragement sufficient to perform a quality educational mission within Louisiana's black community.

The most historically significant event that occurred in Baton Rouge during the early 20th century—perhaps ever—was the intersection of the town's destiny with that of John D. Rockefeller's immense Standard Oil Company of New Jersey. Indeed, within two years, Louisiana and Standard Oil influenced each other profoundly, in one instance by a decision rendered by a Louisianian and in the other by a decision reached by the company's high command.

The only Louisianian to serve as Chief Justice of the United States was Edward Douglass White (1910–1921), a Confederate private, Ku Klux Klansman, and accommodating politician who reached the top because of good friends, good luck, and third-rate competition along the way. Although still dismissed by many as "the Chief Justice whose opinions are never cited," White drafted at least one important judgment: his 1911 "rule of reason" decision that dissolved Rockefeller's oil empire into its component parts. Thus did a Louisianian profoundly affect the future of Standard Oil.

Two years earlier Standard's directors had made a decision that profoundly affected the future of Louisiana, certainly that portion of it containing Baton Rouge. An oil refinery would be constructed in Louisiana's capital city under the management of yet another Standard-controlled company, Standard Oil of Louisiana. Just as everything was coming together for Baton Rouge, the situation suddenly became—miraculously better! But why had an increasingly prosperous though still obscure little Southern river town become the site of a modern and significant installation, managed by perhaps the mightiest corporation in the world?

A local booster waxed enthusiastically six years later, in 1915, over the town's obvious attractions that, he was convinced, were the sole criteria for Standard's selection of Baton Rouge:

Situated high on the bluff over the greatest natural commercial waterway in the world, [Baton Rouge] presented a harbor for the largest ocean steamships without

Above
Starting initially with very meager facilities at its new location in Baton Rouge, Southern University had eight buildings valued at over $65,000, a power plant, and an artesian well within the first year. By the 1920s, when this panoramic view was taken from the Mississippi River, the physical plant had grown considerably. On the extreme left is the Administration Building and on the far right is seen the president's home. Between these were two trades buildings, two dormitories, Parker Dining Hall, three teachers' cottages, a cafe, the water tower, and a power plant. Courtesy, Department of Archives, Southern University, Baton Rouge.

Top left
Southern University officially opened on March 9, 1914. The original physical plant consisted of one large frame dwelling, some 12 renovated cabins, and two temporary buildings constructed to receive students and instructors. This photograph taken during the transition shows some of those early structures on the campus. Courtesy, Department of Archives, Southern University.

Bottom left
Praised in local newspapers as the "leader of the Negro race," Booker T. Washington came to Baton Rouge on April 15, 1915, at the invitation of prominent blacks in the state. After first inspiring students, teachers, and visitors in a speech on the Southern University campus, Washington addressed a crowd of blacks and whites estimated at 5,000 at the public square. Both races participated in the ceremonies downtown, with B.V. Baranco, Sr., presiding. This rare photograph taken on the Southern campus shows Dr. J.S. Clark, fifth from the left on the front row and Washington on his immediate left, with other civic and educational leaders from the parish and state. Courtesy, Department of Archives, Southern University.

There have been only four presidents of Southern University since it opened its doors on the Baton Rouge campus some 67 years ago. On the top row, left is Dr. Joseph S. Clark (1914–1938) and to the right is his son, Dr. Felton G. Clark (1938–1968). On the bottom row, left is Dr. G. Leon Netterville (1968–1974) and to the right, Jesse N. Stone, Jr. (1974–present). Courtesy, Office of Public Relations, Southern University, Baton Rouge.

danger from storms or tidal wave. Within easy access of the greatest oil and gas deposits in America, and situated at the natural gateway from the southwest to points north and east, it offered exceptional advantages for an oil refining plant as it does for many other industries. Its only disadvantage lay in the fact that it had never previously been discovered by the captains of finance and industry.

No doubt Standard's "captains" had indeed considered Baton Rouge's "exceptional advantages," but they were not the only reasons why the company selected a town in *Louisiana* as the location for a new refinery, as John L. Loos disclosed in his history of the Interstate Oil Pipe Line Company:

[Standard Oil wanted] to provide an economical outlet for the great and increasing crude production of the Mid-Continent area and to improve the competitive position of Standard Oil in that region. . . . Because of legal attacks on the Standard companies in Texas and the imminence of their eviction from that state, any further Jersey activity there was out of the question. It was only after long and careful consideration of several eligible sites elsewhere that the directors determined to build the refinery at Baton Rouge.

Texas's misfortune, at least in 1909, turned out to be Baton Rouge's good fortune, and Standard Oil Company of Louisiana was duly chartered in East Baton Rouge Parish on April 13, 1909, in accordance with the provisions of Louisiana's Corporation Act of 1904. The company was capitalized in the amount of $5 million divided into 50,000 shares worth

$100 each. One thousand shares were owned by the five company directors, while the remaining 49,000 shares—a substantial controlling interest—remained the property of Standard Oil Company of New Jersey.

The local press marveled at the amount of money to be injected into the Baton Rouge economy by construction wages alone—a sum "equivalent to at least two-thirds of the total money value of the entire cotton crop of East Baton Rouge for the year 1909." By such comparisons did the old express its awe of the new. The *State-Times* editor who wrote the above lines may have been moved to even further rapture had he been able to foresee that the value of products from the refinery would soon far exceed the "money value" of every plant raised in the soil of East Baton Rouge Parish, and that Baton Rouge would shortly change almost overnight from a town serving agriculture to a city flourishing with industry.

The refinery in its initial year of operation could process only 1,800 barrels of crude oil daily; manufacture only gasoline, kerosene, and heavy fuel oil; and employ about 700 persons. Seventy-two years later the installation turns out 500,000 barrels per day, manufactures more than 600 different products, and is the nation's largest refinery of its kind. Today almost 3,000 persons are employed by the facility.

By 1915 Baton Rouge was feeling its oats. Prosperity had arrived, fitted well, and was in town to stay. Four local banks held about $3 million in deposits, a "progressive" commission form of government had been substituted the previous year for the old mayor-council system, and

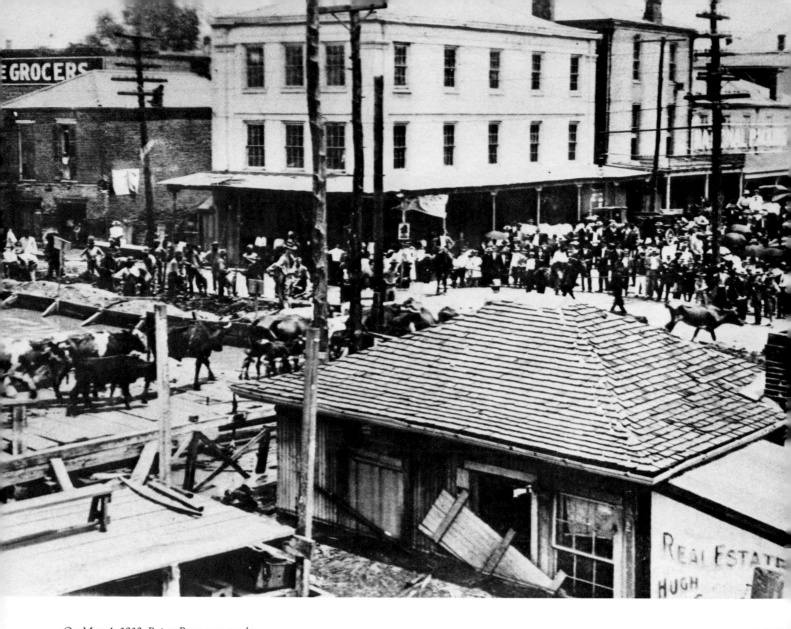

On May 4, 1912, Baton Rougeans awoke to find hundreds of refugees from the flooded countryside pouring into the city. Many had not eaten for days and had lost everything. Steamers, flotilla gasoline boats, U.S. Navy lifeboats, and every imaginable vessel plowed through the high water to rescue victims. Thousands of homeless and thousands of cattle disembarked at the landing. This photograph shows livestock being unloaded at the foot of Main Street. To the far left, workers at the water's edge strengthen the levee. Courtesy, Mr. and Mrs. A.M. Hochenedel.

Since Baton Rouge was incorporated in 1817, there continually has been some sort of law enforcement provided. Until 1859, the city was policed by a town constable. During the Civil War and Union occupation, a force patrolled the community until 1865, when the first chief of police was appointed. In the early years, the three material requirements for each law-enforcement official were his own weapon; a horse; and fodder for the animal. This 1932 photograph shows the entire police force for the city. The "elite" motorcycle brigade stands in front. Courtesy, Sergeant M.B. Cantu.

Left
Pioneer photographer Jasper G. Ewing moved to Baton Rouge in mid-1911 and operated a photographic business there until shortly before his death in 1972. Ewing is perhaps best remembered for his marvelous panoramic views taken with a "circuit camera." This camera, which he designed, had the capability of traveling over a quarter of a circle. This photograph shows Ewing with one of his cameras on the levee at Baton Rouge. Courtesy, Bentley B. Mackay III.

a country club was on the drawing boards with prominent merchants, financiers, lawyers, physicians, and educators as charter members. All of this had also produced respectability at last. According to the *Chronicle,* "The percentage of arrests has not been large, proving that the city is composed, for the most part, of law-abiding citizens and the regulations regarding the handling and sale of intoxicating liquors are enforced in a satisfactory manner, with the result that drunkenness is rare and unusual." A police force consisting of a chief, assistant chief, and "twelve patrolmen whose beats cover the entire city" saw to it that the public peace was not disturbed.

Two years later, in 1917, the United States entered World War I for the purpose, as President Woodrow Wilson stated, of making "the world safe for democracy," and in 1917 Baton Rougeans were no less determined than other Americans to defeat what was perceived as dangerous German imperialism. The effect of the war on the town was brief—the nation itself, after all, was actively involved for only 17 months—and impermanent. (World War II, by contrast, would impose revolutionary changes upon Baton Rouge.)

But on Armistice Day, November 11, 1918, the citizens of Baton Rouge also matched, if they did not exceed, the wild enthusiasm of their fellow countrymen in bringing down the Kaiser. News of the cease-fire arrived over the telegraph at two A.M. From then until the following midnight, the town celebrated with parades, noise-makers, automobile horns, and music. Not until almost one in the morning of November 19, until "the last weary celebrators were still bunny-hugging up Third Street to the tune of Toot Johnson's Jazz band," did the revelry fade away. As only a Baton Rougean could describe it, the *State-Times* editor wrote of the celebration the next day:

It was the Fourth of July and Christmas even, and Mardi Gras, and election night, and a Tiger football victory—all compressed for a generation and rolled into one—one big overwhelming election in which the people took control and celebrated.

Following the "boomlet" that attended World War I, conditions in Baton Rouge seemed almost heavenly. "This is a community that is practically free of crime," boasted the *Sunday News* in 1921. "Our jails are empty, while the criminal court meets only to adjourn. . . ." With an expanding public school system, a new business college, more than 3,000 refinery employees, and a drainage system that was "almost perfect," the city and the parish had become "two of the most delightful places in the world to live."

And so Baton Rouge remained throughout the 1920s and to a limited extent into the troubled 1930s, the oil-based local economy already demonstrating some of its "recession-proof" qualities that would cushion

Above
During World War I, Louisianians contributed greatly to the war effort. Women at home engaged in various projects and sacrificed to help the country and its fighting men. Many of these men marching down Third Street with others from the area likewise gave their all to the cause. Courtesy, Mr. and Mrs. J.E. Snee.

Left
In the mid-1920s, Third Street (now Riverside Mall) was the primary business area of Baton Rouge. The streets were paved and teeming with automobiles. Store signs were visible for blocks and some office buildings "towered" above the streets. The tall white structure on the left near the foot of Third is the recently completed Louisiana National Bank. Courtesy, Louisiana State Library.

Above
Public-health regulations in Baton Rouge gradually developed in the early 1900s. Ordinances were passed to assure cleaner milk, meat, bread, markets, and laundries. After World War I, the focus was on the improvement of individual health habits. As part of this emphasis, each of these young LSU coeds from Alpha Delta Pi sorority around 1918 became "Cho-Cho the Clown" and assisted health personnel in educating school children in personal hygiene and other topics by telling stories. Courtesy, Mrs. Catherine Herget Huckabay.

Right
This broadside advertised a grand fete given in 1918 by the United Daughters of the Confederacy to benefit the Red Cross Society and its then multifarious programs. During World War I ladies of Baton Rouge, primarily through the Red Cross Society, busied themselves in various projects to help the war effort. In addition to serving at a canteen near the State Capitol, women sold war savings bonds, sewed garments for the soldiers, and manned a "melting pot" to collect old gold and silver items. A plea was issued particularly for old silver thimbles. Courtesy, Department of Archives and Manuscripts, LSU, Baton Rouge.

GRAND FETE
For the RED CROSS Society

UNDER THE AUSPICES OF

Henry Watkins Allen Chapter
U. D. C.

CAPITOL GROUNDS
WEDNESDAY, JUNE 12, 1918

Above
This interesting photograph taken in the early 1920s shows many of Baton Rouge's most historic buildings at the time. With a few notable exceptions, all have vanished. Reading left to right are: 1. Bonnecaze-Duncan House; 2. Garig House; 3. St. Joseph's Cathedral; 4. Methodist Church; 5. St. Joseph's Academy; 6. Heroman (Singletary) Building; 7. Presbyterian Church; 8. St. James Episcopal Church; 9. old Post Office; 10. old Masonic Hall; 11. old City Hall; 12. old City Market; and 13. Andrew Jackson Home. Courtesy, Dr. and Mrs. Henry W. Jolly, Jr.

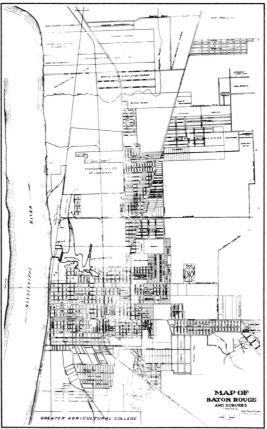

Left
This map shows how relatively small the city of Baton Rouge had remained to 1920. In 1923, the date of this map, most expansion had been to the several newer subdivisions in the east and especially to the north around the Standard Oil Company of Louisiana. South of the city the location for the ''Greater Agricultural College'' is indicated but there is very little development shown between it and the corporation limits. Within the next decades, however, the change would be nothing less than phenomenal. Courtesy, Louisiana Room, LSU Library.

Above
There are probably few photographs surviving from the 1920s that have a more impressive assemblage of leaders of the Baton Rouge community than this group picture of the Baton Rouge Bar Association taken in July 1922. All 27 men are identified: 1. J.Y. Sanders, Jr.; 2. Judge Burgess; 3. T.J. Cross; 4. A.R. Albritton; 5. Judge Sam G. Laycock; 6. W. Carruth Jones; 7. L.B. Aldrich; 8. Herman Moyse; 9. W.O. Watson; 10. Fred S. LeBlanc; 11. Oliver Bouanchaud; 12. Shelby Taylor; 13. Jess Johnson; 14. Fred G. Benton; 15. Bob Day; 16. C.C. Bird, Jr.; 17. Joe Brunot; 18. P.G. Barron; 19. B.B. Taylor, Sr.; 20. J.F. Odum; 21. H.P. Breazeale, Sr.; 22. C.W. Kernan; 23. C.A. Holcombe; 24. Tom Ed McHugh; 25. Deputy Sheriff Rodriguez; 26. Gillie Sides; 27. Judge H.F. Brunot. Courtesy, B.B. Taylor, Jr.

Right
For many years virtually the only descriptions and studies of residences in Baton Rouge were devoted to the larger and grander homes. Recently, however, that interest has broadened to the simpler dwellings and preservationists have turned their attention to the restoration of such architecture. These cottages, probably located in the vicinity of Canal Street, are shown during a flood in the early part of the century. Courtesy, Mr. and Mrs. A.M. Hochenedel.

Baton Rouge against national economic slumps in future years. But before management-minded Baton Rouge had to cope with the economic stresses of the Great Depression, the town's leaders were accosted by an equally depressing psychological phenomenon—Governor and United States Senator Huey P. Long, whose presence off and on in Baton Rouge between 1918 and 1935 was extremely unsettling to local tranquility and confidence.

Long was born in rural Winn Parish in north central Louisiana in 1893 at the beginning of the Populist crisis, in which Winn and many of its residents were deeply involved. Huey's family, however, was neither rich nor poor, but comfortable by contemporary standards. From boyhood, Long demonstrated abilities in both public speaking and leadership, essential for a successful politician in a democratic society.

Young Huey dropped out of high school in his senior year, never really attended college, and crammed a year of legal studies into his receptive brain after supporting himself for a while as a traveling salesman. In 1918, at the age of 25, he was elected to north Louisiana's seat on the state railroad commission, since 1921 the public service commission. For the next six years Commissioner Long vigorously defended utilities consumers, railroad customers, and small pipeline companies, becoming an emerging spokesman and leader of Louisiana's rural masses and common folk. In the process Long also became the feared and despised enemy of utility companies, railroads, and, especially, of Standard Oil, the backbone of Baton Rouge's economy and value system.

Long ran for governor and lost in 1924. Four years later, however, he ran again and was elected. From 1928 until he was murdered in 1935, Huey P. Long not only revolutionized Louisiana, but also became America's foremost radical politician. At home, Long's power and influence derived from his performance—paving roads, providing free textbooks to schoolchildren, upgrading public education and state hospitals, and generally bettering the lives of Louisiana's humbler citizens. Nationally, Long attracted a large following by promoting a scheme called, "Share Our Wealth," which would have taxed the super-rich to provide a free college education for all qualified students, guaranteed family incomes, and similar controversial benefits.

Long was not a "gentleman" to most of those who believed themselves to be such. He was a "hillbilly," was not himself college-educated, and paid minimal attention to genteel amenities in his dealings with other people, whether friend or foe. Long was aggressive, determined, blunt, and often unscrupulous. He accomplished great reforms in Louisiana that were decades overdue, but at the high price of believing that the ends—especially his own—justified the means. Long's insensitivity ultimately cost him his own life at the age of 42—his assassin was Dr. Carl Austin Weiss, Jr., the son-in-law of a state judge whom Long was

Above
Governor Henry Luce Fuqua, Baton Rouge's own son, died at the executive mansion in October of 1926. Educated at Magruder's Collegiate Institute and Louisiana State University and a veteran of the Spanish-American War, he organized the Fuqua Hardware Company and developed it into a major business establishment. Under both Louisiana governors Pleasant and Parker, Fuqua served as general manager of the state penal system before resigning to enter the gubernatorial race in 1923. His campaign motto, "For United, Quiet, Useful Administration," was spelled with the letters of his last name. This rare campaign button was distributed during Fuqua's candidacy for governor. Courtesy, private collector.

Right
In 1940, almost four years after Huey P. Long's death, the monument on the State Capitol grounds marking his grave was erected. Designed by Charles Keck, the bronze statue of the former governor and United States Senator stands with his left hand resting on a model of the Capitol of Louisiana. On the marble base are reliefs depicting some of his accomplishments with inscriptions to Long. This rare photograph dated March 22, 1940, shows the monument shortly after it was raised. Courtesy, Department of Archives and Manuscripts, LSU, Baton Rouge.

conspiring to have gerrymandered out of his office.

To the self-assured, conservative, and tax-shy leaders of Baton Rouge, therefore, the presence of Huey P. Long in their midst created a squalid and oppressive nightmare. The dynamic, unorthodox young governor from rural, neo-Populist Winn Parish seemed to be everything that they were not, or pretended not, to be: rude, inconsiderate, devious, unprincipled, irresponsible, and vulgar. But most of all, he was powerful—far more so than they—and his use of power often dismayed and even terrified them.

Long decided important matters quickly and unilaterally, often without consulting others involved and sometimes gratuitously insulting them. He frequently changed his mind, disrupting plans and previous commitments. He raised taxes, or threatened to, almost constantly. Among Baton Rouge leaders only LSU administrators got along well with Long, and only because Long was devoted to the university.

Local newspapers despised Long, and let him know it. Baton Rouge voters always endorsed the opposition by comfortable majorities, and

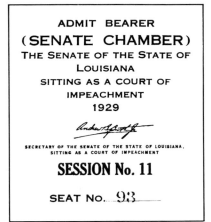

ADMIT BEARER
(SENATE CHAMBER)
THE SENATE OF THE STATE OF LOUISIANA
SITTING AS A COURT OF IMPEACHMENT
1929

Andrew J. Smith

SECRETARY OF THE SENATE OF THE STATE OF LOUISIANA,
SITTING AS A COURT OF IMPEACHMENT

SESSION No. 11

SEAT NO. 93

Above
Louisianians focused their attention on Baton Rouge when the state senate's court of impeachment against Huey P. Long convened in May of 1929. At the rear of the chamber bleacher-like seats accommodating 120 spectators were erected and tickets were issued for each seat. This extremely rare item was one of the tickets printed for the trial. Courtesy, Department of Archives and Manuscripts, LSU, Baton Rouge.

Left
Much excitement was generated at Baton Rouge in January, 1935 when members of the Square Deal Association, an anti-Long organization, seized the courthouse. Martial law was declared for the parish and units of the national guard arrived. On January 26, state police and national guardsmen carrying rifles, machine guns, and tear gas routed a force of some 100 Square Dealers at the municipal airport. When spectators jeered at the troopers, they were dispersed with a volley of tear gas. This incident became known as the "battle of the airport." Courtesy, Louisiana State Museum.

Below
This is one of the few remaining photographs of the governor's mansion prior to the 1930 building. The rambling white-frame house was built by Nathan Knox about 1857 with slave labor. In 1887 it was purchased by the state and remained the executive mansion until it was torn down in 1929. The mansion was located on the western corner of the block on North Boulevard bounded by St. Charles and Royal streets. The remainder of the area was used for servants' quarters, a garage, and gardens. Courtesy, Mrs. Donald A. Draughon.

leading citizens of Baton Rouge muttered nasty things about Long when he was not around. One of the greatest disappointments in recent local history was the state senate's refusal to convict Long during his 1929 impeachment trial.

Between the time Long was shot on September 8, 1935, and his demise two days afterward, "the churches of Baton Rouge," according to a prominent local opponent, "were filled with people praying that he would die." There was no love lost between corporate, urban-establishmentarian Baton Rouge and rural-radical Huey P. Long.

Long's tenure as governor coincided with a world phenomenon that affected each and every Baton Rougean regardless of political sentiment. The totality of Baton Rouge's experience during the Great Depression has yet to be comprehensively studied; but historian Sidney Tobin uncovered some important developments that occurred during the early New Deal years.

Both volunteer and government efforts arose in 1933 to aid the unemployed and needy, whose plight had been steadily worsening since

Left
This valuable photograph, taken on September 12, 1935, features some of the floral offerings at the funeral of Huey P. Long on the Capitol grounds. It was estimated at the time that the total value of flowers sent exceeded $25,000—not a mean sum for that day. The awning in the center of the sunken garden marks the grave and throngs of mourners may be seen on all sides. Courtesy, Louisiana State Library.

Right
The true and full story of the assassination of Governor Huey P. Long will probably forever remain in question. This photograph of the alleged assassin, Dr. Carl A. Weiss, Jr., seems to convey a sober and studious young man. The son of a prominent Baton Rouge physician, Weiss continued his medical studies in Paris and Vienna after graduation from Tulane University. He then returned to the city to practice medicine with his father. Courtesy, Louisiana State Museum.

Above
This former Christian church on the corner of East Boulevard and Louisiana Avenue was purchased in 1921 by the Housewives League. This group was formed two years earlier to participate in activities of interest to housewives and it grew so rapidly that it required a larger regular meeting place. The Woman's Club, Inc., created in 1921, met such a need and was operated by a board of managers elected by stockholders. These women ran the clubhouse for the benefit of affiliated clubs who paid annual fees for use of the facility as well as others who occasionally held meetings there. The building was demolished around 1940 and the present structure was erected on the site. Courtesy, Department of Archives and Manuscripts, LSU, Baton Rouge.

Louisianians benefited greatly from WPA projects sponsored by the Federal government. In Baton Rouge, Louisiana State University was a major recipient of funds for construction and other improvements. One large expenditure was the enlargement of the northern end of the stadium and the dormitory space underneath. This photo, taken on November 28, 1936, focuses on National WPA Administrator Harry L. Hopkins, who delivered the main address at the dedication of the stadium. Governor Richard W. Leche stands to the right of Hopkins. A fitting conclusion to the event was LSU's victory over Tulane, 33–0. Courtesy, Department of Archives and Manuscripts, LSU, Baton Rouge.

Charles P. Manship, Sr., was a prominent publisher and civic leader in Baton Rouge for over 40 years. Assuming control of the State Times *in 1909, he later absorbed the* New Advocate *and in 1925 established the city's first successful morning newspaper, the* Morning Advocate. *He founded the first radio station in Baton Rouge, WJBO, in 1933 and in 1941 he created WBRL, the first frequency-modulation radio station in the Deep South. Manship, always active in civic and charitable affairs, served on the board of the Chamber of Commerce and encouraged industries to locate in his town. Under his aegis, the Good Fellows organization, which provided gifts to needy children at Christmas time, was established. Manship died in 1947. Courtesy, Capital City Press.*

1929. Many citizens began cultivating their own gardens to compensate for shortages of purchasable fruits and vegetables. Two hundred local unemployed set up the Unemployed Workmen's Association, which ran a cannery, garage, store, shoe shop, and beauty parlor. As observed in the *Morning Advocate*, formerly wealthy matrons no longer able to afford servants, who had "never done their own housework . . . learned to leave bridge tables for the more exciting job of keeping a home."

The local office of the Federal Emergency Relief Administration had employed 1,314 black and 715 white jobless men by June of 1933. Among the tasks they performed were construction of concrete sidewalks on the campuses of LSU and Southern, road construction and repair, the expansion of City Park Lake, and a variety of other local construction and maintenance jobs. The Civil Works Administration provided similar employment. A Transient Bureau was created to feed, clothe, house, and medically treat the homeless and unemployed drifters.

Sadly, no government office could prevent the fact that 686 pieces of property were sold at sheriff's sales in 1932 for non-payment of taxes, followed by further sales of 498 pieces in both 1933 and 1934. Like many communities elsewhere in the afflicted nation, Baton Rouge suffered a severe banking crisis soon after President Franklin D. Roosevelt's "bank holiday." Only the Louisiana National Bank could reopen; the four state banks in town failed to survive. One of them, the Louisiana Trust and Savings Bank, merged with Louisiana National. The Louisiana Bank and Trust Company combined with the Citizens Bank and Trust Company to form the City National Bank, while the Bank of Baton Rouge disappeared completely. But between later New Deal emergency relief programs, Huey Long's infant welfare state (many of whose salaried employees lived in Baton Rouge), LSU, the refinery, and strong local leadership, Baton Rouge apparently weathered what remained of the Depression better than many other municipalities and escaped its worst effects. (The town's mayor during these years was businessman Wade Bynum, a seasoned veteran of public service. Bynum served as mayor of Baton Rouge longer than anyone else; his two stints in city hall extended from 1903 to 1910 and again from 1923 to 1941.)

Law-abiding, middle-class Baton Rouge was given another shock shortly after Huey Long had passed from the scene, which amply recharged the town's political cynicism before matters improved after 1940. Elected governor in 1936 was state court of appeals judge Richard Webster Leche, an impressively good-looking 38-year-old New Orleanian. Although the candidate of the Long machine, which still controlled Louisiana at the time, Leche possessed dignity, intelligence, and ability, and was moderately pro-business in outlook. He seemed too good to be true. In 1939 Leche suddenly resigned, stating that severe arthritis prevented him from continuing as governor. (Lieutenant Governor Earl K. Long,

Above
In 1938 a United States law made Armistice (now Veterans) Day a national holiday. In this picture taken in the late 1930s, thousands join Governor Richard W. Leche on the Capitol grounds to observe the signing of the World War I Armistice and to honor the nation's war dead. Included in the crowd are part of the LSU band, cadet corps, and color guard; boy scouts; and members of the American Legion and other patriotic groups. Both courtesy, Department of Archives and Manuscripts, LSU, Baton Rouge.

Left
During the difficult years of the late 1930s, Governor and Mrs. Richard W. Leche hosted a farmers' day at the executive mansion. Inside the building the crowd was even greater than that seen on the front lawn. A welcome sign is prominently displayed at the entrance to the old Governor's Mansion built by Huey P. Long in 1930.

Huey's younger brother, completed Leche's term.)

A federal grand jury indicted Leche on several charges and he was subsequently convicted of using the mails to defraud and violation of the federal "hot oil" act. Soon he was in residence in Atlanta's federal penitentiary. At about the same time, LSU president James Monroe Smith was convicted of embezzlement and went to the Louisiana State Penitentiary at Angola as the most educated inmate in the institution's history. Other prominent Longites were indicted, convicted, imprisoned, fined, or they killed themselves. Among the author's earliest memories as a youngster were the paperboys running down his street hawking "extra" editions with news of the latest arrests.

On the more positive side, Baton Rouge possessed an oil-refining facility of worldwide importance that by 1940 directly supported at least one-third of the local population, which had grown from about 8,000 in 1882 to approximately 34,700 by 1940. By the late 1930s three additional major industries were located in Baton Rouge—Solvay Process, Consolidated Chemicals, and Ethyl Corporation—with others due to arrive in the near future. The first bridge across the Mississippi River at Baton Rouge, and the second spanning that mighty stream within Louisiana, was completed in 1940.

Louisiana's only two state universities remained in Baton Rouge: black Southern University on Scott's Bluff above the river, and white LSU in its majestic new location south of town. The expanding state bureaucracy created by Huey P. Long had also become a permanent ingredient of the Baton Rouge economy as well as a major source of increasing population.

Suburbs had begun to proliferate as early as 1915. Among them were Fairfields and Istrouma to the north, where refinery employees made their homes; Tiger Town, College Town, and University Hills adjoining the new LSU campus to accommodate the institution's growing faculty (many of whom, like the refinery brass, were out-of-staters with different perspectives on life); and Roseland Terrace, Kleinert Terrace, Ogden Park, and Goodwood, east of the old city limits. Here the town's numerous business and professional people began to settle, along with members of the mushrooming state labor force. Many new homes also appeared eastward along Main, Laurel, Florida, Convention, and Government streets.

Several public buildings, two hospitals, an efficient bus transit system, a fine water supply drawn from deep and pure artesian wells, 12 good public schools (along with two equally sound parochial ones), and dozens of miles of paved streets rounded out the outstanding civic improvements made since the turn of the century.

Baton Rouge blacks, however, remained totally segregated from whites, their neighborhoods inferior in quality and their prospects narrowly circumscribed by the "second-class citizenship" of Jim Crow laws

The monumental Baton Rouge State Capitol was designed, planned, and administered by the New Orleans architectural firm of Weiss, Dreyfous, and Seiferth. Epitomizing the end of the Beaux-Arts architectural tradition in the United States, it was begun on November 16, 1930, and dedicated on May 16, 1932. This photograph shows the exterior of the Capitol after it has taken form and is awaiting the finishing touches. Courtesy, Louisiana State Library.

The formal dedication of the present Louisiana State University campus and its initial buildings was celebrated in front of the campanile on April 30, 1926. Special events were scheduled for three days and over 3,500 people attended. Soon to become one of the landmarks most associated with LSU, the bell tower was dedicated at the same time as a memorial to Louisiana's sons and daughters who died in service during World War I. Today it houses the Anglo-American Art Museum. Courtesy, Office of Public Relations, LSU, Baton Rouge.

Facing page
Top
Oil production in and outside of the corporation limits of Baton Rouge has bolstered the city's economy since the late 1930s. This exultant group, which included representatives from the Knox, Amiss, and Farrnbacher families, held an oil field picnic in August 1939. Statistics for November of that year show that the Baton Rouge Field contained over 40 wells pumping nearly 7,000 barrels a day. Courtesy, Miss May Lynn Amiss.

Bottom
This aerial view of the eastern part of the city prior to 1940 shows the vast rectangular area containing the Community Club Pavilion, the swimming pool, and Victory Park. Most conspicuous in the park is the reflecting pool with its two semicircular formal gardens. Baton Rouge Junior High and Gymnasium are immediately to the east. Courtesy, Dr. and Mrs. Henry W. Jolly, Jr.

Above
Governor John M. Parker rests on the shovel while Thomas D. Boyd, LSU president, looks on during the 1922 groundbreaking ceremony for the present Louisiana State University. Courtesy, Office of Public Relations, LSU, Baton Rouge.

Left
In 1937 construction began on a combined railroad and highway bridge across the Mississippi River north of Baton Rouge. Three years later the nearly $10 million project was completed and an elaborate dedication ceremony was held on August 10, 1940. This picture was taken approximately three months before completion of the 2.5-mile-long structure. Courtesy, Department of Archives and Manuscripts, LSU, Baton Rouge.

Right
The first state-approved high school for blacks in East Baton Rouge Parish was established in 1912 on Perkins Road. McKinley High School, pictured here, was the successor to that earlier institution and was built in 1926–1927 on East Boulevard. It remained an educational landmark for the black community for many years. Courtesy, Department of Archives and Manuscripts, LSU, Baton Rouge.

Left
Louisiana was one of the leading producers of Spanish moss in the early 20th century. This rare photograph from the late 1930s shows employees working at Sidney B. Webb's moss factory. It was located in a black residential section in the southern part of the city near the railroad. Courtesy, Department of Archives and Manuscripts, LSU, Baton Rouge.

Right
WJBO, Baton Rouge's first radio station, began broadcasting on December 12, 1934. The studio, transmitter, and tower were located on Magnolia Street and programs could be heard within a radius of 50 to 60 miles. Sitting before its microphone somewhat later is Orene Muse Huckabay, former radio and television personality and newswoman. She and her husband J. Elton Huckabay founded The Register some 32 years ago. The slick-paper magazine devoted to Baton Rouge society and people was written, edited, and published by Mrs. Muse and her son Lovell. The popular annual "Mad Hatter's Brunch" and style show benefitting local charities was the idea of this creative woman. Courtesy, The Register.

forced upon them since Reconstruction. But overt violence against blacks, a commonplace during the violent 1890s, had all but disappeared. As would be true of blacks elsewhere in the South and nation, black Baton Rougeans had to await the postwar "Civil Rights Revolution" before their opportunities and circumstances significantly improved.

But on the eve of World War II Baton Rouge was no longer the "sleepy little river town" remembered today by a dwindling number of senior residents. It was still a town, but a large one on the verge of "cityhood." A community infused with the corporate business mentality, it included as well some of the truly creative and exciting academic minds in the nation. Finally Baton Rouge had much additional room in which to continue growing, another blessing, among others, shared with a similar expanding community, Houston, Texas. All in all Baton Rouge in 1940 had put on several entirely new faces, all looking toward the future rather than the past. That future was both grim, in the short run, and full of promise in the long run.

Having overrun Poland the year before, Adolph Hitler's modern and mechanized Wehrmacht crashed into Holland, Belgium, and France in May of 1940. By the end of that year, London was prey to nightly bombing attacks. On December 7, 1941, Japanese naval forces at last drew the United States, Louisiana, and Baton Rouge into the maelstrom that had become World War II. An unprecedented catastrophe for much of mankind, the horrendous global conflict also unleashed economic forces and demands resulting in greater and sustained well-being for Baton Rouge, which eventually became, in the words of a local official, "Boomtown USA," by the 1940s.

Wade H. Bynum, prominent banker and member of a distinguished old Baton Rouge family, was mayor of the city for almost 25 years. During his tenure at City Hall, he undertook major improvement projects, including the 1923 bond issue that funded additional paving and sewage and provided for the municipal docks and City Park. Bynum witnessed the town grow far beyond his expectations and furnished able leadership during the turbulent years of the Depression. He died in 1946 after many decades of service to his community. Courtesy, Mrs. Herbert Courtney.

For many years, various professional men's and women's organizations in Baton Rouge have contributed immensely to the city and its progress. One of the oldest and most influential is the Business and Professional Women's Club, organized in 1925. Since its establishment, its membership has promoted women's rights, fostered various educational and service programs and drives, and crusaded in some political matters. The advertising and trades display and sale in 1928, sponsored by the BRB&PW and photographed here, netted $600 for an educational fund to help women students. Courtesy, Department of Archives and Manuscripts, LSU, Baton Rouge.

The completion of the expressway at Baton Rouge was a monumental task and when first begun it seemed virtually impossible to many local inhabitants. This view of the I-10 and I-110 highways was taken in March of 1970. The major link following the path to the left leads to the Mississippi River Bridge. The other stretch of interstate passes to the east of the downtown area and on to Plank Road, Scenic Highway, and north. Courtesy, Louisiana State Department of Transportation and Development.

THE ENERGETIC DECADES

With the Japanese surprise attack on Hawaii, December 7, 1941, the United States formally entered World War II, which had raged in Europe and Asia for more than two years. An editorial in the Baton Rouge *State-Times* on December 8 expressed a widely held American view at the time—that Hitler had ordered or at least persuaded his Japanese allies to force the United States into the war by bombing Pearl Harbor and neighboring installations without warning. By 1941 many Americans could foresee war with Germany, and even though most Americans also knew that our relations with Japan were strained, few could imagine the Japanese brutally assaulting United States military and naval facilities on their own. Subsequently it was learned, however, that Japan had indeed acted unilaterally, and that the Pearl Harbor attack had surprised Adolph

Hitler no less than it did Franklin D. Roosevelt or any of his countrymen. But within several days the United States also declared war on Germany and Italy.

Hundreds of Baton Rouge men and women served in the armed forces during World War II. (Mrs. C. Maranto who lived at 1628 North Boulevard in 1942 already had five of her nine sons in uniform by that time.) One of the earliest Baton Rouge casualties was navy Ensign Rodney S. Foss, killed in the Pearl Harbor attack. A destroyer escort was later named the U.S.S. Foss in his honor.

Among many other Baton Rougeans who gave their lives in battle was army Captain Leonard C. Saurage who was posthumously awarded the Distinguished Service Cross, the nation's second highest decoration, for heroism on Bougainville in the South Pacific. Baton Rouge produced at least one winner of the Congressional Medal of Honor, army Staff Sergeant Homer L. Wise whose extraordinary heroism in an engagement with the Germans in Italy brought him his country's highest tribute.

Two men still prominent in local banking also served with distinction and valor in the war. Ralph Sims of the Fidelity National Bank won three Air Medals and a Distinguished Flying Cross, while Mack H. Hornbeak of City National was awarded the Legion of Merit, Bronze Star with oak leaf cluster, and the French Croix de Guerre with palm. Marine Lieutenant Colonel Charles F. Duchein, a future legislator from Baton Rouge, won an Air Medal and a Distinguished Flying Cross. Duchein eventually became a major general in the Marine Corps Reserve.

LSU, because it originated in 1860 as a military academy and continued to stress military training after it became a land-grant institution, has long been known affectionately as the "Old War Skule." Thus it was not surprising that by 1943 15 former students or graduates of the "Old War Skule" had become generals in the armed forces. But the most outstanding general from Baton Rouge in World War II never attended LSU, although he had served on its faculty and would return after the war to become its president. This was Lieutenant General Troy Houston Middleton.

"Rugged, tough-minded and a hard cusser," as a military historian has described him, Middleton was born in Mississippi in 1889 and attended Mississippi A & M College, later Mississippi State University. Choosing the army as his career, Middleton rose meteorically in rank to command a regiment in World War I. (Years later, Army Chief of Staff George C. Marshall would recall that Middleton was our "outstanding infantry regimental commander on the battlefield in France.")

Interwar duty brought Middleton to LSU as commandant of cadets between 1930 and 1936. After a year in the Philippines, he retired from the army and returned to LSU, to which he had become devoted, serving as dean of administration, and later as vice president, from 1937 to 1942.

Above
Distinguished soldier and educator Troy H. Middleton (1889–1976) served Louisiana State University for 38 years in six different administrative positions, including 11 years as its president. As a regimental officer in the United States Army, he was the youngest colonel in the American Expeditionary Forces during World War I. Middleton, during the Second World War, became renown after he, as American Commander, made the key tactical decision to hold Bastogne during the Battle of the Bulge. Following retirement from LSU, he continued in public service by heading the state's Commission on Human Rights and helping to establish the Louisiana Coordinating Council of Higher Education. Courtesy, Troy H. Middleton Room, LSU Library, Baton Rouge.

Above
There were countless ways Baton Rouge civilians helped their country during World War II. In addition to participating in scrap iron, tin foil and book drives and war-bond sales, they grew victory gardens, organized for civil defense, and served as radio operators and airplane spotters. One active group in the area was the Civil Air Patrol, composed of volunteer civilians who used their own aircraft and equipment for various wartime tasks. This photograph shows members of the C.A.P. refueling at the old Parish, or Downtown, Airport in 1942. Courtesy, Fonville Winans.

Right
King Harding Knox, scion of an old and honored family of Baton Rouge, was a businessman, banker, and civic leader. In 1946, he was awarded a citation by the local American Legion post for publishing and delivering at his own expense Home News. This newspaper, printed from May of 1942 to October of 1945, was sent to thousands of men and women from the Baton Rouge vicinity in service during World War II, and included information on people in the armed forces as well as hometown news. Over 247,000 copies were circulated during its three-and-a-half-year existence. Courtesy, Mrs. Donald A. Draughon.

*This view of Baton Rouge looking south
was taken around 1940, probably to publi-
cize the new Mississippi River Bridge. The
oil refinery at that time was on its way to
becoming one of the largest in the world;
in this picture it seems to spread endlessly.
Little development is visible between the
industrial area and the new State Capitol.
Courtesy, Department of Archives and
Manuscripts, LSU, Baton Rouge.*

While the United States was still "neutral" but friendly to the Allies, one of the most popular and hardworking organizations in the country was Bundles for Britain. The Baton Rouge chapter, headed by Mrs. H. Payne Breazeale, Sr., contributed greatly to the program from 1940 until after Pearl Harbor, when most of its energies were diverted to the homefront and American fighting men. Gifts of money, new and used clothing and blankets, knitted articles, surgical and medical supplies, cots, and even the purchase and maintenance of an ambulance were forwarded to British hospitals, civilian war sufferers and military personnel. In addition to club- and group-sponsored benefits, one of the most successful single fund-raising events was a baseball game between the Esso and Norco teams on May 14, 1941. Courtesy, Mrs. H. Payne Breazeale, Sr.

Back in uniform soon after the nation was at war, Middleton again distinguished himself as an effective combat commander, first at the head of the 45th Infantry Division during the Sicilian campaign and subsequently as commanding general of VIII Corps in France, Belgium, and Germany. Between these two commands, Middleton became afflicted with an arthritic knee that resulted in his being sent back to Walter Reed Army Hospital and foreshadowed the end of his field career. But the general was much too valuable to be sidelined. Communicating with General Marshall from England, Supreme Allied Commander Dwight D. Eisenhower stated bluntly, "I don't give a damn about his knees; I want his head and his heart. And I'll take him into battle on a litter if we have to."

Middleton was in command of VIII Corps when that unit, among others, was struck by the German Ardennes offensive, remembered by Americans as the Battle of the Bulge. Although his staff "virtually collapsed," Middleton remained "steady as a rock," later receiving credit from General Omar Bradley for having halted the German advance.

After the war the much-decorated general returned to his beloved LSU as comptroller from 1945 to 1951. In the latter year he was appointed president of LSU and served until 1962, almost three years past the legal retirement age of 70. Old-timers on the Baton Rouge campus affirm that General Middleton was the institution's best president in living memory able, dedicated, hard-working, and a gentleman of absolute integrity. He presided over LSU's greatest period of growth and its expansion from a single campus to a multicampus system. As LSU's president emeritus from 1962 until his death in 1976, General Middleton continued to involve himself in the affairs of the university and of the community, and was as much Baton Rouge's "First Citizen" as anyone could possibly have been.

But Baton Rouge's contribution to the nation's victory in World War II went far beyond the human condition, and often the self-sacrifice, of many of its citizens. Modern wars have been called "quartermaster's wars" because the personnel who fight them require so many supplies, weapons, and provisions. Already a major oil-refining center, Baton Rouge expanded that aspect of her local economy for the war effort and became a principal chemical producer as well.

On the day after the Pearl Harbor attack, Governor Sam H. Jones announced that the Standard Oil refinery would spend at once the sum of $17 million for plant expansion, principally to produce aviation fuel. (Within one year the Baton Rouge refinery was manufacturing 76 percent of the nation's output of that crucial product.) In addition the company's new Chemical Products Division began to produce synthetic rubber once the nation had gone to war and sources of natural rubber, in the Dutch East Indies, had been seized by the Japanese.

Such a crucial military-industrial facility required protection from enemy attack and the result was Harding Field, a fighter base constructed north of town almost overnight. (An undergraduate instructor of the author disclosed several years ago his vivid memories of "war" service at Harding Field. After circling the town in his interceptor during the day, the young pilot invariably relaxed each evening in the Heidelberg Hotel's Hunt Room. After more than a year of this pleasant but enervating routine, the pilot was at last given a combat assignment and arrived in Europe in mid-1943.)

The rapid increase of new employees at the growing refinery, plus army personnel stationed at the airfield, expanded the local payroll significantly. They and their families had to be fed, clothed, housed, and amused; their children had to be schooled and their ailments attended to. The boom was on! After the war, as private investment replaced federal wartime spending in Baton Rouge, the refinery spawned a rapidly expanding petrochemical industry. Harding Field became the East Baton Rouge commercial air facility and was renamed Ryan Airport. (Only privately owned planes had served Baton Rouge prior to World War II. The parish airport reserved for that purpose was converted to other uses by 1979.)

From 1945 on Baton Rouge's fortunes, already on the upswing, became even better. Along with a growing private sector, the area's public employment also commenced its present sustained expansion. Additional employees earning ever-higher salaries stimulated retail, construction, service, and leisure industries. Most importantly Baton Rougeans, like millions of Americans elsewhere, purchased automobiles and headed for dozens of new suburbs that landowners, homebuilders, and real-estate developers were only too happy to provide.

The last four decades have seen change of such a sweeping nature that a Rip Van Winkle awakening from the Baton Rouge of 1940 would have difficulty placing himself in the community today, while a resident from a more remote era might not recognize the city at all. This is because so much of Baton Rouge is totally new. It would require little effort to take strangers into selected areas and convince them on the basis of what they saw that Baton Rouge simply did not exist prior to 1950, 1960, or even 1970.

One could easily be seduced into summarizing the last four decades of Baton Rouge's history in the purely statistical categories of "how much" and "how many." There is certainly enough of that kind of data to fill an entire thick volume. While such an approach would be of great interest to specialists, the general reader might wish to know only the principal statistics indicating the amount of growth, prosperity, and expansion that Baton Rouge has achieved since 1940.

The most inclusive and, for that reason, the most important category

A walk down Third Street in its heyday was a memorable experience. This photograph dating from the 1950s and looking from North Boulevard shows how dense both lanes of traffic could become and how neon signs at this point seemed to extend into infinity. Courtesy, Bill Vega.

of growth has been the steady increase in population, both within the city itself and within the parish. Figures depicting this fantastic explosion are given in the accompanying chart.

	City	% Increase	Parish	% Increase
1940	34,719	—	88,415	—
1950	125,629	262%*	158,236	79%
1960	152,419	21%	230,058	45%
1970	165,963	9%	285,167	24%
1980**	219,164	32%	368,468	29%

  * = City limits were greatly expanded in 1949.
** = Official preliminary figures, United States Census of 1980. Courtesy Louisiana State Planning Office.

As will be readily seen, the most dramatic increases in city population occurred during the first and last decades of the period. Many outsiders came to Baton Rouge during the 1940s, attracted by job opportunities in defense and related industries. But expansion of the city limits in 1949 had an almost equal effect on the city's growth because thousands of

Left
A familiar sight to most denizens of Baton Rouge prior to 1968 was the white-robed holy man of the riverbank, commonly called the "Prophet." He preferred "Messiah of Jesus," and stood near the edge of the Mississippi earnestly praying and preaching total baptism through immersion. Most of his "congregation" consisted of those crossing or waiting to board the ferry boats to Port Allen. Here, the holy man stands near the boat landing. His Bible rests near the log. Courtesy, Capital City Press.

Below left
Of the various social groups in Baton Rouge, two of the most prominent are Delta Sigma Theta and the Matrons Club. The latter, originally Junior Matrons, was organized in 1941 with Mrs. Marjorie Dumas Lawless as founder and first president. The organization focused on numerous social and civic activities with an earlier emphasis on presenting young ladies as debutantes in the Baton Rouge community from 1946 to 1971. Celebrating its 40th anniversary, the club has altered its purpose to meet the demands of the times in the black community. This picture shows the group in 1943, two years after it was established. Courtesy, Matrons Club.

Right
Built in the 1920s at the southernmost corporation limits then, the municipal terminals were equipped to handle freight from oceangoing vessels, river packets, and barges, as well as the interchange between them. By 1930, the city docks were composed of three basic units: a transfer barge, floating barge, and the docks proper. However, even by then it was predicted that they would soon be inadequate for the burgeoning river traffic. The 20-foot-wide runway leading over the levee to a storage area and the river is shown in 1965. Courtesy, W.W. "Woody" Dumas.

parish residents became "Baton Rougeans" overnight. The principal ingredients of the 1970–1980 expansion were significant increases in the number of government employees, both state and municipal, together with expansion of smaller local industries. Growth in employment within the major industrial sector was less spectacular. Only between 1940 and 1950 and again between 1970 and 1980 did the population of the city increase at a higher rate than the parish population.

At present more than 150 major industries in the Baton Rouge area employ 26,000 workers and generate an annual payroll of $450 million. The largest among these are petrochemical and construction firms, but utility companies, equipment suppliers, and transportation industries are also locally important.

River traffic has been crucial to Baton Rouge's economic development from the beginning. Further stimulated by the presence of the Standard Oil refinery and growing even more dramatically as the result of the war boom, river traffic in Baton Rouge has gone far beyond the handling of oil and chemicals, although those products remain significant. Since 1952, when the Greater Baton Rouge Port Commission was created by the state legislature, the abundant water transportation facilities in Baton Rouge have been developed to the extent that Baton Rouge currently ranks third in the nation in grain exports and fourth in general cargo. As the country's farthest inland deepwater port, Baton Rouge handled 79 million tons of

cargo in 1979 from ships flying the flags of more than 30 different countries.

Public-sector employment currently exceeds major industrial employment in Baton Rouge, a trend that will likely continue as the demand for public services and information increases. The state of Louisiana employs some 18,000 Baton Rougeans, the city-parish government about 4,400, and LSU and Southern combined account for about 7,000 jobs. Whether employed in the public or private sector, Baton Rouge residents purchased the awesome amount of $1,986,982,000 worth of retail goods and services in 1980.

Area schoolchildren attend more than 100 public schools, several parochial schools maintained by four religious denominations, and six nonsectarian private institutions. Among the larger public high schools are Istrouma, Robert E. Lee, Tara, Belaire, Glen Oaks, McKinley, Capitol, and Scotlandville. Baton Rouge has retained more than the vestiges of a segregated public school system over the years—McKinley, Capitol, and Scotlandville are overwhelmingly black—and a desegregation suit more than a quarter-century old is finally heading for a decision in the local federal district court of Judge John Parker.

Catholic High School and Redemptorist High School annually vie for the local "Vatican championship" in several sports, while Episcopal High School and the two laboratory schools maintained by the colleges of education at LSU and Southern are three of Baton Rouge's better non-public coeducational secondary institutions. St. Joseph's Academy is an old and excellent Roman Catholic high school for young women.

Increasing support from the mineral-rich state of Lousiana continues to expand the scope and raise the prestige of academic research programs at Baton Rouge's two institutions of higher learning, LSU and Southern. LSU was recently designated a "sea-grant university" by the federal government, while its press, created in 1935, has become one of the best publishers of scholarly works in the nation. Southern presently offers several master's degrees and the degree of juris doctor in addition to a full complement of bachelor's degrees. The survival and growth of Southern from 1913 to 1968 owes much to the leadership of its presidents, Joseph S. Clark (1913–1938) and Felton G. Clark (1938–1968), who guided the institution through lean and troubling times. As in the area of public education, however, a highly controversial lawsuit currently pending seeks to merge some of the programs, if not the institutional identities, of LSU and Southern.

More than 250 churches serve the religious needs of Baton Rougeans, four television and a dozen radio stations entertain them, and three general hospitals, one woman's hospital, and a single state hospital treat their illnesses and injuries.

Literally hundreds of residential subdivisions from large to minuscule have been developed since 1940, mostly from 1965. Downtown Baton Rouge, once the community's retail center, has been abandoned by shoppers for numerous suburban shopping centers. The two largest ones, Bon Marche and Cortana Mall, are located on Florida Boulevard East, which essentially bisects Baton Rouge on an east-west axis and carries the center of population eastward to Amite River.

As more people arrived in Baton Rouge, the volume of sales and property taxes skyrocketed. This steady increase in local government revenue met the need to raise additional funds for expanded public services and facilities. Even allowing for inflation, the growth of city revenue from $784,000 in 1943 to $39,764,000 in 1976 was astounding. Expeditures for the two principal municipal services, fire and police, grew from $104,000 each in 1943 to $5,373,000 for the fire department and $7,035,000 for the police force in 1976.

The watershed period for Baton Rouge was the 1940s, a decade during which wartime prosperity transformed the entire state from one with a rural population base (59 percent in 1940) to an urban majority of 54.3 percent 10 years later. Locally the same trends unfolded. In 1947 parish voters approved a proposal whereby the parish governing body (called a police jury in Louisiana) would be abolished and a consolidated city-parish government established in its place. The plan also did away with the Baton Rouge commission-mayor form of government. Since 1949 a mayor-president has served as the city-parish chief executive and a city-parish council functions as the parish legislative body. (Curiously the incorporated towns of Baker and Zachary retain their own mayors and town councils.)

The city-parish consolidation evolved from the recommendations of a planning commission sponsored by the Baton Rouge Chamber of Commerce, which in the 1940s was headed by J. Theron Brown. Objectives of the consolidation were to increase the efficiency of local government by cutting costs and eliminating duplication of services by the city and parish (county), and to create an ongoing master plan of government for the city-parish. Similar operations in other cities were studied and professional consultants were hired.

Voters within both the city and the parish had to approve the proposal, which narrowly passed on August 12, 1947, by a vote of 7,012 to 6,705, most yes votes coming from the city and most no votes from rural areas within the parish.

Opponents attacked the plan on several levels. One of the major bones of contention was removed prior to the election and may have made passage possible. This was the original provision within the plan for an appointed city manager as the parish chief executive. When many citizens complained that such an official would be a "dictator" not directly responsible to the electorate, an elected parish mayor-president was sub-

Facing page

Top

Aside from the new State Capitol (not shown), just before World War II, only two "skyscrapers" dominated the skyline: the Louisiana National Bank, facing the river, and the Heidelberg Hotel, shown from the back. This aerial view of the city covers from the northern side of Laurel Street to part of the corporation limits on the south and southeast. Courtesy, Baton Rouge Room, East Baton Rouge Parish Library.

Bottom

In Baton Rouge in the late 1950s and early 1960s, businesses began to cluster in shopping centers away from the downtown area. These eventually enticed many of the older commercial establishments from their original sites on Riverside Mall and its connecting streets. The largest such shopping facility in the city today is Cortana Mall, which was dedicated in 1976. Pictured here at the ribbon-cutting are Mayor-President W.W. Dumas, partners of the mall, store managers, and other dignitaries and guests. Courtesy, The Register.

stituted. Other voters complained that expansion of the city limits (one of the plan's more controversial features) would likely increase their taxes inequitably above the quality of proposed improved services. Some rural voters did not want to be "swallowed" by the "little Chicago" while still others simply wished to retain the status quo.

But after some mild transitional difficulties and brief financial dislocations, the city-parish consolidation settled in and now hardly anyone remembers what kind of government Baton Rouge had before.

The last mayor of Baton Rouge under the old system, Powers Higginbotham, was also the first mayor-president. He was defeated in 1952 by Jesse L. Webb, Jr., son of the then parish tax assessor. Mayor-President Webb lost his life in an airplane crash in May of 1956, and was succeeded on an interim basis by his wife, Baton Rouge's only woman mayor, who was designated by the city-parish council to serve out her husband's unexpired term. Jack Christian served in the office for the next eight years, to be followed by Woodrow Wilson "Woody" Dumas, a parish councilman from Baker, who was reelected three times before choosing to retire in 1980. His 16 years as mayor-president spanned the period of greatest prosperity and expansion in the city's history, due in no small measure to "Woody" himself, a blunt but dedicated public servant of integrity, determination, and abundant common sense. Baton Rouge's current mayor-president, Pat Screen, native New Orleanian, attorney,

Above
After 12 years as councilman and 16 years as mayor-president in Baton Rouge, W.W. "Woody" Dumas chose to retire from public office in 1980. While his administrations were marked by unprecedented growth in population and expansion in government, business, and industry, they were nonetheless not completely free of racial and labor problems. This unusual button was distributed during Dumas' last mayoral campaign in 1976. Courtesy, Jean Harwell Smith.

Left
Work began on the Centroplex after the United States Department of Housing and Urban Development agreed to contribute money toward the purchase of its site as an urban renewal project. In May of 1973, construction of the $13 million Governmental Building was undertaken by Charles Carter Construction Company. Four years later, the new structure was completed and dedicated. Here Mayor-President "Woody" Dumas is shown signing the contract for the Governmental Building. Courtesy, W.W. "Woody" Dumas.

and former LSU quarterback, has a tough act to follow.

Baton Rouge finally got a civic auditorium during the Dumas administration, after relying for decades on private facilities, high-school auditoriums, and the LSU Union. Part of an immense complex of public buildings called the Centroplex, located opposite the Old State Capitol on North Boulevard, the auditorium is accompanied by exhibition and convention facilities, city-parish government offices, extensive parking garages, and a library. The total cost of the Centroplex was $78 million, $38.2 million of which came from the federal government in revenue sharing and Housing and Urban Development funds. It has been suggested that the center be unofficially designated as the "Woodyplex" in honor of the mayor-president whose vigorous and sustained efforts made it possible.

On the state-government level during the 1940s and afterward, when Louisiana politics was largely dominated by the bifactionalism between the heirs of Huey Long and his opponents, Baton Rouge remained a center of reform anti-Longism, supporting for governor Sam H. Jones (1940–1944), Jimmie Davis (1944–1948 and 1960–1964), and Robert F. Kennon (1952–1956). Governor John J. McKeithen (1964–1972) met with a mixed response from the city. The two "maverick" governors were Earl K. Long (1948–1952 and 1956–1960) and Edwin W. Edwards (1972–1980); Baton Rougeans supported their opponents with sometimes heavy

Below
The dedication of the Riverside Centroplex and Governmental Complex in November of 1977 represented a major victory for Mayor-President Dumas and numerous citizens' organizations. From 1941, in fact, groups had lobbied for a city auditorium and arena. When these two facilities were finally opened, with the other components of the Civic Center, they far exceeded the expectations of their early promoters. This picture taken in 1976 shows Dumas in the foreground with the framework for the Governmental Building going up and the foundation of the Centroplex. Courtesy, The Register.

Above

On September 25, 1952, the new Lafayette Street Extension just above North Street was opened across state-owned land to Boyd and Third streets. Constructed in less than two months at a cost of about $23,500, it was expected to alleviate much of the traffic congestion in the downtown area. Present for a brief dedicatory ceremony were Mayor-President Powers Higginbotham (third from left on the back row), city councilmen Henry Louis Cohn and Pete Goldsby, Senator Charles Duchein, President of the Chamber of Commerce Andrew Bahlinger, and other state and city employees. *Courtesy, Mrs. Theodore Rosenberg.*

Left

Mrs. Fred C. Dent of Baton Rouge, known throughout the state as Miss Lucille May Grace, was the first woman elected to statewide office and the first to seek the governorship. Serving as register of state lands beginning in 1931, she was elected six times to continue the work of her father, Fred J. Grace, who previously had held her position from 1908 until his death. It was she who helped to open the way for women in Louisiana to campaign for state office. *Courtesy,* The Register.

Above
One of the first public reading rooms in the city was at the Athenaeum, built by the Young Men's Library Association in the 1850s. However, the real library movement in Baton Rouge began around 1900 when the local Joanna Waddill chapter of the United Daughters of the Confederacy set up a facility on the second floor of the old Washington Fire Company No. 1 Hall on Church Street (North Fourth). Later, the East Baton Rouge Parish Library was created in 1939 and that year dedicated its first building on the corner of Laurel and St. Anthony (North Seventh). Today, its main branch is situated on Goodwood Avenue and its newest one is at the Centroplex. In this 1978 photograph the construction of the latter building is seen with a view of Riverside Mall. Courtesy, W.W. "Woody" Dumas.

Right
After a heated campaign, Pat Screen was victorious in his race for mayor-president of Baton Rouge in 1979. A New Orleans native, he attended Louisiana State University in the 1960s and was on the varsity football and baseball teams before obtaining his law degree there. Prior to his election as head of the city-parish government, Screen had practiced law in the capital and had served on the East Baton Rouge Parish School Board. Courtesy, Office of Mayor-President, Baton Rouge.

majorities.

Earl Long, Huey's youngest brother, was a flamboyant, tax-and-spend neo-Populist, the last Louisiana chief executive born in the 19th century (1895). More flexible than his brother—Earl preferred to "rent" legislators rather than "buy" them as Huey had—the younger Long was no less unattractive to the Baton Rouge elite and to government reformers generally. Like Huey, Earl looked to business and industry for much of his tax revenue, handled state money on a cigar-box basis (thus infuriating proponents of modern cash management and accountability), and often embarrassed members of the city's urban middle class by his erratic and un-country-club-like behavior.

In retrospect Earl Long's alleged faults were in many cases simply the normal characteristics of a folksy, rural politician who had survived his own era and most of his contemporaries. It was difficult to dislike a man, even if one disagreed with him politically, who when asked why he had no bodyguards replied, "Hell, they'd only get in my way if I had to run."

Edwin Edwards was the exact personal antithesis of Earl Long—sophisticated, urbane, and well-dressed. (When criticized on one occasion for his sloppy clothing, Earl Long is said to have snorted, "If you think personal appearance is so important for this job, why didn't you elect Rock Hudson?") But Edwards appealed to much the same constituency as the Longs—ordinary average citizens, plus the large numbers of blacks who had returned to politics following the 1965 Voting Rights Act—and his broad-based tax-and-spend philosophy was strikingly similar to earlier Long programs. Thus voters in corporate-oriented Baton Rouge favored those who opposed Edwards in his first, and only, challenging bid for the governorship in 1971–1972, Shreveport Democrat J. Bennett Johnston, who went on to the United States Senate, and Metairie Republican David Treen, who served in Congress for eight years before succeeding Edwards in 1980. Governor Treen is Louisiana's first Republican chief executive since Reconstruction, a fact that illustrates how politics has changed statewide in recent decades. (Baton Rouge itself has been represented in Congress since 1974 by Republican W. Henson Moore, the first GOP congressman from this district in more than a century.)

Increasing discretionary income and additional leisure time have produced a tremendous expansion of recreational and cultural pursuits in Baton Rouge. Heading the list have been athletic activities at LSU, especially football and basketball. Before Governor Leche moved to Atlanta, he filled in the north end of the football stadium, which became a bowl in the 1950s and received an upper tier of additional seats in the late 1970s. Capacity crowds have frequently witnessed the performances of many outstanding players in recent years: Steve Van Buren and Y.A. Tittle in the 1940s, Jim Taylor and Billy Cannon in the 1950s, and a succession of stars who played during the following two decades under

Above
The son of a businessman and civic leader in Baton Rouge, in 1968 Joseph A. Delpit was elected the first black councilman to serve in the capital city and was returned to that position the following term. He is now beginning his second term as state representative from District 67. Delpit has received wide recognition for contributions to his community. Courtesy, Joseph A. Delpit.

Right
Louisiana's senior senator, Russell B. Long, has for many years maintained a permanent residence in Baton Rouge. Some of his earliest associations with the city date from his late father Huey P. Long's presence in the capital as governor, and during his own days as a student at Louisiana State University. One of the most influential men in Washington, Senator Long has served Louisiana in Washington since 1948 and has held seats on some of the most important committees in that august body, particularly the powerful chairmanship of the Senate Finance Committee. Courtesy, Department of Archives and Manuscripts, LSU, Baton Rouge.

ONE AMERICAN PLACE
GROUNDBREAKING... MAY 23, 1972
A JOINT VENTURE OF
GREAT AMERICAN CORPORATION

Above
While serving as Louisiana's governor and as an official resident of the city, Edwin W. Edwards has been actively involved in numerous events in the recent history of Baton Rouge. This 1972 photo finds the former governor participating in the ground-breaking ceremony for an impressive $15 million bank and office building called One American Place. The building was formally opened on December 7, 1974. Courtesy, The Register.

Head Coach Charles McClendon, the winningest coach in LSU football history.

Basketball at LSU first became a popular sport locally during the Bob Pettit era in the 1950s. "Pistol Pete" Maravich stirred local fans a decade later by breaking NCAA scoring records. Under Coach Dale Brown, who arrived in 1972, the LSU basketball team has further progressed by winning two SEC championships and one SEC tournament, making the NCAA playoffs twice, and emerging as a perennial national contender.

Hunting and fishing have increased in popularity as Baton Rouge pastimes, not only in the surrounding environs which continue to sustain many species, but in distant areas as well. The sight of numerous boat trailers and campers entering and leaving town in the spring and summer months is a familiar one in Baton Rouge. For a city its size Baton Rouge has an outstanding municipal sports and recreation program conducted by BREC—the Baton Rouge Recreation and Parks Commission. Thousands of Baton Rougeans, young and old, enjoy the experience of playing on BREC baseball and softball teams.

Until recently Baton Rouge projected an image that was the reverse of New York City—a nice place to live but not to visit. A profusion of new restaurants and nightspots has significantly improved the city's capacity to entertain not only its own residents, but increasing numbers of visitors as well. Unlike many other cities, Baton Rouge's eating and amusement establishments are not all concentrated in one area, but are spread out in clusters in the various suburbs.

In the past two decades Baton Rouge has also acquired a fine symphony orchestra, a superb planetarium, several outstanding museums, and numerous other cultural offerings. No longer can it be said that Baton Rouge remains a cultureless satellite of New Orleans.

What can be said about the "character" of Baton Rouge? In assessing that character, it is necessary to first specify which Baton Rouge, for there are several. As the *Enterprise* put it, there is north Baton Rouge, south Baton Rouge, and black Baton Rouge. North Baton Rouge retains its close connection with the city's older industries, and is predominantly "blue collar" and conservative in matters political, moral, and racial. South Baton Rouge includes most of the city's newer and classier subdivisions, a majority of the area's technocracy, and the expanding and diverse LSU community. Black Baton Rouge, with few exceptions, remains poor.

A good case can be made, therefore, that Baton Rouge is no longer a city at all, but a federation of suburbs, each of which is an almost self-contained community with its own perceptions of what "Baton Rouge" is, what the particular suburb is, and how it relates to its neighbors.

The current center of population in Baton Rouge, which moves inexorably eastward, rests in the Broadmoor-Sherwood Forest area along Florida Boulevard. A largely middle-class district with some upper mid-

Left
Nationally known author Lyle Saxon was a native of Baton Rouge and spent much of his youth poring over volumes in the bookstore of his grandfather, Michael Chambers, on Third Street. Beginning his literary career writing reviews of vaudeville shows at the old Columbia in Baton Rouge, Saxon later served as a reporter on the Times Picayune. *In his last years, Saxon wrote several well-known books including,* Father Mississippi, Fabulous New Orleans, *and* Children of Strangers *in addition to being state director for the Louisiana Writers' Project of the W.P.A. Saxon died in 1946 and was buried in Magnolia Cemetery. This photograph shows the author with a copy of the Louisiana Writers' Project guidebook to the state published under his supervision in 1941. Courtesy, Louisiana State Library.*

Above
In the black community, two of the oldest men's social clubs in Baton Rouge are the Purple Circle and the Bonanza. The latter, organized in 1939, is comprised of many prominent civic and social leaders in the city. This photograph was taken at one of the formal affairs of the Bonanza Men's Social Club in 1953. Courtesy, Dr. Russell Ampey.

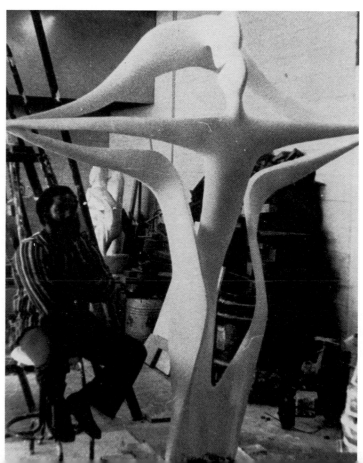

The Baton Rouge Symphony Orchestra has been in existence for over 30 years and continues to enhance greatly the musical life of the community. Following the appearance of the Philharmonic Orchestra and later that of the university's orchestra and other musical productions on campus, the Community Concert Association was organized in 1931. Courtesy, Baton Rouge Symphony Association.

Left
Louisiana-born sculptor and Southern University professor of art Frank Hayden has his works prominently displayed in the city and the state, as well as in other parts of the nation. Perhaps he is best known locally for his bicentennial monument, the "Red Stick" at Scott's Bluff and his sculpture at the Civic Center. Courtesy, Frank Hayden.

Far left
Retiring in 1979, Charles Y. McClendon had served 18 years as head football coach at LSU in addition to several years as assistant coach. During his employment there he compiled an enviable record: 13 post-season bowl games, 17 first-team All-Americans, 51 first-team All-SEC, 77 academic All-SEC, in addition to being named National Coach of the Year, and twice SEC Coach of the Year. Courtesy, Office of Sports Information, LSU, Baton Rouge.

Since coming to Baton Rouge in 1953, Dr. Valerian Smith has amassed an incredible list of accomplishments in the cultural field. A leader in creating the Community Chorus and Baton Rouge Community Playhouse, he later instituted the first Afro-American Cultural Week and Arts Festival in the city. In 1972, Smith premiered his play, **Black Vuai,** *at the Baton Rouge Little Theater and later saw it presented in New York, Washington, Houston, and California. He has likewise written scores for at least two musical plays (one of which has run in New York) and originated the soul/jazz band, Black Blood and Chocolate Pickles. Courtesy, Dr. Valerian Smith.*

dle-class enclaves, these subdivisions house professional people, petro-chemical employees, successful salesmen, and a handful of LSU professors.

Baton Rouge's more affluent citizens dwell in such subdivisions as Bocage and Stone's Throw, close to the Baton Rouge Country Club along Jefferson Highway, or on extensive spreads outside the city limits, especially along Perkins and Highland roads in south Baton Rouge.

LSU's faculty tend to herd together in the older suburbs of College Town and University Hills and in the newer developments south on Highland Road—Plantation Trace, Kenilworth, and Magnolia Woods.

With few exceptions Baton Rouge's blue-collar population still lives "north of Choctaw" and in the adjacent Baker-Zachary area. The city's black population has spread districts but remains concentrated into many of the older center-city in Scotlandville near Southern, in Eden Park, and in old south Baton Rouge just north of LSU.

Like other rapidly growing communities, Baton Rouge has its share—some traditionalists say more than its share—of apartment complexes and condominiums. They range from lavish to basic and speckle the city from interior to periphery.

As stated previously many Baton Rougeans tend to live within their subdivisions, attending the local church, sending their children to the neighborhood school (if possible or desirable), patronizing the nearest shopping center and convenience store, even going to dentists and phy-

Above
One of the major social events in the capital each year is the formal presentation of young women to their families and friends by Cercle de Bacchus, Bal de Noël, and The Baton Rouge Assembly. The oldest of these groups dates to about 1956. Pictured here making her bow, and escorted by her father, is the former Antoinette Brunot Duchein, daughter of Major General and Mrs. Charles Francis Duchein. The Baton Rouge Assembly, founded in 1960–1961, was initially composed of members whose families had resided in the city for over 50 years. Courtesy, Major-General and Mrs. Charles F. Duchein.

Left
Baton Rouge was not totally immune from the student activism that pervaded the United States in the 1960s. This group of Louisiana State University students and visitors joined with those from other colleges in Louisiana in October of 1969 to peacefully observe a national moratorium on the Vietnam War. Following an all-night prayer vigil, individuals gathered on the LSU Parade Ground to begin a full day of events. Many wore white arm bands or small stickers saying, "Work for Peace, Oct. 15," with the picture of a dove bearing an olive branch in its mouth. Courtesy, Office of Public Relations, LSU, Baton Rouge.

sicians whose offices in many cases are no more distant from home than several blocks. Baton Rouge is truly a dispersed, varied, and pluralistic system of subcommunities.

While "antagonistic" or "alienated" are excessive terms to describe the relations between Baton Rouge suburbs in all cases, there is little communication or positive interrelation between them except through the medium of school competition in sports. The salesman residing in Villa Del Rey may never have been to Plantation Trace and might get lost attempting to go there, as might an LSU professor living in Plantation Trace attempting to find Villa Del Rey.

The reality of this assessment is revealed by the manner in which the city-parish council is elected, and how its members often approach their duties. Because they are not elected at large but from districts within the parish, members do not think "at large" either, but rather in terms of what will benefit those who elected them. Consequently members of the council somewhat resemble members of Congress whom Woodrow Wilson described as "ambassadors from distant lands who meet to exchange favors."

When, during the autumn high-school football season, Broadmoor plays Lee, or Tara takes on McKinley, or even when urban Catholic travels to suburban Woodlawn, not merely schools but communities are contesting with each other. (One of the most objectionable features of

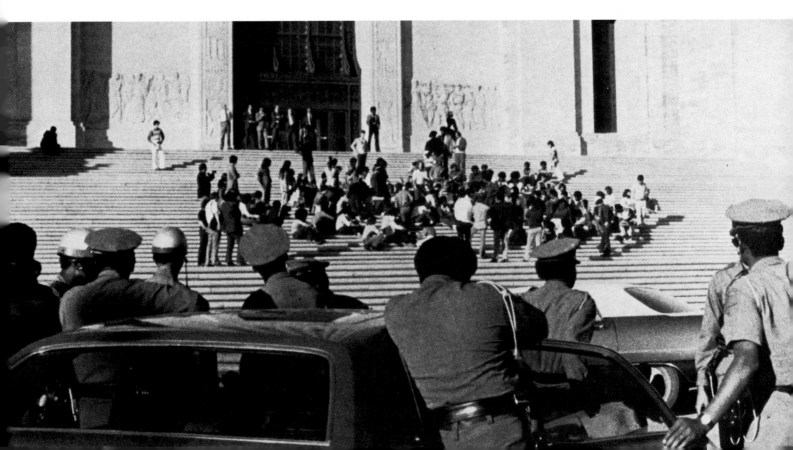

the pending massive desegragation of Baton Rouge public schools from the point of view of many parents is not that white and black children will sit in the same classrooms—that has been common for a long time—but that their children will be bused from one "Baton Rouge" to another.)

Perhaps the only areas of common loyalty or concern with which most Baton Rougeans identify are the fortunes of LSU and Southern athletic teams, and the hope or assumption that "their" Baton Rouge, whatever it may be based on, will continue to thrive.

Historically, "thriving" Baton Rouge came into existence only recently. Discovered by the French long ago in 1699, but almost ignored during the balance of French tenure in Louisiana, Baton Rouge possessed strategic value for its next tenants, the British and Spanish, but remained little more than a hamlet until 1820, shortly after the town became part of the United States.

Growth and development proceeded slowly during the rest of the 19th century. Although river trade and commerce had made Baton Rouge a prosperous little community by 1860, and the location of Louisiana's government in town had added to Baton Rouge's prestige and sophistication, much of this progress was retarded by the Civil War during which the town was nearly destroyed and the state capital temporarily moved elsewhere.

Baton Rouge as it is today really dates from the construction of the Standard Oil refinery in 1909. That event proved to be so important that it almost eclipses everything that occurred before and much that took place afterward, except for the prosperity initiated by World War II, which in turn made possible the subsequent development of the Port of Baton Rouge, the local petrochemical industry, and the modernization of local government and public services. The postwar Sunbelt boom has incalculably benefited Louisiana generally, resulting in further enhancement of local prosperity from growing state employment and the expansion of LSU and Southern University.

While many of the physical reminders of Baton Rouge's past have been lost to the onslaught of office buildings and general renewal efforts (especially in the old downtown area), many structures have been saved, restored, commemorated, or converted to other uses. Since 1963 most of this work has been done by the Foundation for Historical Louisiana, a private, nonprofit organization chartered to promote the preservation of buildings, sites, and objects significant to Louisiana's heritage, and to encourage an awareness of this unique heritage through educational programs. The Foundation restored, and now conducts tours through, Magnolia Mound Plantation and Grounds; operates the Louisiana Lagniappe Sightseeing Service; has a docent program for the LSU Rural Life Museum; and hosts a preservation workshop, in addition to giving out awards to outstanding Louisiana preservationists. Among its many no-

Murphy W. Bell, born and educated in Baton Rouge, has been a leading black attorney since he was admitted to the Louisiana State Bar. Perhaps he is best known for his role as counsel in various civil-rights cases from 1960 to the present time. Serving as the lead attorney, he has handled desegregation cases against various Louisiana parish school boards in addition to important trials involving sit-ins, Southern University demonstrations, and cases involving the state NAACP and Black Muslims. Courtesy, Murphy W. Bell.

table accomplishments that have added so much to Baton Rougeans' appreciation of the city has been the preservation and restoration of much of Beauregard Town and Spanish Town, in the historic Riverside area.

Many of Baton Rouge's old public and private buildings have been placed on the National Register of Historic Places, and one—the Old State Capitol—has the honor of being listed as a National Historic Landmark. Its Gothic architecture, which has inspired admiration and affection (as well as Mark Twain's disgust) is of particular interest, as are its stained–glass dome and massive spiral staircase.

Other buildings of historical significance, including privately owned homes, churches, and government or military buildings, include the Warden's House (which dates from 1837–1840 and was used as a receiving station for the penitentiary), the splendid antebellum Stewart–Dougherty house, the Potts house (built in the mid 19th century by master brick-mason Nelson Potts), and, from the same period, St. Joseph's Cathedral (which, however, has a modernized interior).

From more recent times, Huey Long's Governor's Mansion has been restored to the 1930s period of its construction and furnished with antiques. It also contains a collection of personal and governmental memorabilia from the state's most controversial political figure.

Also serving as fascinating reminders of the area's long and exciting history are Mount Hope and Magnolia Mound plantations (a social his-

tory of which follows in the Appendix). Magnolia Mound, furnished in the style of the early 1800s, tells modern visitors not only about the masters' lives inside the house, but also how work was done: a cutaway view of the wall shows how Spanish moss was used in the mortar, and a basketful of brown cotton and the products made from it add another dimension to our understanding of the daily life of long ago.

The Pentagon Barracks, a collective architectural feature of Baton Rouge for 140 years, have been put to good use almost continually since their construction. The four remaining buildings, with their majestic Doric colonnades, have served as army barracks, LSU dormitories, offices for state government, and as apartments for state-government employees.

Finally, the Historic Marker Program, given impetus from the Foundation for Historical Louisiana and begun in 1969 with funding from the city-parish government, has installed markers containing historical information at many sites around the city. The markers identify the original locations of everything from the Indian mounds to the Battle of Baton Rouge to the first air–mail flight between U.S. cities. The buildings and historical sites that have been so commemorated, as well as the writings of historians, provide forward–looking Baton Rougeans with the certain knowledge that a community has existed here for a very long time, and will continue to exist—whatever the future brings.

Above
One of the rooms at Magnolia Mound Plantation, where visitors can see the exposed timber and bousillage *(mud and moss) used in the house's construction. Photo by Dave Gleason.*

Right
The Louisiana State University Memorial Tower is situated in the heart of the campus and is perhaps better known as the "Campanile." Erected as a monument to Louisianians who died in service during World War I, it was funded largely from public subscription. The structure was formally dedicated on April 30, 1926. The wings of the building today are used as a museum to house the Anglo-American Art Collection.

Above
The Louisiana state seal and the flags under which the state has served may be seen in the main rotunda of the Capitol.

Left
This beautiful chamber decorated with marble and other types of stone is the meeting place for the Louisiana House of Representatives. The furniture is made of inlaid walnut and laurel and the wall behind the rostrum is paneled in walnut.

Above
St. James Episcopal Church, on the north-east corner of North Fourth and Convention, is the second church to occupy that location. The Gothic Revival building was completed in 1895 under architect W.L. Stevens, Sr. and contractor W.H. Miller. The Tiffany glass windows over the altar in the chancel are among the most beautiful in the city.

Above right
Designed by Father John Cambiazo, and erected between 1853 and 1856 on land donated by Don Antonio Gras, St. Joseph's Cathedral is the oldest church in Baton Rouge.

Right
This two-story, Classical Revival house located on North Street was built by Nelson Potts between 1846 and 1850. A master brick mason, Potts built many of the finer homes in Baton Rouge.

Above
Magnolia Mound Plantation House, now on the National Register of Historic Places, is one of the few surviving frame houses of mud and moss construction in the East Baton Rouge Parish area. Dating from the late-18th century, the land on which it is situated was originally granted to James Hillen in 1786. Purchased in 1791 by John Joyce, the plantation passed at his death to Constance Rochon, his widow. The house was restored to the period of occupancy by Constance and Armand Allard Duplantier, whom she married after the death of her former husband.

Left
The plantation house rooms have been authentically and beautifully furnished in the early Federal style.

Facing page
Top
Located high on a knoll near Capitol Lake and somewhat to the east of the new State Capitol, the Governor's Mansion, with its 21 white Doric columns, is reminiscent of the grand plantation homes of old Louisiana. Begun in 1961 and completed two years later at a cost of about $1 million, the mansion was first occupied by James "Jimmie" H. Davis during his second administration as governor.

Bottom left
Part of the folk architecture section of the LSU Rural Life Museum, the Acadian (or Creole) House is a reproduction of the wood and bousillage houses that French settlers in southern Louisiana once built. The building shows both French and Caribbean influence.

Bottom right
This house on North Street is one of the most outstanding examples of classical architecture standing in the city of Baton Rouge. Built circa 1850 by Nathan King Knox, it has remained in the hands of the Stewart-Dougherty families and their heirs since they first occupied it. During the Civil War the house was used as a hospital by Union soldiers.

Left
Built in the Classical style in 1845, the Bailey House on North Boulevard is the headquarters of the Foundation for Historical Louisiana. This organization, founded in 1963, not only has worked for preservation and beautification of historical structures and sites, it also was instrumental in the establishment of the Historic Marker Program.

Below left
Reminiscent of Baton Rouge's military days, this cannon stands atop an Indian mound on the Old Arsenal grounds overlooking Capitol Lake.

Below
This marble monument made by Enochs of Philadelphia, Pennsylvania, is one of the most imposing in Magnolia Cemetery. The three children on the statue represent those of William H. and Mary Crenshaw, all of whom died in 1858. A fourth child, "The Nameless One," was buried in 1855. Tombstones such as this remind one of the extreme fragility of life in the 19th century.

Facing page
This spectacular panoramic view looking south toward downtown was taken from the top of the Capitol.

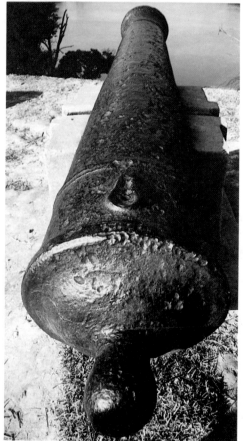

The 19th and 20th centuries merge in this view of Baton Rouge today. A far different city than it was when the cathedral's spire—dwarfed by downtown skyscrapers here—was first completed, Baton Rouge has grown into its role as a thriving, dynamic city of the modern South with remarkable speed. And as the 21st century approaches, there is no sign of a slowdown in Louisiana's energetic capital.

PARTNERS IN PROGRESS

From its origin as the site of an Indian village, through many years as a sleepy river town, to its emergence as a major educational, governmental, and industrial center of the South, Baton Rouge has been a city of change and diversity.

Beginning as "Istrouma," a boundary between two Indian tribes where a red stick *(baton rouge)* once stood high on the bluffs above the river to mark a territorial division, the area soon attracted early settlers, who recognized that the high fertile land would be safe from the river's annual floods. That land first made cotton and then sugar cane "king," as the agricultural community survived the territorial claims of several nations, the eventual trauma of the Civil War, and the difficult changes of Reconstruction.

In the late 1800s, as Natchez and Bayou Sara prospered as river port towns to the north and New Orleans reigned as the queen city of the southern delta, Baton Rouge retained its flavor as a small farming community. But soon, significant changes began to occur in the quiet town by the great river. Louisiana State University, originally founded in Pineville in the central part of the state, moved to Baton Rouge; Louisiana's state government selected the city as its permanent home; and Standard Oil arrived in the early years of the twentieth century to begin what would become one of the great industrial developments of any area in the United States.

Today, one can still drift along this part of the Mississippi and see the history of Baton Rouge reflected there. At the north end of the river, high on the bluffs where settlers first spotted the red stick, stands Southern University, recognized as the largest institution of higher education for black students in the country. Below the school, the city's older industrial plants are outlined in the water, including the Exxon refinery, the world's largest oil refinery complex and a reminder of the era when cotton fields yielded to the city's first influx of industrial growth. In the center of the reflection rises the Louisiana State Capitol, the nation's tallest capital building and perhaps the most beautiful. And below the capitol, the modern downtown business district melds with the city's oldest historic structures to recall the community's earliest days.

Moving south, the old state capitol still stands in all its Moorish-Gothic splendor. Baton Rouge's handsome new Riverside Centroplex conveys the city's pride in its downtown area. And next to Riverside is Louisiana State University, a traditional leader among the nation's institutions of higher learning.

Yes, it's all reflected in the flow of the river—an educational, governmental, and industrial center of international renown and importance. Within its boundaries can be found a diversity of people who are proud of their city and its rich history. We can only guess what Baton Rouge will be like tomorrow, but from the following accounts it seems certain that the future will be filled with bright promise and an unending dedication to growth and progress.

Alessi Jewelry

This is the story of Marion J. Alessi, who as an entrepreneur and merchant has recorded his name into the colorful history of the Capital City. Alessi was born in 1929 in the small town of Independence, Louisiana, located forty-five miles northeast of Baton Rouge. An only child, Alessi and his parents weathered the Great Depression as most Americans did, making ends meet as best they could. It was the worst of times and economic hardship abounded, yet it taught the child valuable lessons about family loyalty, dogged perseverance, and trust in a better future.

At the outset of World War II, Alessi's parents moved to Alexandria, Louisiana, where they entered the drive-in restaurant business. The Pelican Drive-In quickly became a popular spot with the local citizens. About this time, Dominic Alessi, Marion's father, began tinkering with a machine he had designed and built that would peel potatoes for deep frying with a peculiar twist to the cutting.

In 1943, the family moved to Baton Rouge and opened Alessi's Drive-In. The new restaurant became a stunning success overnight. People from miles around motored to the corner of Florida Boulevard and JayBird Lane (now Foster Drive) for a hamburger, cola, and a steaming basket of Alessi's "Kurly-Q" french-fried potatoes. It was not uncommon to sell over 1,600 pounds of potatoes a day. Even today, the drive-in is fondly remembered by native Baton Rougeans who

recall its quaint charm and indisputable reputation for good food.

Operating the restaurant was truly a family affair. Dominic was cook; Juanita, Marion's mother, was head cashier; and teenaged Marion darted about serving as carhop. It was during this period that young Alessi began to hone his skills as a businessman. He discovered that hard work and assertiveness were the keys to success. He designed the building layout of the restaurant during math class at Catholic High School; there was no holding this youngster back.

After graduating from high school, Alessi channeled his energy into the family business. He spent one year working and studying at the chic Dolores Drive-In in Los Angeles. Upon returning home, Alessi modernized the restaurant's operation and opened two additional locations to provide better service to bustling Baton Rouge. Constantly involved throughout the 20-year history of the family restaurant (the business was closed in 1963 to make way for the glut of fast-food franchises that were mushrooming), Alessi began to expand his business acumen as the city entered the 1950s.

In the mid-fifties, Alessi helped organize and form Guaranty Federal Savings and Loan Association. He is a former member of the board of directors and an original stockholder of that institution. He became involved in civic affairs and served as president of the East Baton Rouge Optimist Club. He worked tirelessly for the Chamber of Commerce and even had time for dramatic acting, working with the late Lee Edwards at the Baton Rouge Little Theater. In 1956 Alessi acquired Production Services, Inc., a firm that marketed "motiva-

tional" background music to area businesses. His reputation as an ambitious and innovative young businessman was beginning to grow.

In the mid-1960s, Alessi and his lifelong friend, Dr. Charles G. Walker, purchased Pierce Foundry, a business established in 1854. Rich in heritage, the old company once held contracts to manufacture cannon balls for the Confederacy during the Civil War. The foundry had cast and poured the iron that is now the impressive fence surrounding the old state capitol. Alessi and Dr. Walker upgraded the plant's operations, and today Pierce Foundry is the leading producer of gravel and field irrigation pumps used by industry throughout the United States. Alessi was equally ad-

ept in other matters and further enhanced his fortune with real estate speculation and other investments. As the sixties came to a tumultous close, Marion Alessi began his quest for the business he most desired . . . diamonds.

From an early age, Alessi had been fascinated by the beguiling mystery of precious gems, particularly diamonds. He marveled at their brilliance and beauty and promptly cultivated a keen appreciation for their aesthetic value. In 1972, Alessi purchased Campus Jewelry, situated on Highland Road near the gates of Louisiana State University. He knew from the start that the jewelry business would be his greatest challenge and his highest reward. By 1975,

Alessi had made the decision to open in Baton Rouge the finest jewelry salon in the Deep South. Alessi Jewelry was born.

In November 1978, the finishing touches were placed on the new showroom at 8700 Florida Boulevard in Alessi Square. The unique "Alessi Touch" was evident throughout. The building, employing a modified Roman arch theme on the exterior, was personally designed by Alessi. Not one detail of the construction was left unattended. The interior display cases were custom crafted by a San Antonio-based carpentry shop. The stainless steel vault, where customers are treated to private showings, was purchased from a bank. There is even an enclosed garage to house the 1976

Silver Cloud Rolls-Royce that Alessi purchased for his customers' use. The new store was the culmination of a dream, one that took over thirty years to materialize.

Alessi's business legacy has ranged from "Kurly-Q's" to the rarest South African diamonds. As a business leader and involved citizen, he has become an example of opportunity blooming into prosperity. And as the city races toward a new era, Marion J. Alessi continues to contribute his drive and determination to the betterment of the Baton Rouge community.

Below
The striking Alessi Jewelers facility located in Alessi Square features Romanesque arches.

Allied Chemical Corporation

Allied Chemical Corporation goes back a long way in Louisiana. Paradoxically, the company was doing business here even before it existed. Allied Chemical was formed in 1920 by a merger of several chemical firms, but some of its predecessor companies evolved in the nineteenth century. The Union Texas Petroleum Division of Allied, for example, began as the Union Sulfur Company, and it was mining sulfur in Louisiana as far back as 1896.

Union Texas does not mine sulfur any longer, but it is a growing worldwide producer of oil, natural gas, and related energy products, with four producing locations in the state. Three other Allied business areas—agricultural, plastics, and chemicals—also have major plants in Louisiana, three of which are located in the Baton Rouge area.

The Baton Rouge South Works, located at Lupine and Ontario streets, was built during World War II to supply refineries with the HF alkylation process for producing the high-octane fuel so necessary for the American military effort. Elemental flourine produced at the plant was used as an experimental fuel in the space program during the late 1950s and early 1960s. Another South Works product, Genetron®, a flourine-based compound, is used by a wide variety of customers, from refrigeration wholesale distributors in Baton Rouge to oil refineries in Montana, from government complexes in New Mexico to chemical producers in Italy.

The Baton Rouge Polyolefins Plant, located in East Baton Rouge Parish, was acquired from W.R. Grace & Company in 1966. The facility, which produces high-density polyethylene for fabrication into plastic containers and industrial shapes, has been expanded several times. The world's largest reactor for this material is currently being constructed on this site. Allied Chemical transferred all people related to this business to Baton Rouge in 1972, and now employs more than 400 plant and business personnel at this location.

Allied's Geismar Complex production facilities began operations in 1967. The 3,600-acre site, located fifteen miles south of Baton Rouge on the east bank of the Mississippi River, consists of four production units and support facilities. The plants manufacture and ship nitrogen fertilizer solution, sulfuric acid, ammonium polyphosphate fertilizer solution, hydrofluoric acid, ethylene, propylene, and many other products.

Allied Chemical's investment in Louisiana is substantial, valued at $320 million in 1978. In 1979, the company spent $79 million in capital funds in Louisiana, and in 1980 spent $90 million, much of it on an expansion of the Baton Rouge Polyolefin Plant.

The corporation has more than 1,250 employees in the state, and in 1978 the payroll exceeded $30 million. In addition, Allied Chemical has from 500 to 850 contract workers on the job at any given time—drilling wells, doing construction work, carrying out maintenance, and so on.

Louisiana has been a good place for Allied Chemical to grow. And Allied Chemical's growth has been good for Louisiana and its residents.

Below
The Baton Rouge Polyolefins Plant, which produces high-density polyethylene for fabrication into plastic containers and industrial shapes, has been expanded several times since it was acquired in 1966.

Left
Allied Chemical's Geismar Complex production facilities began operations in 1967. The 3,600-acre site consists of four production units and support facilities.

American Bank

American Bank in Baton Rouge has a history rich with significant accomplishments for this area, because of the determined efforts of a group of local businessmen who joined together in April 1946 to form a community bank.

Within three years of its founding, American Bank had acquired the distinction of having the largest percentage gain in deposits over the previous year of all other banks in the nation. During the next two years, the bank introduced the drive-up window at its original Plank Road location, which was followed by the city's first walk-up window. In 1954 American Bank opened an office downtown, giving Baton Rouge its first branch bank.

By the end of 1962, American Bank had more than $81 million in assets and a third location in the mid-city area. That same year J. Clifford Ourso was elected chairman of the board. By the end of the 1960s, American Bank had added three new locations to its branch system, and its assets exceeded $248 million.

In 1970, a holding company called Great American Corporation was formed to give the bank flexibility to move into other areas of financial service. These included Ambank Mortgage Company, American Data Processing Company, Ambank Acceptance Corporation, American Equipment Leasing Company, and American Investment and Management Company. That same year,

American Bank became the first in Baton Rouge to have assets surpassing $300 million, establishing it as the largest state-chartered bank in Louisiana.

American Bank moved into its new headquarters at One American Place in downtown Baton Rouge in December 1974. The company now has eighteen locations throughout East Baton Rouge Parish, including the city's first "stand-alone" automated teller. J. Clifford Ourso served as chairman of the board and president of Great American Corporation until March 1981. Joe Traigle succeeded Ourso at that time. Max Pace is chairman of the board of American Bank.

Though American Bank's neighborhood origins have been left behind, the ideals of its founding members remain. Even today, that neighborhood feeling and concern for each customer has been carefully preserved. Concern for the customer and the community is an ideal that has always been stressed by J. Clifford Ourso, one of American Bank's founders and leaders. Mr. Ourso has used his business experience to help his community prosper. There is scarcely a segment of civic life, a charitable or religious effort, or an educational endeavor that has not felt the strength of his or his company's support. He is a Papal Knight of St. Gregory and a member of the Catholic High School Hall of Fame. He served as a member of the school board for three terms, and was named as one of the ten men who "move Baton Rouge." One of the highest commendations he has received is the Golden Deeds Award, which was presented to him by the citizenry of Baton Rouge in recognition of his tire-

less and unselfish contributions to the community. Much of his success in business is attributed to his own personal depth of character.

Top
American Bank moved into its new headquarters at One American Place in downtown Baton Rouge in December 1974.
Bottom
Max Pace (left) is chairman of the board of American Bank; Joseph N. Traigle serves as chairman of the board, chief executive officer, and president of Great American Corporation; and J. Clifford Ourso, Sr. (seated), serves as chairman emeritus of Great American Corporation.

Anco Insulation

When the Aber Company of Houston, Texas, decided to discontinue operations in Baton Rouge in the early 1960s, R.L. "Sonny" Anderson, Jr., of the industrial insulation firm decided it was a good time to start his own company in the area. He saw the industrial growth in Baton Rouge's future and knew his experience with insulation would satisfy an important need for corporations planning to build or expand plants there. In November 1962, Anderson, with the help of H.F. Johnson, Charles Verrett, and Geneva Ivey, formed ANCO Insulation, Inc.

They expected that ANCO, like any new company, would start slowly and only gradually build a solid reputation for quality and service. They were amazed and excited when ANCO did almost $1.3 million worth of business the first year—$.5 million more than anticipated. In fact, the company's growth throughout the 1960s was much more rapid than expected, due partially to the vast amounts of reconstruction work necessitated by Hurricane Betsy's devastation of southern Louisiana.

Bolstered by its immediate success, the company expanded its operations in the 1970s, opening Louisiana offices in New Orleans, Lake Charles, and Monroe, and out-of-state offices in Mobile and Birmingham, Alabama; Tampa, Florida; and Houston, Texas. Today, ANCO serves a widespread market area covering the entire Gulf Coast, the southern portions of the East Coast and the Midwest, and has overseas operations in Trinidad, Panama, Aruba, China, and Saudi Arabia.

Although ANCO contracts with several different types of industries, it has come to be nationally recognized for its work with the petrochemical and power industries and is now one of the nation's largest in-

dependent insulation distributors and contractors. From 50 employees in 1962, the company now averages from 2,000 to 2,200 workers employed on a month-to-month basis according to construction activities. And the enterprise that hoped to do a mere $.75 million in business just eighteen years ago now does an annual volume of $50 million.

Under the direction of president R.L. Anderson, Jr., ANCO makes a large contribution to the area's employment opportunities. The company will continue to be a major force in the Baton Rouge business community and in the national industrial insulation industry.

Left
ANCO Insulation is nationally recognized for its work with the petrochemical and power industries. This photograph shows an oil tower and refinery which the company insulated.
Below
ANCO Insulation is located at 1896 Woodale Boulevard, serving a worldwide market as one of the country's largest independent insulation distributors and contractors.

Scaffolding Rental and Erection Services

As part of today's construction procedures, scaffolding has become crucial to both the proper implementation of the project design and the safety of construction personnel. Fourteen years ago, R.L. "Sonny" Anderson, Jr., recognized that Louisiana was on the road to significant industrial expansion and that that expansion would entail extensive plant construction. And so he founded Scaffolding Rental and Erection Services, Inc., to meet the scaffolding design needs and to solve the erection and dismantling problems of the state's burgeoning construction industry.

In 1966, the first year of operation, business totaled $63,000—with just two men on the company payroll. In 1980, with more than 850 field and office personnel, the firm's volume exceeded $33.5 million, making the company the leading scaffolding supplier and contractor in the country.

During its first few years of operation, the firm concentrated on scaffolding rentals for small, specialized applications. Gradually, however, the company shifted to contractual work on much larger industrial jobs, and today 75 percent of Scaffolding Rental's revenue is derived from labor contracts.

Recently, the company has added annual maintenance contracts to its repertoire of services. And the current practice of establishing scaffolding as a separate subcontract on major new construction has also stimulated further growth for the firm.

Scaffolding Rental and Erection Services now specializes in large-scale industrial projects for such diverse industries as petrochemical, power, aluminum, and cement. A "coast-to-coast" enterprise in the fullest sense of the term, the company has completed projects in more than half of the fifty states. Headquartered at 4717 Adams Avenue in Baton Rouge, the firm can provide service in a matter of hours to all parts of the country.

Throughout its history, Scaffolding Rental and Erection Services has emphasized growth and service for Baton Rouge and for the entire state of Louisiana and will continue to do so for years to come.

Left
Although Scaffolding Rental and Erection Services first performed applications for small contracts, the company is now the foremost scaffolding supplier and contractor in the nation, specializing in projects for the petrochemical and construction industries.
Right
This crew with its fleet of modern equipment helps to ensure that Scaffolding Rental and Erection Services will continue to be a major force in the Baton Rouge business community.

Area Wholesale Tire Company

Twenty years ago, The Dayton Tire & Rubber Company was in dire straits. The firm had just been acquired by Firestone and Dayton Tire warehouses across the country were being closed. A father-son team, C.S. and C.R. Potter, decided to invest $25,000 and try to get the operation on its feet. The Baton Rouge wholesale operation (Dayton Tire Company of Louisiana, Inc.) had only three employees and one delivery truck, and business was so light that half of the warehouse was leased to other companies.

For five years, C.S. commuted from his "retirement" in New Orleans to oversee the business; finally, in 1966, son C.R. (a 1958 Texas Christian University graduate) left his job with Texaco to manage the company. Changing the firm name to Area, expanding the product line, and selling retail as well as wholesale, by 1972 the company was able to enlarge the once neglected warehouse and add a service department to handle the retail business.

In 1975, AWT opened a wholesale facility in Alexandria, and in 1977 modern corporate offices were completed at the firm's main location at 5930 McClelland Drive in Baton Rouge. Further expansion occurred throughout the 1970s—the company opened another facility in Lafayette and a retail store in Alexandria, tripled space in its Airline Highway location, and increased its market penetration. Today, AWT supplies every major tire store in Louisiana, southern Mississippi, and eastern Texas.

Top
Area Wholesale Tire Company has been located at 5620 Airline Highway since 1960.
Bottom
The Area Wholesale Tire Company complex today offers all the modern conveniences and services necessary to supply the greater Baton Rouge area.

The firm's 1966 sales of $180,000 have skyrocketed to more than $10 million in 1980. And its three-employee staff has grown to sixty. The original lone delivery truck has been replaced by a fleet of twenty-five vehicles that supply Baton Rouge and surrounding areas with Remington, General, Alliance, Somitomo, and Empco tires and tire products. The company has strongly penetrated the replacement tire market and started importing off-the-road and large truck tires from Israel and Japan. AWT's trucking subsidiary delivers synthetic processed rubber from Baton Rouge's Copolymer Rubber Plant to Huntsville, Alabama, where it is manufactured into Remington tires and then sold by AWT.

As for the future, Shreveport and/or Hammond will be the next site for expansion. And soon, Area Wholesale Tire plans to install a new computer system to enhance distribution and accounting efficiency.

Baton Rouge has found that time and change can make a great difference in the fortunes of a southern city. Likewise, twenty years and a change of management have certainly turned the fortunes of this optimistic, growing company.

Associated Grocers, Inc.

Ten years after its formation, the Associated Grocers had created for the Baton Rouge area a cooperative grocery supplier that had proven itself to be a worthwhile venture. From fourteen farsighted grocers who started the enterprise in May 1950, the cooperative had grown by 1960 to include forty-eight stores. Sales in 1950 amounted to $207,000, utilizing 2,500 square feet of warehouse space. In 1960, the warehouse had grown to 10,000 square feet and sales had increased to more than $1.7 million.

By that year, an advertising campaign in local papers was making the association's name and policies familiar to area consumers. The cash-and-carry procedure used initially gave way in 1955 to the group's first truck, when free delivery to member stores was initiated.

Plans for a new warehouse in 1960 were realized with the completion of a $200,000 steel-framed edifice containing over 30,000 square feet of space. By January of the following year, the facility was in use and a more extensive line of groceries, meats, and nonfood items was offered, as sales climbed above $2.25 million. Two years later, the warehouse saw expansion to 53,000 square feet, while member stores had increased to a total of 119.

For ten years the association prospered in this location, but in 1973 the demand for an even larger and more modern facility necessitated the purchase of the present 55-acre tract on Anselmo Lane. The board of directors gave final approval for construction of a 217,000-square-foot structure that cost in excess of $4.5 million. Spanning seventeen acres, the new facility combines modern warehouse technology with efficient office management to supply the more than 250 member stores in twenty Louisiana parishes.

Since moving into the Anselmo Lane facility in 1975, the association has increased its service capabilities with the installation of a cart delivery method and a new computer system allowing members to take advantage of direct ordering, accounting and payroll control, custom pricing, and scanning assistance. The firm's store engineering, printing, and equipment purchasing departments are available to members.

The tremendous expansion and growth that Associated Grocers experienced under the leadership of past president Sam S. Politz is continuing today through the management of Hillar C. Moore, Jr., as the cooperative strives to offer to its members the best in service to provide low prices, quality products, and reputable operating standards that will please local consumers.

Left
Associated Grocers experienced prosperity and growth under the guidance of past president Sam S. Politz.
Right
Spanning seventeen acres, Associated Grocers' new facility on Anselmo Lane combines modern warehouse technology with efficient office management.

Bank of the South

Bank of the South, recognizing and responding to the tremendous growth in recent years in the southern sectors of Baton Rouge, became the city's seventh banking institution on April 2, 1979.

James A. Desselle, Jr., was the motivating influence behind the bank's formation and now serves as chairman of the board and chief executive officer. Frank J. "Jim" Greely is president and cashier.

Members of the board of directors are: Arton A. Bertrand; James A. Desselle, Jr.; Jan W. Duggar, Ph.D.; Frank J. "Jim" Greely, Jr.; William C. Haile, M.D.; George D. Haynes; Marjorie B. Mackey; Harold "Fritz" McNemar; Philip J. Muscarello; James L. Pope, Jr.; Frank G. Rieger, M.D.; Milton W. Shepard; Lawrence E. Tujague, M.D.; John B. Tyner; George St. Julien; and Charles D. Sylvest.

It was with great pleasure and pride that Bank of the South joined the healthy financial community of Baton Rouge and began to meet the need for increased banking facilities in a city that continues to expand at an amazing rate. Selecting the bank's location with regard to convenient and accessible service for this area of the city, Bank of the South is the only financial institution in the Baton Rouge area with main headquarters located in the outlying section. The bank opened its doors with paid-in capital of $2.5 million and is offering the latest in a wide variety of banking services, such as drive-up hours from 7:00 a.m. to 10:00 p.m. Most importantly, Bank of the South's pledge to the Baton Rouge area is to provide financial service tailored to meet the needs of its clientele on a person-to-person basis.

Top
Bank of the South's new facility, located at 9800 Airline Highway, was designed for the convenience of its Baton Rouge patrons.

Center
On August 27, 1979, the Honorable Edwin E. Edwards presided over Bank of the South's ribbon-cutting ceremony.

Bottom
James A. Desselle, Jr., actively involved in the formation of Baton Rouge's newest banking institution, serves as its chief executive officer and chairman of the board.

Barnard and Burk, Inc.

Designing the city's streets and highways, engineering its deep water port, and constructing a wide range of industrial facilities up and down the Mississippi, Barnard and Burk, Inc., has for many years created landmarks that symbolize the strength and development of Baton Rouge. Now a national engineering and construction firm, B & B began as an engineering partnership established in the city by Charles C. Barnard and Jack S. Burk in 1943.

The company initially undertook municipal and public works projects such as the construction of byways and water supply treatment, sewage, and drainage systems. B & B also handled assignments involving electric power generation, transmission, and distribution. And the firm later expanded its professional services to include the engineering of ports and marine terminals, natural gas transmission systems, and facilities for the refining, chemical, and petrochemical industries.

In its early years, B & B prepared the master plan for the Port of Baton Rouge, issued the preliminary engineering and economic feasibility reports for five successive bond issues, and designed and supervised construction of the facilities. A letter, dated January 16, 1956, from Ernest D. Wilson, president of the Greater Baton Rouge Port Commission, states: "Certainly, Barnard and Burk has every reason to be proud of a difficult job well done in a complicated field of engineering."

The company engineered a 1,000-mile section of a natural-gas pipeline from Baton Rouge to Miami for the Florida Gas Company, long sections of Interstates 10 and 12, and numerous other municipal streets and rural roads.

Over the years, offices were opened in several states and in South America. Headquarters remained in Baton Rouge in a new facility built on a six-acre landscaped lot off Highway 61 on Mayfair Drive. Services were expanded to include pipe fabrication and plant maintenance work. Today, through its Plant Services and Southeast Fabricators divisions, B & B is one of the largest contract maintenance firms in the United States and a leader in pipe fabrication.

In 1973, Barnard and Burk was acquired by Aerojet-General Corporation and is now operated as a wholly owned subsidiary. Under the direction of president James Nugent—only the second president in the company's history—B & B has increased its involvement with the chemical/petrochemical industry. The company also embarked on a program of geographical expansion

An East Coast office was opened in 1975 and since that time major projects have been completed for many industrial leaders.

In January 1978, B & B moved its corporate headquarters to Pasadena, California. The move was made to further decentralize the organization and to allow the individual operating divisions to function more independently. A Western Division was also set up in Pasadena, and engineering and construction operations in Baton Rouge were consolidated as the Gulf Coast Division.

Today, Barnard and Burk, Inc., through its Gulf Coast, Northeastern, and Western divisions, provides engineering, procurement, and construction services on a nationwide basis. The company is consistently ranked among the larger engineering-construction organizations in the country. Headquarters are now in California, but Baton Rouge remains home.

Top
Barnard and Burk provided a wide range of engineering and construction services at this Stauffer Chemical Company agricultural chemical complex at St. Gabriel, Louisiana.
Bottom
The master plan for the Port of Baton Rouge was prepared by B & B.

Baton Rouge Chamber of Commerce

Right from the start, the Baton Rouge Chamber of Commerce was among the most active and vital groups of its kind in the country. For the local chamber the start occurred more than a half century ago, when it joined the United States Chamber of Commerce in the early 1920s, conducted its first membership campaign, and hired a full-time staff manager. Although the new organization recognized that Baton Rouge was already a rapidly expanding and industrializing city, the chamber did not view its function as merely a promotional one; rather it set out at once to stimulate more business growth and to improve the city's quality of life.

The list of projects in which the chamber participated during its formative years illustrates the significance of the organization in the history of Baton Rouge: development of the Baton Rouge port, intracoastal waterway links, airline service, and river channeling; improvement of city streets, flood control measures, and municipal docks; construction of the first bridge across the Mississippi River, new industrial plants, downtown street lighting, and the Baton Rouge airport; and organization of dedications, shows, conventions, and expositions for new industries, 4-H Clubs, political inaugurals, and the new Louisiana State University.

Today, the Baton Rouge Chamber of Commerce holds a position of leadership in a modern, multifaceted community—the center of Louisiana state government, one of the largest inland deep-water ports in the nation, the home of two major universities and a giant petrochemical complex, all combining to create one of the most impressive records of municipal prosperity in America. The chamber's business and professional men and women work together to better the area's economic stability; to increase social, cultural, and government services; and to convey to visitors and newcomers Baton Rouge's unique style of life.

Since 1957, the local chamber has had its headquarters at 564 Laurel

Street, a modern facility hailed as one of the most outstanding chamber buildings in the country. Designed by architects Bodman, Murrell & Smith, the building contains 6,800 square feet of office space and is accented by 20-foot ceilings and windows. The structure replaced a familiar downtown landmark, the Louis G. Stirling house, a transition that highlights the chamber's connection with the historic roots on which Baton Rouge was founded.

The Baton Rouge Chamber of Commerce, a completely nonprofit organization, is financed voluntarily by dues-paying business and professional people who recognize the importance of the chamber's role in their community. Ask any of its 2,700 members if the city needs an active chamber and they will all give you the same answer—you bet your future it does!

Left and Below
Since 1957, the Baton Rouge Chamber of Commerce has had its headquarters at 564 Laurel Street, a modern facility hailed as one of the most outstanding chamber buildings in the country. Designed by architects Bodman, Murrell & Smith, the structure contains 6,800 square feet of office space and is accented by 20-foot ceilings and windows.

Baton Rouge Lumber Company

A group of prominent Baton Rouge citizens formed what is today known as the Baton Rouge Lumber Company in May 1885. Among them was William Garig, whose family later became sole owner of the enterprise. Named after the firm's original manager, the company was located on the bank of the Mississippi River at 702 South First Street in an area known as Catfish Town.

In the beginning, the lumber company was strictly a milling operation. Rafts of logs were floated down the Mississippi from forests upriver and corralled along the bank near the downtown business district of Baton Rouge. After their removal from the river, the logs were sawed into finished lumber products and loaded onto rail cars for shipment throughout the Southeast.

There was no levee along the Mississippi in those early years; this not only facilitated removal of the logs from the river, but also allowed for ready access to low-lying areas along the river during its annual spring flooding. The lumber company operations were flooded on a yearly basis at the original location.

At the turn of the century, the company began to diversify, gradually phasing out its wholesale logging operations and becoming a wholesale-retail yard, able to supply lumber as well as other building materials. Baton Rouge was outgrowing its sleepy little river town image, and contractors and others in the building trades were seeking materials in rapidly increasing quantities.

In March 1906, full ownership of the lumber company was purchased by Mrs. William Garig. For the sum of $106,000, this purchase included the sawmill and its land, the lumber company logo, its open accounts and logging contracts, and all other properties. At that time, the firm's name was changed from the Burton Lumber Company to the Baton Rouge Lumber Company.

Since 1906, ownership has remained in the Garig family's hands. Each of the owners—Mrs. Garig, William P. Connell, Mrs. Eleanor Connell Witter, and present owner Phillips Connell Witter—has played an important role in the development of not only the Baton Rouge Lumber Company, but in the city for which the business is named.

Baton Rouge is no longer a sleepy little river town, but has grown into one of the South's most important industrial centers, experiencing an exciting new era of prosperity and progress.

Baton Rouge Lumber Company's managers—William Burton, William P. Connell, Millard W. Dixon, Mark H. Souter, and today's St. Clair Bienvenu—have all contributed dramatically to the company's continued growth and success. Under Bienvenu's guidance, the business moved in February 1968 from its historic downtown site into spacious, modern facilities on South Choctaw Drive.

Top
The Baton Rouge Lumber Company was originally located on the bank of the Mississippi River, on South First Street.
Bottom
Logs floated downriver were easily pulled from the Mississippi for processing in the pre-levee days of the late 1800s.

Baton Rouge Savings & Loan Association

The Baton Rouge Building and Loan Association was organized on January 10, 1923, with assets of only $50,000. The association's first president was W.S. Holmes, who served until 1926. Under his guidance, the company increased its assets sevenfold.

In the latter part of 1926, Security Building and Loan Association was purchased. At that time, Holmes was succeeded by O.O. Ogden as the association's president. By the time of his death in 1927, Ogden had increased assets to $806,000.

The association's name was officially changed to Baton Rouge Savings & Loan Association in 1954. Under the leadership of W.A. Gotschall, the firm's third president, assets increased dramatically to $11.3 million. Upon Gotschall's death in 1957, Matt G. Smith became the association's fourth president.

By 1958, customer facilities had expanded to three offices and company assets had almost doubled. Smith became chairman of the board on December 19, 1962; he was succeeded as president by Clyde P. Didier, who had joined the association in 1954 as a comptroller.

Smith served as the board's chairman until his death in 1971. At that time, Ben R. Miller was elected to succeed him, a position he held in turn until his retirement in 1976. Didier was then appointed chairman of the

The board of directors of Baton Rouge Savings & Loan Association operates from the main office at 400 North Boulevard.

board and David O. Stanley was named executive vice-president. Stanley, who had joined the association in 1958, was promoted in 1980 to the posts of president and chief operations officer. Didier retained the positions of chairman and chief executive officer.

Continued growth and progress have been experienced throughout the more recent history of Baton Rouge Savings & Loan. Six branches now serve Baton Rougeans through the parish of East Baton Rouge. The firm's main office has remained at 400 North Boulevard since 1954.

Total assets of the association are now over $100 million. Offering easily accessible facilities, Baton Rouge Savings & Loan has also determined that necessary assistance in area housing has been provided. Millions of dollars in dividends have been paid to savers over the years.

Diligent efforts to serve homeowners, builders, and savers in the Baton Rouge area more effectively continue to be made by Baton Rouge Savings & Loan Association. This old and progressive firm has always enjoyed innovative ideas. It was the first savings and loan in the state to offer VISA credit cards, to engage in secondary mortgage marketing, to develop a service corporation to offer more complete service to its members, and one of the first to be fully computerized.

Baton Rouge Water Works Company

A contract dated November 8, 1887, records the earliest known effort by local citizens to secure a reliable water supply. E. Smedley and John H. Wood were contracted to "construct, build, maintain, operate, and own a system of water in the city of Baton Rouge and to supply said city and its inhabitants with water."

The water was drawn from the Mississippi River and treated through a filtering system before being delivered to area residents. Most people

had their own cisterns; consequently, customer demand for river water was not high.

That first year, a standpipe 100 feet high and 15 feet in diameter was erected on Lafayette Street. The tower, still standing though no longer in use, is on the National Register of Historic Places. Today it is recognized as historically vital, but in 1888 the river water was deemed unfit and in 1889 the first well was drilled to a depth of 109 feet.

Residents in the Baton Rouge area currently enjoy the distinction of living in one of the few cities in America to have perfectly soft water. That first well in 1889 was the beginning of this local luxury.

In April 1910, the company changed hands and became the Baton Rouge Water Works Company. Mr. C.C. Bird served as president from offices located on Natches Street (now Front Street). Meters in those early days were read by men who traveled from house to house in horse-drawn buggies. Bills were prepared each night

Left
This standpipe of riveted wrought iron plates was built in 1888 and placed on the National Register of Historic Places in 1973. The old state capitol is in the background.
Below
The offices of the Baton Rouge Water Works Company are located at 4615 Government Street.

and hand-delivered the next day. As local demand grew, so did the company, with offices moving up the hill to 131 Lafayette Street.

Water for Baton Rouge is obtained from fifty-one deep wells ranging in depth from 1,000 to 3,000 feet. The water supply probably enters the ground in the area near Vicksburg, Mississippi, moves through sand strata, and eventually reaches Baton Rouge where it is drawn off by wells, emerging from the ground bacteriologically pure. It is chlorinated and then pumped to distribution lines now totaling 1,200 miles in length. Because of this superior supply and distribution system, Baton Rougeans enjoy one of the lowest fire insurance rates in the nation.

Moving to its present Government Street location in October 1961, the Baton Rouge Water Works Company is now housed in a modern building of glass, aluminum, and brick. Its drive-up window and night depository were designed for customer convenience. The company now employs more than 200 persons under the guidance of president Raymond E. Pillow.

The water, from deep wells throughout the service area, is collected and transported by the Baton Rouge Water Works Company. The company determines that the water's safety for human consumption is assured and delivers it to the Baton Rouge area on a continuous basis. Few people stop to consider how drastically their lives would be affected should the supply of water cease. Baton Rouge Water Works Company strives to ensure that Baton Rougeans never have to experience such a difficulty.

The Bedford Corporation

The Bedford Corporation, originally chartered in July 1962, was formed for the purpose of apartment construction. During the next six years, extensive experience in that field was gained as the Baton Rouge area enjoyed a period of rapid growth. Reorganized in 1968 for general construction purposes, the company is now capable of handling complete turnkey projects and all forms of general contracting. The corporation also is a dealer for pre-engineered metal buildings.

With skilled employees known for their abilities to handle a diversity of construction projects, the best way to understand Bedford is to get to know its main officers. Odis Haymon, a native of Vernon Parish, graduated from Louisiana State University in 1947 with a Master of Science degree.

In the late 1950s and early 1960s, Haymon built and sold more than 100 local residences. His first apartment complex was built in 1946; he later built more than 1,000 rental units in Alabama, Florida, Tennessee, and Louisiana. A licensed general contractor, he serves as president of The Bedford Corporation.

Michael Schulz, a New Orleans native who also finished at LSU, is secretary-treasurer of Bedford. A registered civil engineer and land surveyor in the state of Louisiana, Schulz has had extensive experience in all phases of design and construction. Serving in his present capacity since 1968, his duties have involved him in all aspects of construction. His work has included more than 1,000 apartment units, several thousand houses, and numerous commercial and industrial structures.

The Bedford Corporation is proud of the variety of work it has done for its clients. The firm has worked for state and local governmental agencies, such as the parish of East Baton

Rouge; the Ascension Parish Police Jury; and numerous school boards, including those of East Baton Rouge, Ascension, and Livingston. National clients include Allied Chemical, Bausch & Lomb, C.F. Industries, Ciba-Geigy, Dow, Exxon, Georgia-Pacific, Gulf Oil, Kaiser Aluminum, Ormet, Shell Chemical, Stauffer, Texaco, and Uniroyal. Projects undertaken have varied from schools, medical clinics, warehouses, office buildings, feed mills, a slaughterhouse, a soap factory, retail stores, apartment houses, restaurants, computer facilities, a sewage treatment plant, a refuse transfer station, laboratories, and foundations for industrial structures.

Devoted to the continued growth of the area, The Bedford Corporation is proud of its participation in the past and present development of Baton Rouge and looks forward to an even greater role in the future.

One of The Bedford Corporation's many recently completed projects, the Parkview apartment complex now serves the growing demand for housing in the Baton Rouge metropolitan area.

Blue Cross of Louisiana

In 1929, Americans were only a decade or two away from horse-and-buggy medicine. Technology was still at the Model-T stage, with hospitals offering little more than room, board, and sympathy. It was the first year of the Great Depression.

Justin Ford Kimball, Ph.D., was vice-president of Baylor University in charge of its medical unit in Dallas. Aware of the financial problems facing the citizens in his community, especially the school teachers, Kimball initiated a program to assist them by providing twenty-one days of care in the Baylor Hospital for the prepaid amount of fifty cents a month. More than 1,500 teachers joined the Dallas Plan and interest generated in the idea was great.

Similar plans began forming across the country, each associated with a particular hospital. By 1932, community plans had emerged, offering members a choice of hospitals. The following year, the American Hospital Association began to encourage the development of plans and began regulating them. That same year, the plan in St. Paul, Minnesota, began to use a blue cross to identify itself. In 1939, the American Hospital Association adopted the blue cross with its seal superimposed as the official emblem of approved plans.

Community plans in Baton Rouge, New Orleans, Shreveport, and Alexandria were initiated in the 1930s. In 1938, the plans in Baton Rouge, Shreveport, and Alexandria were consolidated into Louisiana Hospital Service, Inc. T.B. Bennett of Baton Rouge was named executive director and Wallace E. Franck of Alexandria was named assistant director. Louisiana Hospital Service, Inc., served fifty-nine of the state's sixty-four parishes.

The Hospital Service Association of New Orleans was established in 1934. Under the direction of Edward Groner, the plan served the five parishes in the metropolitan New Orleans area. In 1962, Edmond J. Vallon was named the plan's chief executive officer and served in that capacity until his retirement in 1974.

Both Louisiana plans experienced dramatic growth in the decades following World War II. In 1966, the plans were named fiscal intermediaries for the hospital part of the medicare program. In March 1967, Howard L. Reitz was named president of the Baton Rouge plan. The following year, the plan moved into its present building on Florida Boulevard.

In January 1975, the Louisiana plans consolidated and became Blue Cross of Louisiana, with corporate headquarters in Baton Rouge. Reitz was named president of the new statewide plan and Earl J. Wilde, Jr., who had succeeded Vallon in New Orleans, was named executive vice-president. Blue Cross of Louisiana serves over one million people in the state. Claims paid to Louisiana citizens exceeded $.5 billion in 1979. Blue Cross of Louisiana is, and will remain, the leader in the prepayment of health care in the state.

Left
Corporate headquarters of Blue Cross of Louisiana are located on Florida Boulevard in Baton Rouge.
Below
Howard L. Reitz has been president of Blue Cross of Louisiana since March 1967.

Braud Glass, Inc.

The year was 1930 when Noah P. Braud began his glass and mirror business at 234 North Boulevard. The enterprise was known as American Glass and Mirror Works and the phone number was simply 780. The new company's undertakings included picture framing and beveling; and glass and store fronts, auto glass, and mirrors.

A self-educated man with little formal schooling, Braud came to Baton Rouge from his native Iberville Parish. In Louisiana's capital city, he married another Iberville native, Inez Cecilia Harrell, on December 23, 1930. They would have four children—Noah Jr., Barbara, Nancy, and Cynthia.

An active member of the Baton Rouge business and social community for almost fifty years, Braud was distinguished by his generous nature and ability to deal with people. He served as the company's president from its founding until his death in 1979. Mrs. Braud served as company treasurer until her death that same year.

In 1940, Braud sold his interest in American Glass and formed Braud Glass Company, which relocated at the corner of Main and Front streets. From four employees and 6,000 square feet of floor space, the business grew by the late 1950s to thirty-two employees and 20,000 square feet of floor space. Mirror resilvering, upholstery, and electroplating departments were

Left
Noah P. Braud opened his glass and mirror business in 1930, the same year this photograph was taken.

Right
Located at 969 North Eighteenth Street, Braud Glass offers a wide selection of glassware products and services.

added later to provide more complete customer service.

In 1958, with the widening of Front Street, Braud moved into new facilities at 969 North Eighteenth Street. He realized that the new downtown Interstate Loop would soon pass right by this site, providing easy access to all parts of the city.

The company, incorporated that same year, continues to serve the Baton Rouge area with the honest, dependable, quality work that has marked the business throughout its many years of operation. One of the few firms in this area to resilver antique beveled mirrors, Braud Glass, Inc., also installs plate glass, mirrors, storefronts, and aluminum doors. Available in the company's modern showroom are window glass, plate glass, furniture tops, custom mirrors, art and colored glass, and handblown glassware.

BASF Wyandotte Corporation

Founded in 1890 by 80-year-old Captain John Baptiste Ford, Wyandotte Chemicals began its history in the city of Wyandotte, Michigan, the site chosen by Ford because of the availability of vast salt deposits underlying the area. With an abundant supply of water from the nearby Detroit River, the salt and water provided the basic resources for the manufacturing of soda ash, a vital ingredient in the production of glass.

In 1970, BASF Wyandotte Corporation was formed with the merger of BASF Corporation of New Jersey into Wyandotte Chemicals of Michigan. BASF Wyandotte is an American member of the BASF Group, a worldwide leader in chemicals, with over 300 affiliates and subsidiaries recording annual sales of more than $15 billion. The BASF Group dates from 1865, when it was founded in Germany.

Today, the company is comprised of three principal product groups, Industrial Chemicals, Colors and Fine Chemicals, and Polymers, and manufactures and markets industrial chemicals, organic intermediates, Styropor® expandable polystyrene, urethane chemicals and systems, dyestuffs and pigments, textile and leather auxiliaries, crop protection chemicals, vitamins, and magnetic recording media.

The Industrial Chemicals group operates the Geismar manufacturing complex twenty-five miles south of

Top
The Industrial Chemicals group of BASF Wyandotte Corporation operates the Geismar manufacturing complex twenty-five miles south of Baton Rouge.

Bottom
The surroundings of the Geismar works are dominated by magnificent oak trees, many over 300 years old.

Baton Rouge. The company's initial introduction into Louisiana occurred in 1955, when a 1,200-acre site along the Mississippi River was purchased. The location of the plant had been carefully studied to ensure that it was situated in an area offering direct access to water transportation, an abundance of raw materials, and sufficient land for future expansion and devel-

opment. Geismar was the decided choice.

The BASF plant was one of the first industrial complexes to be located on the Mississippi between Baton Rouge and New Orleans at Geismar. On what had been the fields of Cottage Farm Plantation, the company's first products—chlorine, caustic soda, ethylene oxide, and ethylene glycol—were produced by 1958. The site now includes two chlorine/caustic plants, and toluene diisocyanate, polyol, butanediol, and Basagran herbicide plants. The newest additions are the tetrahydrofuran and diphenyl methane diisocyanate plants. The company's original $11-million investment has grown many times over, and today amounts to about $400 million. The site has expanded to 2,300 acres with more than 1,000 employees.

The Cottage Farm Plantation family cemetery is located on the company property and it is faithfully maintained while the complex continues to grow. Proud of its pioneering efforts in the industrial development of the Mississippi River south of Baton Rouge, BASF Wyandotte appreciates the area's rich and storied past and looks eagerly toward what is certain to be a bright and progressive future.

Capital City Press

"In my opinion you've got to regard newspapers as living creatures and treat them as such. To me, very early in its life, a newspaper assumes a personality of its own. Editors may occasionally come along whose egos are strong enough to modify a paper's personality for a space of time, but it's often the newspaper that molds its writers and editors. I feel my job as publisher is to seek out the personality of each of the newspapers, sharpen and define it, and help the staff realize that no matter where they work—pressroom, composing, newsroom, wherever—they all contribute to this newspaper's total personality. You really have to watch a newspaper all the time or it'll wander off and become something different."

This quotation of Douglas L. Manship, the third member of his family to serve as publisher and editor of both the *State-Times* and *Morning Advocate*, was printed in the November 12, 1977, issue of *Editor & Publisher*. The article was a profile of Manship as he began a year as president of the Southern Newspaper Publishers Association, also the third member of his family to hold that office. His father, Charles P. Manship, was SNPA president for two successive terms, 1941-43, and his brother, Charles P. Manship, Jr., served in 1958-59.

Each of the two Baton Rouge newspapers does have a unique personality and when seen against their histories the differences are understandable. Baton Rouge's site on the first high ground on the Mississippi River made it a natural gathering place for the Istrouma Indians and then the European settlers. From the first non-native settlement to the present day, all written records show a stormy history of controversy between people of passionate political convictions—a natural matrix for newspapers. Dozens of newspapers appeared during the city's early years, all advocating a cause or a particular political party. Fiery editorials, libelous attacks against the opposition, and high-flown rhetoric make the few remaining examples of these early newspapers fascinating reading even now. Editors frequently wore guns and at least three documented duels were fought between editors and irate readers.

The newspaper that was to survive in one form or another and become the present *State-Times* began publishing in December 1842, as *The Democratic Advocate*, a morning newspaper. For a half century there were mergers, changes in ownership, and changes in the frequency of publication until, in 1904, *The Democratic Advocate* was bought out by the *Baton Rouge Times*, an evening publication. In 1907, the *Times* merged with the *State* and began publishing as the *State-Times*.

In 1909 the newspaper was purchased by Capital City Press, with Charles P. Manship as publisher and James Edmonds as editor. A few months later Edmonds left Baton Rouge and Manship became editor and publisher. In 1912 Manship bought Edmonds' remaining interest and acquired complete control of the *State-Times*.

On the first day of publication under the masthead of Capital City Press, the *State-Times* carried a front-page policy statement which was a dramatic departure from the earlier party-partisan newspapers. This policy, still in effect today, reads in part: "It is our intention to print a newspaper whose editorials are not for sale, and whose news items cannot be suppressed, a newspaper commensurate with the hopes and plans of Baton Rouge, provided the businessmen of Baton Rouge measure their patronage by the same standard. To no politician, no officeholder, no director of public patronage are we under obligation—and looking the world in the face, we dare tell the truth of any man living."

Under the firm guidance of Charles Manship, the *State-Times* steadied.

Still innovative, still colorful, daring in its editorial stance when necessary, the Baton Rouge newspaper gained depth, quality, and credibility. It weathered the first World War, the Great Depression, and the tumultuous political wars of Louisiana.

In 1925 Charles Manship began the *Morning Advocate*, which covers out-of-the-city news in depth, has a younger staff, and is generally friskier than the *State-Times*. In 1934 he established Baton Rouge's first radio station, WJBO-AM, and in 1941, the first FM station in the South, W45BR, now WFMF-FM.

During World War II Manship di-

Left
Capital City Press' new $20-million facility, the Bluebonnet Production Center, will house the newspaper presses and one of the most modern distribution operations in the United States in 1982.
Below
Charles Manship, founder of Capital City Press, was publisher from 1909 until his death in 1947.
Center
Charles Manship, Jr., publisher from 1947-1970, is now president of Capital City Press.
Right
Douglas Manship has been publisher and editor of the State-Times *and* Morning Advocate *since 1970.*

rected the American Office of Press Censorship in the European Theater of Operations, stationed in London in 1943-44. After his death in 1947, his elder son, Charles P. Manship, Jr., became publisher and editor of the two newspapers. The younger son, Douglas, became secretary-treasurer of Capital City Press and guided the development and building of WBRZ-TV.

During his years as publisher and editor, Charles Manship, Jr., expanded the newspapers from a small company to a large, financially stable organization. He guided the newspapers through the upheaval of desegregation and the violent labor problems that developed around the booming industrial growth of the city. In 1950-53 he built a fine new structure at 525 Lafayette Street to house the growing company.

In 1970 Charles Manship, Jr., retired as publisher and editor of the *State-Times* and *Morning Advocate* and is now president of Capital City Press. His brother, Douglas Manship, became publisher and editor of the newspapers. Under his guidance, a

revolutionary change in production methods was completed in 1974-75, when the newspapers converted entirely to cold type. Capital City Press, innovative in the use of electronic equipment, pioneered a new computer program which electronically schedules and lays out all advertising in the newspapers; this program has been sold to newspapers all over the world.

Keeping pace with Baton Rouge's booming growth, Capital City Press is building the $20-million Bluebonnet Production Center to house the presses and one of the most modern distribution operations in the United States. Page images will be microwaved from Lafayette Street across the city to the Bluebonnet Production Center.

In an era when inheritance taxes have forced many independently owned newspapers to sell to large conglomerates run by distant managers, the Baton Rouge newspapers are still locally owned, distinguished by the quality and commitment of their staffs, and still deeply involved with the community of Baton Rouge.

Capital Savings Association

Founded in 1909 by John Hereford Percy, the Capital Building and Loan Association has been a significant part of the Baton Rouge business community for more than seventy years. Percy had operated a small savings and loan and insurance company in neighboring St. Francisville, north of the capital city, before embarking on the move. At that time, a savings and loan was sorely needed in Baton Rouge, so Percy, aided by several prominent businessmen, began organization of Capital. W.C. Whitaker, B.B. Taylor, Robert Hart, and others were instrumental with Percy in the formation of the new corporation. Capital Building and Loan Association, a state-chartered institution, opened with Whitaker as president and Percy as secretary-treasurer.

At its original location on Third Street near Florida, the association grew slowly during its formative years. Under the capable leadership of O.M. Thompson, who had joined the company in 1922, the association weathered the depression and then began to enjoy the growth that the entire area was experiencing. Capital was the first local loan association to offer VA loans.

In 1929, the association purchased the site of its historic location from the First Presbyterian Church. Capital remained at this site for over fifty years, doubling the building's original size in 1954. The state's first branch office was opened by Capital the following year. The firm's name

Left
J.H. Percy (left), founder and first secretary of Capital Savings, later served as president and was chairman of the board until his death in 1959. O.M. Thompson, who joined the firm in 1922, later served as president and is now chairman of the board.
Right
This 1863 photograph looks north toward the intersection of Florida and Fourth. The structure at left is the Heroman building, present site of Capital Savings' home office. At right is the First Presbyterian Church, later the site of Capital Savings from 1929 to 1980.
Bottom
Completed in 1980, Capital Savings Association's modern new six-story building in downtown Baton Rouge stands across the street from the location where the organization operated for fifty years.

was formally changed in 1974 to Capital Savings Association. Today, that site of Capital's location from 1929 to 1980 is just across the street from the present building, a magnificent new addition to the downtown skyline.

Thompson retired in 1965 and Edmond Salasi assumed the presidency until his retirement in 1977. The company is now prospering under the able direction of Paul Reeves.

Capital, with assets in excess of $245 million, serves the entire Baton Rouge area by arranging home loans and providing a safe place for the investment of funds. Capital Savings is proud to be a part of the downtown business community and eagerly anticipates the coming years of continuing progressive service to the Baton Rouge community.

Cayard's, Inc.

"I've come in to get acquainted and to see how we can help each other," said Robert Cayard to each potential customer he visited in 1945.

Cayard believed that if he helped others with their businesses, they would help him with his; and he pioneered the first restaurant- and bar-supply house in Baton Rouge with that philosophy. Area restaurant owners liked the approach, and soon many were buying their supplies from him. Cayard had shown that he could provide them with units designed expressly for use in public eating places.

Beginning the business meant long hours working out of a one-room extension Cayard had built onto the back of his garage. The family car was used for sales trips; and Mrs. Cayard and the children helped when they could. But the company's growth demanded more help and larger quarters.

After several moves, the business settled at 1545 South Boulevard. Cayard continued to increase his inventory until he was able to outfit the beginning or established restaurateur with virtually any piece of equipment needed. Heavy ranges, fryers, large baking ovens, dishwashing machines, large refrigerators, cold-storage rooms, ice machines, counters, and booths were just part of the wide range of supplies offered by Cayard's. Proper installation of each item sold was an integral part of the service provided by the company.

Above
Cayard's, Inc., was located at 1545 South Boulevard until 1964.

Left
Robert Cayard pioneered in the establishment of the first restaurant- and bar-supply house in Baton Rouge.

Throughout the years, Cayard gained the nickname of being Baton Rouge's "largest restaurant proprietor." This appellation was awarded because of the generous financial aid and moral support he gave to novice restaurant owners.

After seventeen years as a newspaperman and businessman in Illinois and another twenty-five years in Baton Rouge, Robert Cayard decided it was time to retire in 1962. When the business was announced for sale, two factory salesmen who had supplied Cayard's were particularly interested. Robert Dellafiora and Chuck Blair became the majority stockholders, recently adding Grady Hickman as a new partner.

In 1964, the business moved to expanded facilities at 4215 Choctaw Drive, with more space subsequently added to that location.

Today, Cayard's is one of the largest restaurant suppliers in the Gulf States, continuing to grow with Baton Rouge and the wide area the business services. From a small group of local restaurants, the company's clients have diversified to include hospitals, state institutions, schools, and even kitchens on offshore oil rigs. The staff has now been expanded to offer not only supplies and equipment but employees skilled in the planning, layout, and design of modern kitchen facilities.

Century 21 Central

After twenty years in the brick business, Joe Grisaffe decided to take the advice of friends and customers and go into the construction of top-quality homes. It was a logical move, because he had learned a great deal about home building from his father, a builder in Grisaffe's native Assumption Parish. Under the name of Belle Alliance Homes, Grisaffe's new enterprise began home construction in 1976.

Approached by another builder, Grisaffe became a partner in J.B. & J. Builders, which developed the Avalon subdivision in Baton Rouge. Its properties were so popular that a need was realized to establish a marketing service for the company's projects; so J.B. & J. Realtors was formed to fulfill that need. In 1978, Grisaffe sold his interest in J.B. & J. Builders, purchasing total ownership of J.B. & J. Realtors and becoming a member of the Century 21 family.

In 1980, Century 21 J.B. & J. Realtors became Century 21 Central. Grisaffe relocated his business to its present South Sherwood Boulevard location. At that time, a restructuring of the firm occurred and Grisaffe's wife, Ellen, was named sales manager. A former registered nurse, she had in 1979 decided to see what her husband's real estate business was all about. In her first year, Ellen achieved more than $2.5 million in sales.

It has been a mere five years since Grisaffe began building homes and wound up in the real estate business.

His first realty office staff was comprised of one part-time secretary and three agents who dealt only in residential sales. Today, three full-time office employees monitor the work of twenty agents who annually handle sales amounting to several million dollars.

Expanding and continually diversifying, Century 21 Central now offers the services of residential, referral and relocation, commercial and investment, and property management divisions.

The real estate business in the Baton Rouge area exemplifies the tremendous growth the area has experienced in recent years. Coming from a small town in Assumption Parish to find his place in the capital city, Grisaffe realized the exciting opportunities offered by Baton Rouge and took advantage of those opportunities to achieve significant success. Today Century 21 Central is an integral part of Baton Rouge's business community, and continues to play an important role in the expansion and development of the greater Baton Rouge area.

Left
In 1980, Joe Grisaffe carefully oversaw the construction of Century 21 Central's new headquarters at 5841 South Sherwood Forest Boulevard.
Below
Under the guidance of Ellen and Joe Grisaffe, Century 21 Central has become an integral part of the Baton Rouge business community.

Charles E. Schwing & Associates, Inc.

Charles E. Schwing & Associates, Inc., has been characterized since its founding by innovative architectural design, as well as by a wide range of services in the fields of planning, site selection, economics, and technology.

Founded by Charles E. Schwing in 1961, the five-person firm offers architectural services for new construction, as well as for restoration and remodeling. Included among those services is the company's expertise in such diverse areas as budget review, feasibility studies, zoning analysis, and energy studies.

Schwing, a practicing architect in Louisiana since 1956, was educated in engineering, architecture, and fine arts at Louisiana State University, Georgia Institute of Technology, and Ecole des Beaux Arts in Fontainbleau, France.

Schwing served as the 1980 president of the American Institute of Architects, when he became the institute's fifty-sixth president in December 1979. He has also served as treasurer of the AIA Foundation and AIA Research Corporation. Elected to the AIA College of Fellows in 1977, Schwing is also an honorary member of the Society of Bolivarian Architects of South America and the College of Architects of Venezuela, and an honorary fellow of the Royal Institute of Canadian Architects.

Joining the enterprise in 1966 as an

Above
After a bomb caused extensive damage to the Louisiana State Capitol on April 26, 1970, Charles E. Schwing & Associates performed careful restoration work, returning the historic rooms to their original condition.
Above Right
Charles E. Schwing & Associates renovated this old rice warehouse for the European Import Gallery in the historic French Quarter of New Orleans.

associate architect, Kenneth B. Campbell was named vice-president in 1972. A practicing architect in Louisiana since 1958, Campbell holds degrees in architectural engineering and civil engineering from Louisiana State University. He is a registered land surveyor, civil engineer, and architect, and spent three years in the U.S. Navy Civil Engineer Corps. Professionally, Campbell has served as president of the Baton Rouge Chapter of AIA and as board member of the Louisiana Architects Association.

Among the many fascinating projects undertaken by Charles E. Schwing & Associates, Inc., was the recent restoration and transformation of an old rice warehouse in New Orleans' historic French Quarter into five apartments and an auction gallery for the European Art Import Gallery. For this exceptional work, the firm received a commendation from the Vieux Carre Commission for outstanding achievement in historic preservation.

Of particular importance in Baton Rouge was the contribution made by the firm toward the restoration of the Louisiana State Capitol Senate Chamber after a bomb blast ripped through the speaker's area of the historic structure. In a round-the-clock effort, the extensive damage was repaired and the room meticulously returned to its original beauty, with care taken to preserve every detail. For the firm's considerable contribution to this project, it was awarded a joint commendation from the Louisiana State Senate and the House of Representatives. The firm also restored the House Chamber and is presently working on an underground addition to the capitol's west side.

Clovis Hendry Industries, Inc.

Lundin-Hendry Company, a partnership of Edward J. Lundin and B. Clovis Hendry, was founded in 1947 to perform residential and commercial roofing and sheet metal work. Two years later, the firm was incorporated. The paid-in capital at that time was $20,000. Between 1949 and 1961, the corporation performed roofing and sheet metal work and also ventured into the architectural plastics field. In 1962, the company diversified and became two distinct enterprises—Lundin-Hendry, Inc., which retained the roofing and sheet metal aspect of the business, and Lundin and Associates, which assumed the architectural plastics work.

On December 28, 1962, the name of the corporation was changed to Clovis Hendry, Inc. It was decided that the principal endeavor would be industrial sheet metal and roofing work. On November 6, 1979, the company name was changed once again to Clovis Hendry Industries, Inc. The firm, specializing in the fabrication of special alloys, has the finest shop of its kind in the area. The company has shown steady growth since 1962; annual sales now amount to $4 million.

B. Clovis Hendry, Jr., president of the corporation, is in charge of industrial sheet metal work. Gary G. Hendry, executive vice-president, is responsible for architectural sheet metal work and roofing. B. Clovis Hendry, chairman of the board, is primarily concerned with company finances.

Because of the large number of petrochemical industrial plants in the Baton Rouge area and the reputation for integrity and quality the firm enjoys with those plants, future growth seems assured. Clovis Hendry Industries, Inc., recently purchased sixteen acres of land on Highway 1 in Addis, Louisiana, and is currently constructing a $1.25-million shop and office. This new facility will greatly increase shop space and will allow the installation of sophisticated new machinery. Office space will be enlarged also, providing quarters to accommodate the continually increasing payroll.

Left
This modern fluid bed dryer, produced by Clovis Hendry Industries, Inc., is fabricated from Type 304 stainless steel. Weighing 50,000 pounds, the unit measures 30 feet in length by 18 feet in height by 12 feet in width.
Right
This photograph taken in 1980 shows a Lafayette, Louisiana, residence on which Clovis Hendry Industries, Inc., installed a copper standing-seam roof.
Bottom
Basil E. Hendry (right), shop superintendent and father of Clovis Hendry, Sr., checks a duct fitting in this 1953 photograph.

Collier Agency

The Commercial Insurance Agency was founded in 1927 by Mr. T.J. Singletary, who served as the company's first president. A prominent businessman, Singletary also founded the Commercial Securities Company and the Commercial Fire & Casualty Company. The latter firm, now known as Audubon Insurance Company, is located at 4150 South Sherwood Forest Boulevard in Baton Rouge, with offices throughout Louisiana and Mississippi.

Commercial Insurance Agency opened its doors in offices located in the old Allen Building, later known as the Singletary Building, which was located at the corner of Florida Boulevard and Church Street (now Fourth Street). The historic old building is prominent in many early photographs of Baton Rouge because of the variety of functions it served. It was used as a hospital during the Civil War, for example.

The fledgling enterprise enjoyed steady progress from its beginning. I.P. "Pat" Collier purchased the business from Singletary in 1953, renaming it the Collier Agency at that time.

In July 1973, Mrs. Lucille Gwin, with more than twenty-six years in the profession, became president of the Collier Agency. She retains that position today. Mrs. Gwin has an impressive record of active participation in community affairs. She is a board member of the Baton Rouge Area Chamber of Commerce and a member of the Council for Presbytery of

South Louisiana. In addition, Mrs. Gwin has served as president of Executive Women, Inc., and of Baton Rouge Insurance Women; she presently heads the Insurance Committee for Presbytery of South Louisiana.

Among the Collier Agency's major companies are Maryland Casualty since 1946; AETNA Casualty since

Mrs. Lucille Gwin has served as president of the Collier Agency since 1973.

1953; Audubon-AMCO since 1954; and CNA since 1977. The Collier Agency today continues the reliably responsible service that has been synonymous with the firm since its early days as Commercial Insurance.

Copolymer

Synthetic rubber has played a major role in the defense and economy of the United States, a function it continues to retain today. The outcome of World War II can be directly related to the development of synthetic rubber, more than to any other manmade or natural material used in wartime efforts. Its evolution can, to a great extent, be attributed to the work of Copolymer Rubber & Chemical Corporation.

The firm was established to operate a manufacturing plant built by the United States government at the inception of World War II. It was recognized that the urgent need to fill the country's cut-off supply of natural rubber had to be satisfied. Until that time, synthetic rubber for tires and other general uses had not been produced on a large-scale commercial basis. It was vital to replace the demand for natural rubber in the manufacture of essential rubber end products. Through a system of cooperative free exchange established among various rubber companies, petrochemical manufacturers, and university researchers, production of synthetic rubber soon began in this country. The first bale of synthetic rubber produced on a commercial scale in a standard design plant rolled off the production line of the Baton Rouge plant operated by Copolymer. From that beginning, many significant accomplishments in the industry were attributed to the Baton Rouge facility.

In 1955, the Copolymer Corporation purchased the plant from the federal government, and the enterprise became the independent Copolymer Rubber & Chemical Corporation. At that time, seven firms composed the constituent group of companies owning Copolymer. Today the constituent group consists of The Armstrong Rubber Company; Gates Rubber Company; and Sears, Roebuck and Co. During the years of government ownership the facility rose to prominence in its field. With the institution of private ownership in 1955, the company has continued its efforts to expand all areas of the plant's operations. A major step in that development occurred in 1966, when plans were announced for a $10-million EPDM plant to be constructed across

the river from Baton Rouge in West Baton Rouge Parish on a 700-acre parcel of land. It began operations in March 1968.

In more recent years, Copolymer has realized great strides in the vital areas of energy and environmental protection. The older Baton Rouge structure has undergone millions of dollars of renovations, making the facility today capable of surpassing the most rigorous federal environmental regulations. The West Baton Rouge plant at Addis was designed with energy-saving and pollution control devices for optimum efficiency.

Conservation of power and the conversion from natural gas to alternate fuels has signified Copolymer's continuing efforts to work toward more effective operations for the plants and for the nation. Copolymer and its employees are an important part of the vast and still-growing Baton Rouge industrial complex.

Left
Copolymer's EPDM plant is located in Addis, Louisiana, on the west bank of the Mississippi River.
Below
The corporate offices and main production facilities of Copolymer are located in Baton Rouge, Louisiana.

Cortana Mall

Cortana Mall, located on the former site of an antebellum plantation, is today Baton Rouge's most unique and prestigious shopping complex. As the largest enclosed shopping mall in the Deep South, Cortana features five major department stores and 128 specialty shops under one roof. With 1.5 million square feet of shopping area, Cortana is the largest single-level mall in the United States. But despite its mammoth proportions, accessibility, comfort, and convenience are carefully maintained, and contribute substantially to Cortana's success.

Cortana's site, located at the intersection of Airline Highway and Florida Boulevard, is almost geographically central to the metropolitan trade area and is convenient to both Interstates 10 and 12. As a major regional shopping center, Cortana serves the needs of a five-parish area containing more than one-half million people.

From t-shirts to tuxedos, Cortana Mall has one of the largest and most diverse merchandise selections in the South. After parking in the 8,000-space lot, a visitor to Cortana can find his shopping, banking, and eating needs accommodated in one stop. Arts, crafts, antiques, cars, and home improvements are just some of the many mall-wide shows that bring additional variety to the mall's year-round appeal.

The present complex, opened in 1976, uses only 110 of the 418 acres in the tract, which will soon see further expansion. Commercial office buildings, a hotel, an inn, an entertainment center, residences, a school,

parks, light industrial facilities, and a convenience-shopping center will add to the complete living environment that will soon surround the shopping mall.

Anchored by five major stores—Dillard's; Goudchaux's; JC Penney; Sears, Roebuck and Co.; and Wilson's—the mall is enhanced by an intriguing assortment of specialty shops. In 1976, Cortana consisted of just eight stores. Within one year, 78 were open for business and by 1978 that figure totaled 96. There are now 133 stores in operation, and the complex is still growing.

Also growing is the tremendous impact the business generated within Cortana has had on the local community. In 1979, estimated sales fig-

Top
Cortana Mall is one of the largest and most prestigious shopping complexes in the South.
Left and Right
Visitors to the mall can fulfill their shopping, banking, and dining needs in the spacious and elegant surroundings of Cortana.

ures were in excess of $194 million. In that same year, Cortana's sales represented 40.3 percent of all apparel sales and 13.2 percent of total retail sales in the Baton Rouge metropolitan area.

Cortana, developed by Mall Properties of New York, is owned by Flor-Line Associates, a partnership of Baton Rouge contractors Frank G. Sullivan, Jr., and Milton J. Womack; New York businessman Morton L. Olshan; and JC Penney Realty.

Dow Chemical Company: Louisiana Division

Planting water oaks and cedars with pecan trees at the corners, Andrew H. Gay raised a grove of trees in the shape of a Maltese cross. The year was 1905, the location near Plaquemine, about ten miles south of Baton Rouge.

Five years later, Gay constructed a home within the grove and named it Union Plantation. The original structure consisted of an entry hall, sitting room, sun porch, kitchen, dining room, four bedrooms, and two baths. The attic was opened in 1923, adding two large bedrooms and baths upstairs. At that same time, pillars were installed along the front of the house.

The plantation itself, purchased by Gay at a tax sale during the Civil War, comprised more than 1,400 acres. The Union tract, with its main crop of sugar cane, was just one of Gay's several large real estate investments. In 1928, a weevil disease caused a serious decline in sugar production and Union Plantation suffered its effects along with its neighbors. Many workers left the fields as acres of fertile cane were reduced to meager plantings intermingled with row crops.

Gay sold Union Plantation in 1942, and the estate changed hands several times prior to Dow's purchase of the tract and home in 1956.

The house, constructed of native cypress, has nearly 6,000 square feet of living space. During Dow's restoration of the home, much emphasis was placed on preserving its unique character; original lighting fixtures, bathroom accessories, hardware, longleaf pine floors, transoms, and mantles were carefully retained. Carpets and draperies now incorporated into the home were made with products from Dow's industrial facilities.

In September 1956, when a group of officials gathered on the Mississippi River's west bank ten miles below Baton Rouge, there were no industrial plants in sight. The only scene for miles along the river's western levee was acre after acre of sugar cane. About 100 employees were busily preparing for the construction of Dow Chemical USA's new Louisiana Division. That event would see the beginning of industrial expansion onto the west side of the river, which until that time had been contained on the other side of the mighty waterway. But the cane fields and established traditions would soon give way to the modern times that have since seen both shores of the Mississippi become the center of a vital, active, and still-growing industrial region known as Louisiana's Ruhr Valley.

Today, Dow's Louisiana Division employs a total work force of nearly 3,000 at its three principal facilities: the Plaquemine manufacturing plant located on the division's original tract on the Mississippi River; the Napoleonville brine-production facility; and the Grand Bayou/Bayou Teche fractionation units. Dow now maintains

Left
The Union Plantation house built by Andrew Gay in 1910 was purchased by Dow Chemical Company in 1956. It has been carefully renovated, retaining its original charm.
Far Right
The original road on the Dow plant site was opened in 1956.
Top
Harvesting of the final sugar cane crop on Union Plantation occurred in November 1956.
Bottom
At the Louisiana Division of Dow Chemical, some 1,100 acres of the original land purchased have been utilized.

seventeen production plants, power and steam generating facilities, a central waste-treatment plant, a research and development department, a technical services department, and an administrative services facility. The largest taxpayer in Iberville Parish, Dow's operations generate a payroll in excess of \$100 million per year, while plant operations create more than \$125 million worth of business with surrounding firms annually.

At the Plaquemine facility, only one-third of the 2,900 acres are in use at the present time, which means that the already sprawling plant has substantial expansion possibilities. In its continuing development as an area leader in industrial production, in fact, the plant has recently completed a \$400-million expansion, which includes the first world scale hydrocarbon- and naphtha-cracker built by Dow in the United States. Recently completed facilities at the same site now manufacture CLOROTHENE solvents and ethanolamines.

While no longer surrounded by cane fields, Dow's Louisiana Division has taken particular interest in maintaining a harmonious relationship with the surrounding environment. The buildings are well designed and scrupulously maintained; and the creatively landscaped gardens add to the beauty that has been incorporated into the industrial area. In addition to the care that is given to the Union Plantation house, which was on the original tract purchased in 1956, the Louisiana Division of Dow Chemical has maintained environmental standards higher than those required by the EPA. More than \$25 million has been spent in recent years to assure that clean air and water surround the Dow facilities, and the company has been the recipient of several national awards for its significant environmental control efforts.

Electrical Maintenance and Installation Company

When H.L. Smith, Jr., founded Electrical Maintenance and Installation Company (EMI) in 1970, he had only an inkling of one day expanding into the industrial sector. At the start he concentrated on providing quality electrical services to residential and small commercial buildings. Through the early 1970s, however, as he saw the rapid industrial growth in and around Baton Rouge, Smith decided to help develop the new plants. Making the leap into industrial work paid off handsomely for Smith, for today EMI is recognized as Louisiana's leading electrical specialist for commercial, industrial, and public institutional projects.

To handle its increased workload in the 1970s, the company purchased a building at 2279 Main Street, substantially increased its engineering and supervisorial staff, and computerized its job-estimating, cost analysis, inventory, and payroll accounting. Expanding into industrial contracts also necessitated the hiring of expert industrial electricians to master the highly technical wiring, site, and control work on the plants. The firm now employs more than thirty technicians, who offer drafting, design, estimating, electrical management, equipment selection, material requisition, and consulting services.

During its first ten years of opera-

Top
H.L. Smith, Jr., founded Electrical Maintenance and Installation Company in 1970.
Bottom
The office staff of EMI is comprised of (from left to right) Glenn Chidester, accounting; Mrs. Pat Robinson, secretary and accounting; R.G. Buckles, purchasing; H.L. Smith, president; Mrs. Smith, payroll; and Jacques Vidrine, purchasing assistant.

tion, EMI has contracted with several private concerns, completing hundreds of electrical installations across Louisiana—grain elevators, shopping centers, bulk plants, schools, hospitals, clinics, nursing homes, and major industrial work. And the company has worked closely with the city of Baton Rouge and the Louisiana state government on several institutional projects, such as pumping stations and treatment plants.

Since its founding eleven years ago, Electrical Maintenance and Installation Company has strived to achieve perfection in its products and services—and to implement those services best suited to individual needs. As prosperity and growth continue to be a part of Baton Rouge's industrial picture, EMI will continue to be an integral part of the city's business future.

Ethyl Corporation

In 1922, General Motors researchers accomplished a major scientific breakthrough when they discovered tetraethyl lead, a lead-based additive that eliminated the troublesome problem of engine knock. As a result of this discovery, General Motors and Standard Oil Company of New Jersey formed Ethyl Gasoline Corporation, later Ethyl Corporation (Delaware), to market the new product to oil refiners. Baton Rouge was chosen as the site for Ethyl's principal antiknock manufacturing facility because of its strategic location in the oil-rich regions of the South.

Ethyl opened its Baton Rouge operation in 1937 on former plantation lands just north of the Standard Oil (Exxon) refinery. Ethyl's experience in chemical technology grew, and the Baton Rouge plant was greatly expanded in the mid-1950s to meet the increasing demand for antiknock compounds.

By the early 1960s, the corporation's research into ethylene-based technology, which related closely to the production of plastics, attracted the attention of the Albemarle Paper Manufacturing Company of Richmond, Virginia. The long-established firm, under the leadership of president Floyd D. Gottwald, recognized the need to enter the field of plastics, which at that time were beginning to replace many traditional uses of paper. In what was widely considered one of the most unusual business deals in U.S. history, tiny Albemarle purchased Ethyl from giants GM and Jersey Standard in 1962. One Wall Street headline proclaimed, "Jonah Swallows the Whale." Albemarle, with annual sales of $49 million, had acquired a company with annual sales of more than $193 million. Upon completion of the transaction, Albemarle changed its name to Ethyl Corporation (Virginia).

Until the 1962 purchase, Albemarle had been a paper manufacturer, but the new Ethyl Corporation, headquartered in Richmond, was structured into separate divisions to reflect its new diversification. With the VisQueen division of Union Carbide acquisition in 1963 and that of IMCO Container Company in 1968, the firm began to widen its manufacture of plastic products. Today, the Plastics Group makes packaging products and films; plastic parts, bottles, and containers; and polyvinyl chloride compounds and resins.

After the purchase of the William L. Bonnell Company and Capitol Products Corporation, the Aluminum Group was formed to supervise aluminum operations. Today, the group produces thermal-barrier windows and doors; curtain and window walls for high-rise buildings; and shapes for storefronts, mobile homes, autos, boats, jet aircraft, and other applications.

Ethyl's Petroleum Chemicals Group produces a wide variety of petroleum chemicals and fuel additives on a worldwide basis. The Edwin Cooper Division produces lubricant additives. The Chemicals Group produces a wide range of hard-to-make specialty intermediates. Coal-related operations are managed by an Ethyl subsidiary, The Elk Horn Coal Corporation, which owns more than 140,00 acres of coal lands in eastern Kentucky.

The company has also been active in exploring for gas and oil in the United States and Canada. With its long tradition of finding innovative solutions to difficult problems, Ethyl Corporation will continue to be a leader in the nation's quest for energy independence in the future.

In 1980, Ethyl had total sales of $1.7 billion and earnings of $90 million. The company employs some 15,700 people at more than sixty locations throughout the world.

Top
The first sale of gasoline containing "Ethyl" antiknock compound occurred in 1923 at this Dayton, Ohio, service station.
Bottom
Ethyl Corporation's U.S. manufacturing facility for gasoline antiknock compounds is shown shortly after it was opened in 1937.

Exxon Company U.S.A.

In 1909, when the Standard Oil Company of New Jersey decided to build a refinery in Baton Rouge, few observers were able to predict the significant effect that decision would have on the city's future. From the company's viewpoint, Baton Rouge was an attractive site for a plant. The city was strategically located on the Mississippi River at a point accessible to large, ocean-going vessels, and upriver the system of inland arteries provided commercial trade routes to a large segment of the country. On the proposed construction site, just north of the city, the tranquil rows of cotton fields were about to undergo quite a change.

On that 225-acre tract, in April 1909, Standard Oil Company of Louisiana began construction of its original Baton Rouge installations. By November of that same year, the new refinery was capable of processing 1,800 barrels of crude oil a day. The plant employed about 700 people and represented an investment of $650,-000. Since its earliest days, continued expansion and modernization of the refinery have been an important part of the company's overall growth plan. Between 1909 and 1927, for instance, Standard Oil spent more than $50 million to expand its Baton Rouge facilities.

From 1927 to 1940, Standard Oil invested another $32 million in the refinery, and during World War II the plant became a significant contributor to the nation's war effort. Since the war, expenditures for further devel-

Right
Exxon U.S.A.'s Baton Rouge Refinery was constructed in 1909. Rows and a few plants of the original cotton field may still be seen. In the background is a neighboring sawmill.
(Above) is a night view of distillation units at Exxon U.S.A.'s Baton Rouge Refinery.

opment at the refinery have totaled more than $500 million, with current investments averaging $70 million annually.

Following a series of corporate changes, involving Standard Oil Company of Louisiana, Standard Oil Company of New Jersey, Esso Standard Oil Company, and others, on January 1, 1973, the Baton Rouge Refinery came under the aegis of Exxon Company, U.S.A.

Today, the Baton Rouge refinery is the nation's second largest. From the initial 225 acres, the facilities now encompass more than 2,000 acres. The plant can process over 500,000 barrels of oil a day and can manufacture more than 600 different products and grades.

Crude oil arrives at the refinery by pipeline from fields in Louisiana, Texas, Mississippi, and Florida.

Oceangoing vessels bring in Alaskan and foreign-source crude. Finished products move out principally by pipeline, tanker, and river barge.

About 2,500 members of the Baton Rouge community are employed at what is generally considered the most complete refinery in the world. From its pioneer days, the Baton Rouge organization has made many valuable contributions to the development and commercial application of the new petroleum-processing techniques. Through its concern for improvement, modernization, safety, and environmental protection, the Baton Rouge refinery continues as a leader in one of the world's most competitive industries.

Exxon Chemical Company U.S.A.

Until 1940, Exxon's Baton Rouge Refinery manufactured only fuels, lubricants, and other petroleum products. Then, in 1941, the first operating facilities that later would become the Baton Rouge Chemical Plant of Exxon Chemical Americas began operations as the refinery's Chemical Products Division.

The first chemical unit to begin production was a Paracril synthetic rubber facility that went on the line in April 1941. A low-pressure steam cracking unit followed in September of that year and the first butadiene extraction unit followed in February 1942.

After the United States entered World War II in December 1941, U.S. production of synthetic rubber became crucial to the nation's war effort, as the Japanese had seized control of all natural rubber supply areas. On request of the United States government, Exxon—then Standard Oil Company (New Jersey)—agreed to supply synthetic rubber to the maximum extent of production capability. At Baton Rouge's chemical operation, the first Butyl rubber plant already was under construction. That plant, plus two additional units, were operated by Exxon under government ownership until April 1955, when the facilities were sold back to the company.

The successful development and production of Butyl rubber by Exxon was considered a major contribution to the victory of the allied forces in World War II. Also, Baton Rouge thus

These recent aerial photographs show Exxon Chemical Americas' Baton Rouge Chemical Plant (left) and Plastics Plant (right).

earned the title of "Cradle of the Synthetic Rubber Industry." During the war years, Exxon also manufactured a number of different chemicals, including ethyl, isopropyl, and oxo alcohols, aromatic distillates, ethylene, propylene, butadiene, isoprene, and isobutylene.

Following the war, recognizing the great potential for petroleum-based chemicals and plastics, Exxon undertook the first of several extensive expansions that have made Baton Rouge one of the country's largest and most versatile chemical-producing complexes. Today, the Baton Rouge Chemical Plant turns out twenty-eight separate product groups (more than 100 products), including synthetic rubbers, chemical raw materials, industrial chemicals, ethylene, propylene, and butadiene.

The Baton Rouge Plastics Plant was built in 1968. There, Exxon produces about 100 different grades of low-density polyethylene, a widely used plas-

tic resin, at a rate of approximately 700 million pounds a year.

The various operations that have evolved from Standard Oil's initial 1909 refinery have maintained close operational relationships based on integration of feed and product streams. For example, the plastics plant obtains its raw materials from the chemical plant, which, in turn, draws on the refinery as a source of feedstocks.

As the Standard Oil Company (New Jersey)—Exxon organization evolved, a number of name changes occurred after chemical operations began. So Exxon chemicals have been marketed under a variety of names, including Esso, Enjay, and Humble. On November 1, 1972, Standard Oil Company (New Jersey) became Exxon Corporation and all United States operations came under the Exxon name. At that time, domestic chemical operations came under Exxon Chemical Company U.S.A. The most recent name change—to the present Exxon Chemical Americas—occurred on July 1, 1980. In Baton Rouge, the organization continues to pursue its role as a responsible industrial citizen.

Franklin Press

Printing today is a far cry from the painstakingly slow process used in the days when Ben Franklin worked as a printer. Because of a fondness for one of this country's most respected statesmen, E.J. and Inez Land named their new printing company Franklin Press. That beginning was in 1922, when Baton Rouge was a tiny river town. State government had not yet had the effect on the capital city that it would in later years. Louisiana State University was just beginning to establish itself as a major institution of higher learning. The tremendous growth of industrial development along the Mississippi River had not yet begun to see significant progress.

Along with the community, Franklin Press grew steadily, maintaining high standards that relied on words attributed to the company's namesake: "'Tis a laudable ambition that aims at being better than his neighbors!"

In 1933, Francis Holliday joined the staff as an apprentice, learning not only the printing trade but also the fundamentals necessary to become a good businessman and community citizen. Soon, Francis became a partner and, when E.J. Land retired, he was named president.

Under Francis' able leadership, the firm continued to adhere to the three basic principles that marked his early years at Franklin—printing excellence, respectable business operation, and significant contribution to the Baton Rouge community.

The commitment to those key precepts today finds Franklin Press en-joying the respect and patronage of a large number of clients from every sector of the Baton Rouge private, public, and business communities.

Ben Franklin's printing methods are certainly antiquated by today's standards, as are those used in the 1920s when the Lands began their company. Today, the printing industry is highly technical and mechani-cally complex. But fundamental values and high ideals never seem to change. And that is the keynote to the real success of Franklin Press.

Top
Methods used in the printing industry are vastly different today than they were during the 1940s.
Bottom
Today, Franklin Press uses the most modern and sophisticated equipment in its 37,000-square-foot operations center.

Gerard Furniture Company

On March 1, 1966, with $750 and the advice and help of several friends, particularly Saul Fried of Vicksburg, Mississippi, Gerard Adam Ruth purchased his own furniture store on North Foster Drive. During his days at Baton Rouge High School, Gerard worked after school for the late Archie L. "Pops" Wachenheim (former manager of Globe Furniture Company) at Lloyd Furniture Company on North Boulevard. After attending Louisiana State University and serving three years' active duty during the Korean War, he decided to go into business for himself. After the service Mr. Ruth worked for the late Frank Hemenway, Jr., at Hemenway's, and for Leon Feldman at Feldman Furniture.

The late Lewis Gottlieb advised Gerard that the Simon Furniture Company was for sale and that its purchase would be a prosperous move for the young man. Filled with enthusiasm and confidence, Ruth borrowed the necessary funds to buy and open Gerard Furniture in the Mid-City Shopping Center on North Foster Drive.

It was truly a family affair in the early days with Ruth being assisted by his wife, the former Selma Rodriguez, and their four children, Marsha, Andy, Larry, and Amy. Initially, he made all the deliveries himself in the company's only truck after store hours.

Gerard Furniture soon established a reputation as a merchandiser of fine quality furniture, accessories, and art, and additional employees were needed to serve the expanding clientele.

In 1976 it was obvious that the 7,500-square-foot building was not adequate as the company experienced continued success. So Ruth redesigned and remodeled the old Boyce Machinery Building originally designed by Ludwig Engineers located on Florida Boulevard across from Bon Marche Mall. The 50,000-square-foot building was given a new exterior with a quartz crystal stucco finish accented with copper canopies and French-inspired showroom windows. The copper lanterns surrounding the building were handmade by Cajun artist Ivan Bourdier and the landscaping and the entry courtyard were designed by noted Baton Rougean O. Steele Burden. Architectural treasures salvaged from Europe were used inside to complete the sense of elegance. David Eisen of New York,

president of the Furniture Industry Publishing Company, said after visiting the new Gerard Furniture showroom that it was now the "finest home furnishings center in the country."

In the vast expanse of the facility, the creative mind of the store's owner was free to express imaginative ideas with his distinctive flair. The store features such exciting departments as the James River Gallery, the Louisiana and European Art Gallery, the Charleston Room, the Patio Shop, the Clock Room, the Florida Room with wicker and rattan furnishings, and the Brass and Copper Room. It also has a complete design center featuring office furniture, leather, fabrics, wall paper, and carpeting.

Ruth is also active in the community where his business thrives. He is a life member of the Baton Rouge Jaycees and a JCI Senator. He is a founder and past president of both the Baton Rouge and the Louisiana Home Furnishings Associations. An avid sportsman, he is the winner of boat racing's Pan American Hall of Fame Trophy and has also received the Baton Rouge Boat Club's highest honor, Life Commodore. Ruth is a charter member of the Red Stick Kiwanis Club in Baton Rouge and continues to be active in sports and hunting clubs and numerous other civic organizations and charitable groups.

Top
Gerard Ruth stands in front of his company's Florida Boulevard store, one of the country's most complete home furnishing centers.
Bottom
Amy, Andy, Gerard, Selma, Marsha, and Larry Ruth (left to right) stand in front of Gerard Furniture's original location in the Mid-City Shopping Center on North Foster Drive.

Goudchaux's

When Benny and Jake Goudchaux opened a small variety store in 1907 in the 1700 block of Main Street, the general consensus was that the new enterprise was doomed to failure. The street was little more than a narrow dirt path leading to the cotton gin and cemeteries. Contrary to popular opinion, however, the brothers' tenacity and determination paid off. The business succeeded and grew.

By 1925, the firm was flourishing and the need for larger quarters resulted in a move to 1500 Main Street. In turn, the store enjoyed much greater accessibility as the city's growth continued and people moved away from the downtown business hub. Jake died that same year and Benny continued to manage the store.

Across the Atlantic Ocean in Aurich, Germany, Erich Sternberg began to feel the undercurrents of change that were starting to affect the quality of life during the early 1930s. Increasing persecution and political pressures caused Sternberg to look for an avenue of escape. America seemed to be the answer. Securing a visitor's visa, he left his family in 1936 and came to the United States.

Upon his arrival in the United States, Erich Sternberg went first to Philadelphia, where he stayed with relatives before traveling to Jackson, Mississippi. From there he moved to New Orleans, where he worked for other relatives who operated the Famous-Sternberg clothing manufacturing company. Benny Goudchaux was one of Famous-Sternberg's clients. Sternberg became acquainted with Goudchaux and was persuaded to move to Baton Rouge to work for him on a trial basis for one dollar a day.

"Mr. Erich" spoke no English, and the abrupt transition to a situation in which he worked with the public was not an easy one to make. But he took over the operations of the men's department and within a very short period of time he had leased that

Left
Erich Sternberg, a native of Germany, chose Baton Rouge as his new home.
Below
This photograph of Goudchaux's dress department was taken around 1946.
Top
Erich Sternberg (center) stands in his newly purchased store during the 1936 Christmas season.
Bottom
Goudchaux's store was located at 1500 Main Street in the 1930s.

department. Sternberg was determined that Baton Rouge would be his family's new home.

With the successful leasing of the men's department in 1936, Sternberg felt that he could send for his family at last; they arrived in 1937. Stern-

berg's success continued. By 1939 he had leased the entire store and by 1945 he had purchased the building itself.

Erich Sternberg quickly established a place for himself and his family in the Baton Rouge community. This

sense of camaraderie was not only important in his personal life, but was extended to his professional life, as well. Instead of using a suite of offices, the management of the store was handled from the center aisle. That tradition of accessibility continues today. A Sternberg is always on the floor, available to customers and employees.

Today, the Main Street headquarters are still located where Erich Sternberg took over Goudchaux's men's department in the mid-1930s. In 1968, the Main Street facility was renovated, the tenth major expansion at that location. Giving the building its present familiar facade, the additions increased the store's floor space by 66,000 square feet within the sales areas. A 65,000-square-foot distribution center was later added. The opening of Goudchaux's award-winning Cortana Mall store in February 1976 marked the first branch expansion.

Following a continuous policy of development begun in 1948, Goudchaux's has added a minimum of 50 percent to the total store space every four to five years, with sales doubling every six years.

Other highlights of the company's history include several facts and figures: Sales per square foot are the highest of any department store in the United States; Goudchaux's is listed among the nation's 100 largest department stores; and a long-standing tradition of interest-free credit combined with the store's reputation for fairness and active involvement in the community explain Goudchaux's enviable record of 75 percent account saturation within the store's primary market area.

Gulf Coast Supply Company, Inc.

The attic of Douglas J. Daly's Galveston, Texas, home was where Gulf Coast Supply Company, Inc., began in 1946. The company's main operation was supplying spare parts to U.S.-flag vessels.

Within six months, it became necessary to move the growing business to a small frame house located across Water Street from the ruins of Moulin Rouge, reputed home of notorious pirate Jean Laffite.

At that time, the young firm's employees numbered two—Daly himself and a secretary. Equipment consisted of one 1939 Chevrolet truck.

By 1954, the company had moved again to larger quarters, added several employees, and begun producing its own supplies. The Inverted Vent Check Valve, the company's first self-produced item, is still manufactured in Baton Rouge today.

A new facility totaling 15,000 square feet was built in 1958. At the same time, a commercial warehouse was added to the growing Gulf Coast plant. In 1961, however, the company experienced considerable misfortune; destruction caused by Hurricane Carla forced suspension of all operations for more than a month during extensive repairs and renovations.

By 1965, the ships of the world's merchant marine trade had become obsolete. The retirement of these ships brought about the introduction of a wide variety of vessels of non-standardized design and construction. At the same time, U.S.-flag ships declined from 80 percent of free-world trade to about 20 percent.

With this turn of events, Daly realized that Gulf Coast Supply Company, Inc., would have to diversify in order to survive. The firm relocated in Baton Rouge in 1968, and began producing and selling stainless steel and marine specialty items.

Today, the company operates from a modern 20,000-square-foot warehouse and office complex, where fourteen employees service an area comprising Louisiana and Mississippi. Although industrial sales of stainless steel account for 80 percent of the company's business, an active supply of vent valves to marine concerns keeps Gulf Coast Supply Company linked with its origins.

Since the death of Douglas J. Daly in February 1980, the company has been under the capable guidance of his son, Douglas J. Daly, Jr.

Top
Douglas J. Daly, Sr., founded Gulf Coast Supply Company, Inc., in 1946 and served as its president until his death in February 1980.
Bottom
Today, Gulf Coast Supply Company is located in a spacious warehouse and office complex at 7976 Commerce Street in Baton Rouge.

Harrison Paint Company

Money was scarce when Holt T. Harrison and his wife Elmira opened Harrison Paint Company in 1942, soon after the United States entered World War II.

The company was originally housed in a building at 631 Main Street, with inventory so limited that there was not enough to fill the large structure. As many small hardware stores were forced to close, Harrison purchased their lines, scouring the surrounding area for more products to enhance his depleted stock. He found discontinued paints, which he purchased to help fill the void. His efforts were so thorough that many out-of-state owners came to Harrison to buy hard-to-find items for their stores.

In those days, color mixing was done strictly by hand and eye. Customers arrived with fabric swatches, a shoe, even the blossom of a favorite flower, and requested its distinct shade in paint. Harrison Paint gained a reputation for being able to mix and match anything.

An unusual event in the company's history occurred when a local contractor came to Harrison requesting help with a government contract he had obtained. The man was to paint landing barges being used in Pacific invasions. The camouflage paint had been shipped to him in five-gallon drums, but the paint was so old that it had settled and was impossible to stir. In a typical display of ingenuity, Mr. Harrison located and brought to Baton Rouge the first paint agitator

to be introduced in the city. With several rocks dropped into each can to facilitate thorough stirring, the shaking of the camouflage paint began. (Today, of course, ball bearings are used in that capacity.) Each can shook for thirty minutes, and the successful results earned the young business fifteen cents per can.

The company grew to include three stores in Baton Rouge and locations in Shreveport, Lake Charles, and New Orleans. After Mr. Harrison's death in 1961, all stores except the Baton Rouge location on Choctaw Drive were closed. With the widening of that street in 1968, it was necessary to relocate and the present main facility at 5425 Choctaw Drive was constructed.

In 1969, under the guidance of a new vice-president and general manager, Alvin A. Patteson, a rebuilding and expansion program was initiated. That same year, a second store was opened in Sherwood Village, and a third addition was completed in 1978 at 4823 Perkins Road.

Significant technological strides have been made in the paint industry since 1942, and Harrison Paint Company has shared in that growth. The development of latex paints and advancements made in tinting procedures have greatly enhanced the versatility offered by Harrison. Tinting is now computerized; the latest equipment can produce color in a gallon of paint in ten seconds. Shakers now handle up to four gallons of paint at a time in spill- and noise-controlled cabinets.

The Harrison family still remains vitally interested and involved in Harrison Paint Company. Today's stores offer customers hundreds of types and colors of paints as well as a wide selection of wall coverings.

Gulf States Utilities

The relationship between Gulf States Utilities and the city of Baton Rouge can be traced back to February 1859, when the Baton Rouge Gas Light Company was established. The company was founded with the express intention of lighting the capital "as it ought to be, in about four months," so quoted the *Baton Rouge Weekly Advocate*.

Several utility companies sprang up between 1889 and 1900, with one buying out the other or going completely under for various reasons. One of the enterprises to emerge in 1893 was the Capital Railway and Lighting Company, which introduced electric streetcars to the Baton Rouge area. In 1900, local business interests formed a new corporation, Baton Rouge Electric and Gas Company, which acquired the electric and street railway business. This firm was later purchased by the Baton Rouge Electric Company.

Present-day Gulf States Utilities' Baton Rouge operations began in 1907 with the formation of the Baton Rouge Electric Company. At that time, the power station was located on North Boulevard; eight years later, a new station was built on Government Street. This location houses Gulf States Utilities' service, metering, and substation departments today.

The city of Baton Rouge had a population of about 12,500 in 1915 and the three new 500-kilowatt generators at Government Street provided a capacity sufficient to carry the load for the next five years. As the city continued to grow, Baton Rouge Electric Company grew with it. By 1930, the firm was operating in Port Allen and as far west as the Atchafalaya River. Service to Baker and Zachary in the north had been added, with transmission lines running all the way to the Mississippi state line. Denham Springs was being served to the east, and with the purchase of the Gonzales Ice Company, Ascension Parish was added to the system. A sure indication of prosperity occurred in the spring of 1928, when the first neon

sign was erected in Baton Rouge by Baton Rouge Electric Company in

front of its main office building on Florida Street.

During the 1930s, operations were initiated to bring natural gas into the city from fields around Monroe. In little more than a month over a hundred gas ranges had been sold by Baton Rouge Electric Company, including thirty-seven to new customers who replaced their old wood- or oil-burning stoves. New gas space heaters were also in sudden demand and the company had a difficult time keeping up with the deluge of orders.

In the firm's transportation depart-

ment, streetcars were slowly being phased out. A ceremony was held to mark the last streetcar ride in April 1936, as the company completed the transition to buses. In February 1938, Baton Rouge Electric Company and Gulf States Utilities were consolidated to form the present-day corporation.

The years ahead will not be easy ones, with the fuels we have relied on in the past becoming more expensive and more difficult to obtain. In order to ensure continued growth and prosperity in the Baton Rouge area, Gulf States Utilities is building coal and nuclear plants while diligently exploring alternate sources of energy. The company's commitment to Baton Rouge is as strong now as it was in 1859, and that commitment is to provide adequate supplies of gas and electricity to the area at the most reasonable cost possible.

Opposite Left
Until the introduction of mechanical hoists in the 1970s, company servicemen climbed up the poles and secured themselves as shown here, in order to work on electrical wires.

Opposite Top and Bottom
Knee-deep in water on Main Street during an 1898 rainstorm, this mule is hitched to a line wagon. When called to work on electric wires, service crews rode to their assignments in this type of wagon until motorized line trucks replaced the earlier vehicles.

Top
This power plant, with a capacity of 2,090 horsepower, was designed and built for Baton Rouge Electric Company in 1915 by the Stone & Webster Engineering Corporation of Boston, Massachusetts.

Center
Gulf States Utilities is working to meet the current and future needs of the Baton Rouge community through the construction of River Bend Nuclear Power Plant north of the city.

Bottom
Barney Calvit (far right), presently assistant general line foreman, poses with a Gulf States Utilities line crew in this 1925 photograph.

Hernandez Ice, Inc.

Emile Hernandez began business in 1930 with one ice truck, which he used to distribute ice door to door for one of the local companies in the Baton Rouge area. In those days prior to widespread use of the electric refrigerator, home delivery of ice was not a luxury, but a necessity. Southern Louisiana summers were just as hot and humid then as they are today.

Since that first summer more than fifty years ago, Hernandez worked to establish a business that would grow steadily over the years, keeping pace with local population and industry growth. This growth continued at such a rapid pace, in fact, that local demand for ice by plant workers and area residents helped to offset the

slump that occurred when refrigerators became available.

In the early 1940s, Hernandez, along with son A. Prince Hernandez and daughter Mrs. J.R. Lieux, formed Hernandez Ice Company and undertook the construction of an ice-manufacturing plant at 6608 Scenic Highway near the center of their market area. By 1945, the facility was in operation and business was thriving.

When Hernandez retired in 1947, his son, daughter, and a company stockholder, C.D. Thibaut, Jr., formed

Hernandez Ice, Inc. This move was marked by the expansion of the Scenic Highway plant. A retail sporting goods and convenience store was added to the plant at this time. The addition of this outlet to the business was very important during years in which declining ice sales were experienced.

During the 1950s and 1960s, a downward trend in ice sales was felt, but with the early 1970s, the desire for ice used for recreational purposes brought about a sharp reversal. Through distribution at convenience-store locations throughout Baton Rouge, the company's market area grew consistently from the original north Baton Rouge ice-plant vicinity to encompass a 40-mile radius today.

Still a family-owned concern, the business in 1977 became the sole property of Mr. and Mrs. R.L. Jeansonne. (Mrs. Jeansonne is the oldest daughter of A. Prince Hernandez.) Hernandez Ice is now a diversified company serving the greater Baton Rouge area and its unique combination of heavy industrial concentration surrounded by a broad diversity of recreational opportunities. From supplying plant workers with drinking water to providing the ice used at picnics and on camping trips, Hernandez Ice, Inc., continues its long-established role in the life of Baton Rouge and its people, both at work and at play.

Top
A fleet of refrigerated delivery trucks ensures that local residents are supplied with ice for all their business and recreational activities.
Bottom
Employees at Hernandez Ice, Inc., are kept busy filling the great demand for ice supplies in the greater Baton Rouge area.

Billy Heroman's Flowerland, Inc.

In 1833, 25-year-old George Heroman emigrated from Germany to the United States, settling in the small community of Baton Rouge. Within four years, he was in business at the corner of Florida and Fourth streets as a book merchant. The population of the city at that time was less than 7,000.

In 1865, after returning from the Civil War, his son, Frederick William Henry Heroman, continued this business, adding flowers, seeds, and related items. Soon, his son joined him and the mane was changed to F.W. Heroman & Son. That son, Frederick I., continued the family tradition of serving the residents of the Baton Rouge area. He and his father moved the business to 364 Main Street, where Heroman's Seed Store added plants and a variety of accessory items. It was at this location that the fourth generation entered the business. Fred I. and Gladys had four sons who incorporated a floral service into their father's business, and from there each formed his own destiny: Fred Jr. in wholesale greenhouses, Harry in retail florist, Billy in florist and gifts, and Al in insurance and investments.

William J. "Billy" Heroman, the third son, married the former Janet Landry, a Baton Rouge native, and they had four children. In 1945, after Billy returned from service in World War II, he joined his father in the family business. In 1955, he purchased a small flower shop at 1946 Perkins Road and set out to establish his own

Top
Billy Heroman's Flowerland's modern facility at 10812 Harrell's Ferry Road was built in 1978.
Above
Fred W.H. Heroman, Anna Gass Heroman, Fred I. Heroman, and two unidentified clerks stand inside the F.W. Heroman & Son store on Main Street in this photograph taken during the 1880s.

position in the local floral business. There, continuing the family tradition, Billy's four children, Cyril Ann, Billy Jr., Ted, and Rickey, became the fifth generation of Heromans to join their father in the floral business.

After they graduated from college, all four of Billy's children elected to remain in the family business, so a second and much larger flower shop was built at 10812 Harrell's Ferry Road in 1979. There, the traditions that began in 1830 continue, making the Heromans the oldest retail merchant serving the residents of Baton Rouge under the company's original name. Today, Billy Sr. is president and chairman of the board of Billy Heroman's Flowerland, Inc. Billy Jr. is vice-president, Cyril Ann Heroman McBride is secretary and Richard is treasurer. The fifth generation, Billy Jr. and Rick, are now managing the two locations and are continuing to promote the growth of the corporation. With more than 35,000 square feet of floor space and thirty employees in the two locations, they continue to see that excellent service, wide selection of flowers, plants, and gifts, and pleasant atmosphere make Billy Heroman's Flowerland an enjoyable place to shop. Billy and Janet and their four children are proud of their family's years of service to the Baton Rouge community.

D. H. Holmes Company, Ltd.

The carriage trade of Baton Rouge has been shopping for the finest in lace goods, jewelry, and fashionable summer, winter, bridal, and traveling wardrobes from D.H. Holmes Company since before the Civil War. Such was the reputation of Daniel Henry Holmes in the Deep South in the mid-nineteenth century that ladies sought out his imported goods which were assured of "coming up to all claims."

Holmes, who founded his store in 1842 in New Orleans, is considered a pioneer in the field of department store operations in America. Many principles of merchandising, now considered normal practice in the industry, were initiated by Holmes and reflected his concern both for his customers and the long-term growth of his company.

His earliest policy was that "goods must come up to all claims." In the nineteenth century, before "consumerism" was in vogue, returning merchandise to any store for any reason was simply not done. However, Holmes' philosophy of doing business was contrary to the retail attitudes and practices of those times. Without hesitation, he would replace an item or refund the money to satisfy a customer. The company's present no-risk shopping policy is an inheritance from the store's founder.

In 1848, Holmes instituted the first home-delivery system in the South and one of the first in the nation. During the Civil War, he was the first to employ female clerks, a practice considered revolutionary at the time. Today, women far outnumber men among sales persons in retail stores in America. After guiding his store through decades of oppressive Carpetbag rule during Reconstruction, Holmes died in 1898 at the age of eighty-three.

In 1905, the business was converted to a publicly held stock corporation and continued to be progressive. It was the first store in the South to have air conditioning; the first to install elevators and escalators; and the first to use metered mail, parcel post, Air Express, and transatlantic service.

D.H. Holmes Company entered the Baton Rouge market in 1955 with its first store and has since added two additional stores. A fourth store will be opened in the fall of 1983. It will be the largest Holmes store in Baton Rouge and will feature full lines of fashion merchandise as well as broad selections in home furnishings departments.

The company maintains its headquarters in New Orleans, where it has five stores and extensive warehouse facilities. It has additional stores in Lafayette, Houma, and Hammond, Louisiana; Jackson, Mississippi; and Mobile, Alabama. Better than 90 percent of its stock is owned by people living in Louisiana. The company's 4,500 employees comprise the single largest block of stockholders.

Top
Daniel Henry Holmes, a Renaissance man of his time, founded his company in 1842. He was fluent in five languages; maintained homes in Kentucky, Louisiana, and Paris, France; and operated offices in New York and Paris.
Bottom
This artist's rendering shows the new Holmes store on Bluebonnet.

Hunt's Flowers and Garden Center

Vernon Hunt, like so many residents of the Baton Rouge area in the 1930s, worked at Standard Oil Company's new refinery in the northern part of the city. In his spare time he grew vegetables and sold them to fellow workers.

In 1935 he erected his first building and by that time was selling seed and plants as well as fresh vegetables. Before long, customers were asking Mrs. Hunt to arrange the beautiful flowers she was growing around the shop. The couple soon found themselves with a growing garden center and flower shop. By 1950 the size of the building had doubled and three greenhouses had been added.

Today, the company is operated by Vernon and Luvinia Hunt's daughters. Yvonne and her husband, Joe Roshto, operate the Flower Shop while Faye and her husband, Sam Rushing,

On the same site where his original vegetable stand was once located, Vernon Hunt (above) constructed this facility and began the seed and floral enterprise known as Hunt's Flowers & Garden Center.

Jr., run the Garden Center.

They have followed in the footsteps of their parents. Yvonne served as president of the Louisiana State Florist Association, the office her father had held twenty years before. Faye and Sam are active in the North Baton Rouge Lions and Lioness clubs, as were her parents.

This small family endeavor has grown to rank among the top 500 flower shops in the Florist Transworld Delivery Association in sales. The garden center not only sells seeds and plants but has a wide selection of outdoor power and garden equipment. Faye has brought her hobby into the business, selling a complete line of miniature furnishings and accessories.

Many years have passed since Vernon Hunt first sold his fresh vegetables near the Standard Oil refinery, but the business he established continues to show a personal interest in its customers and renders excellent service to meet the needs of its many Baton Rouge area customers.

Jules Madere Creative Jewelry

At the early age of twelve, Jules Madere began to acquaint himself with the fascinating profession of the jeweler. Obtaining his initial training from some of New Orleans' top jewelers, Madere was ready at age seventeen to strike out on his own. He decided that Baton Rouge was a city where he could succeed; and in 1948, he opened his first shop on Third Street in downtown Baton Rouge.

The prosperity the business experienced at its original location eventually enabled expansion. A Government Street store was opened in 1962 and the firm's modern new location on Airline Highway was built in June 1978.

For more than thirty-five years, Jules Madere has served Baton Rougeans, becoming affectionately known throughout the area as the city's premiere jeweler. His clients

Top
Still in his teens, an ambitious Jules Madere stands atop his first shop on Third Street in 1948, during one of the city's infrequent snowstorms.
Bottom
The new Airline Highway location of Jules Madere Creative Jewelers, built in 1978, has been cited for its ingeniously functional design.

have included such personalities as Frank Sinatra, Elvis Presley, Pete Fountain, and Dizzy Dean. Yet Madere's attention and interest in the simplest Mother's Day charm remains just as strong.

Jules Madere Creative Jewelry is a family-oriented business; his son and two daughters are active participants in the company. Wayne Madere started working in his father's store each night after school. He attended Louisiana State University for two years and then joined the Navy, where he gained valuable vocational training while working at navy base jewelry stores. After fulfilling his military obligations, Wayne returned to work for his father. An accomplished jeweler and diamond setter, Wayne serves as vice-president in charge of diamond and special-order sales, and does most of the buying and traveling for Jules Madere Creative Jewelry. Jules' two daughters, Marsha Phillips and Celeste Matherne, coordinate the firm's giftware buying.

Madere's is no longer just a retail business, but has specialized for a number of years in the production and repair of custom jewelry. The firm's store at 9345 Airline Highway is a unique concept in jewelry merchandising and display. Designed under a square roof, the circular structure is laid out in such a way that the customer can walk without interruption around the building's constantly changing showcases. Offices and workshops are discreetly hidden within the center so that they do not detract from the shopper's enjoyment of the store's handsomely designed interior. The facility was commended for its innovative layout in the December 1978 issue of *Modern Jeweler*.

Kaiser Aluminum & Chemical Corporation

The day Henry J. Kaiser came to Baton Rouge in 1946 is not recorded. It was probably considered just another business trip. However, the impact of that visit on the aluminum industry and especially on the state of Louisiana may never be fully realized.

It was at the end of World War II and Mr. Kaiser and his associates were in Baton Rouge to inspect the war surplus alumina plant built in 1942 on the Mississippi River. They were known for their successes in dam and roads construction and shipbuilding ventures. Now Mr. Kaiser wanted to enter the aluminum business. He had looked at two other plants in the Northwest—the Mead reduction facility and the Trentwood rolling mill, both in Washington. He placed his bid for the three plants and the War Assets Corporation accepted it. A dynamic new aluminum producer was born.

In its first three years, the company was called Permanente Metals Corporation, the name of a magnesium operation owned by the Kaiser interests at Permanente, California. In 1948, the company offered common stock to the public, and the next year changed its name to Kaiser Aluminum & Chemical Corporation.

To be a fully integrated mine-to-metal aluminum producer required the acquisition of a permanent source of bauxite, the ore from which alumina is extracted. The young company's first of many expansion programs took care of this important necessity in 1950 by acquiring bauxite mining leases and facilities in Jamaica. It was also during the 1950s that Kaiser Aluminum constructed new plants at Chalmette and Gramercy, Louisiana. At Chalmette is the giant nine potline aluminum smelter, or reduction plant, and at Gramercy is a second alumina plant. Later, a carbon coke processing plant was constructed at Norco.

The growth of Kaiser Aluminum has been astounding, but nowhere has it been more dramatic than in Louisiana. From its modest beginning with 350 employees at Baton Rouge, the company's four plants entered the 1980s with a force of 5,000 employees and an annual economic impact on the state of over $.5 billion.

For nearly four decades, Kaiser Aluminum's activities in the aluminum industry have been a period of unprecedented growth and expansion throughout the world. It is the third largest aluminum producer in the nation and is prominent in such diverse industries as industrial chemicals, real estate, agricultural chemicals, refractories, and international trading. The company operates nearly 100 plants and support facilities in the United States and conducts operations in 18 foreign countries through its subsidiaries and affiliates.

Kaiser Aluminum's Baton Rouge plant was the first of the company's four Louisiana facilities. It now provides about 1,000 jobs. Statewide, the corporation has some 5,000 employees.

Kornmeyer's

Kornmeyer's purchased an entire carload of radios in 1916, a move that was unheard of at that time. Featuring new dynamic speakers instead of the old magnetic models, the new units cost as much as $800 each. Despite the considerable cost, the store quickly sold out of the radios. That feel for innovation, and the traits of determination, tenacity, and the willingness to try something new while remaining faithful to long-standing traditions, have all marked the 101 years Kornmeyer's has spent as a cornerstone member of the Baton Rouge business community.

German-born Jacob Kornmeyer had immigrated to the United States in 1849 and five years later he opened a general merchandising store in the sleepy little river town of Baton Rouge. At that time, industry was an unusual word in the plantation-dominated South. It was in this primarily agricultural environment that Kornmeyer focused his first business interests. His interest in general merchandising soon gave way to his love for furniture, and in 1880, Kornmeyer erected a two-story wooden building at the corner of St. Ferdinand and America streets opposite the courthouse square. By the late-1800s, the furniture business was well-established on the ground floor, and the Kornmeyer family utilized the upper story as living quarters.

In 1883, Julius Andrew Bahlinger, Sr., joined the company as a salesman-handyman. Ten years later, he married Kornmeyer's daughter, and the young couple took up residence

Top
This photograph from 1880 shows the original store on the corner of St. Ferdinand and America streets. Kornmeyer's attracted customers with its quality products and service, just as it has throughout the company's history.
Bottom
Great-grandsons of Jacob Kornmeyer—Marion J. Bahlinger; Frederick J. Bahlinger, Jr.; Peter F. Bahlinger; and Harold I. Bahlinger—manage the store's operations today.

above the store with the rest of the Kornmeyer family. Two sons, Andrew Jr. and Fred, were born there. These two young men joined the business in 1917 when their father, the senior Bahlinger, retired. In eight

years, the brothers became co-managers of the store. By the 1940s, Andrew's sons, Marion and Harold, and Fred's sons, Peter and Fred, Jr., were members of the Kornmeyer's force. Today, the four Bahlingers manage all phases of the store's operations.

Throughout the years, the firm has seen its share of hard times. The agricultural depression that hit the area in the early 1900s greatly affected Baton Rouge businesses. No sooner had a semblance of normalcy returned, when a severe yellow fever epidemic struck the area, and Kornmeyer's immediately helped to provide necessary bedding for ailing townspeople. Baton Rouge was placed under quarantine. The great influenza epidemic of 1918 swept through the community, and again Kornmeyer's came to the aid of the city. With the flood of 1927, camps housing the hapless victims of the Mississippi's raging waters were once again supplied by the store.

It has been a long journey from that simple two-story building across from the courthouse. Shipments no longer arrive by steamboat; and the original downtown store was replaced in 1924. Completed in 1966, a 60,000-square-foot store located on Florida Boulevard is now the main operational center for Kornmeyer's. The company's sales volume has tripled since the opening of that store. The firm now employs a work force of approximately 100, including interior designers; Kornmeyer's was one of the area's first stores to offer professional design services to its customers. The company reflects with pride on its accomplishments of the last 100 years, and eagerly anticipates the coming century.

The Lamar Corporation

Charles W. Lamar lost a bet in 1908, and the fortunate result of that event was the founding of The Lamar Corporation.

J.M. Coe of Pensacola, Florida, was granted a charter in 1902 to operate a poster company by the Associated Bill Posters of the United States and Canada. He formed the concern, operating it in conjunction with his Pensacola Amusement Company. The poster company's main function was to supply advertising materials to the Pensacola Opera House, a sideline of the Pensacola Amusement Company. The poster business was managed under the name of Pensacola Advertising Company.

In 1905, Charles Lamar, then president of the American National Bank in Pensacola, entered into partnership with Coe, in both the amusement and advertising companies. Three years later, the two men decided to dissolve their mutual interests; one would receive the opera house, the other the advertising business. Lamar lost, and the advertising business was his. That enterprise, now called Lamar Outdoor Advertising, would become one of the largest outdoor sign companies in the country.

Lamar, still associated with the bank, operated the advertising business as a sideline. But it became increasingly profitable and in 1926, Lamar's two sons, Charles Jr. and L.V., purchased the Baton Rouge Poster Advertising Company and re-

Above
Under the dynamic leadership of president Kevin P. Reilly, The Lamar Corporation has enjoyed significant growth.
Top
In 1908, Charles Lamar, Sr., founded the company that today bears his name.
Bottom
Charles Lamar, Jr., worked from 1926 until his death in 1960 to expand the enterprise begun by his father.

named it the Lamar Advertising Company of Baton Rouge. To keep pace with the increasing growth of the Pensacola operation, another facility was opened in 1938 in Jackson, Mississippi.

Upon graduation from Harvard's School of Business Administration in 1955, Kevin P. Reilly joined the firm as a leaseman, then served in other capacities before becoming managing partner of the Baton Rouge operation in 1958. Charles Lamar, Jr., died in 1960 after spending the majority of his adult life expanding the company his father had begun. Under Reilly's capable guidance, the company entered a period of unprecedented growth. Gross sales in 1960 were nearly $1.5 million; today they exceed $20 million.

The period of tremendous growth really began in 1972 and 1973 with the purchase of seven outdoor properties throughout the South. The Lamar Corporation was organized in 1973 to provide centralized accounting and management services for the increasing list of holdings. Today, The Lamar Corporation owns and operates nineteen companies in nine states. In addition to outdoor advertising, Lamar has a real estate division, an insurance agency division, and a computer service division.

The Pensacola Opera House burned down long ago; today that site is occupied by a parking lot. But Charles Lamar's lost bet has resulted in the emergence of one of the nation's most prosperous and dynamic advertising corporations, an important and integral part of Baton Rouge and its business community.

Levy-Kramer & Associates, Inc.

Room 538 of the old Reymond Building no longer exists, but the young company that was founded in January 1963 and began operations there has survived and prospered. Founded by Raoul L. Levy as a sole proprietorship, this enterprise was established to provide consulting services to architects, private owners, and government agencies in the fields of electrical engineering and illumination.

After moving to larger quarters within the Reymond Building, the company relocated in 1969 to a larger facility on Main Street. This move was followed by two others: first, to the IBM Building on Sherwood Forest Boulevard and finally, to the firm's present location on Colonial Drive.

Raoul L. Levy, Consulting Engineer, became Levy-Kramer & Associates, Inc., in 1971, when F.B. Kramer, Jr., became a partner. He had joined the firm two years before, in March 1969. He presently serves as vice-president and secretary of the corporation.

In January 1976, a mechanical engineering department was added to provide services paralleling those of the electrical department, specializing in heating, ventilating, air conditioning, and plumbing systems for buildings. The mechanical department has recently been expanded to provide energy management and conservation services.

Raoul Levy; Lloyd Fauntleroy, an electrical designer with the firm since

The company that would later become Levy-Kramer & Associates, Inc., was founded in 1963 by Raoul L. Levy (left). In 1969, F.B. Kramer, Jr., joined the firm and now serves as vice-president and secretary.

1966; and Burt Payne, head of the mechanical department, began their careers with Ogden & Woodruff, Consulting Engineers, one of the pioneer companies in the consulting engineering field in Baton Rouge. Founded in the late 1940s, Ogden & Woodruff performed electrical and mechanical engineering services on many major construction projects throughout the state. Raoul Levy joined Ogden & Woodruff in January 1950, and remained with the company until 1957. Kramer in 1966 was an employee with a successor firm, Ogden & Hall, and remained there until joining Levy's enterprise.

In 1963, the year of its formation, Raoul L. Levy, Consulting Engineer, provided services for approximately

85 projects. Today, Levy-Kramer & Associates, Inc., has diversified and grown; its services are utilized on more than 200 projects each year. Some of the principal Baton Rouge projects for which the firm has provided electrical or mechanical engineering services, or both, include St. Joseph Convent and Orphanage; Kornmeyer's Furniture Store on Florida Street; buildings for Gulf South Research Institute; Community Coffee Plant; a major addition to Baton Rouge Main Telephone Building; Cortana Mall; Centroplex Arena; Exhibit Hall; H.J. Wilson Company's corporate headquarters; Capital Bank & Trust Company's Operations Center; Louisiana State University's Center for Engineering and Business Administration; Louisiana National Bank's Operations Center; and Phase Two of the Louisiana State School for the Deaf.

Louisiana Television Broadcasting Corp.

Louisiana Television Broadcasting Corporation was formed in 1953 by Charles P. Manship, Jr. (publisher of the Capital City Press), his brother Douglas L. Manship (president of Baton Rouge Broadcasting Company), and seven other area business leaders. The corporation obtained an operator's license for WBRZ-TV (Channel 2), and on April 14, 1955, WBRZ-TV officially signed on the air as an NBC/ABC affiliate, opening up television reception to thousands of Louisiana and Mississippi residents. Charles and Doug Manship acquired full stock ownership of Louisiana Television Broadcasting Corporation in 1958.

During the first twenty-five years of operation, WBRZ-TV established itself as the leader in local broadcast journalism. Utilizing the Eyewitness News format, in 1980 the station programmed over fifteen hours weekly of locally originated news. Channel 2's news documentaries have been recognized nationally for excellence in journalism.

In September 1970, Doug Manship succeeded his brother Charles as publisher of the Capital City Press. He later relinquished the general management responsibilities of WBRZ to Jules L. Mayeux, an original employee of the station. Under Mayeux's guidance, WBRZ's community image reached new heights.

In the late 1970s another generation of Manships entered the management ranks at WBRZ. In 1977, Richard F. Manship was named station man-

Left
Directors and engineers operate from WBRZ's first master control room.
Right
WBRZ's "Live Eye" was Baton Rouge's first live, microwave transmission unit.

ager. That year general manager Mayeux and he were responsible for WBRZ's network affiliation switch from NBC to ABC, the national ratings leader.

WBRZ-TV was the first local television station to broadcast in color; to purchase self-sustaining radar weather equipment; to utilize a live, field transmission unit; and to convert completely from film to video tape production. Because of innovations such as these and its commitment to quality broadcasting, the station has been repeatedly recognized for professional excellence by the Associated Press, United Press International, the National Association of Television Programming Executives, the Broadcast Promotion Association, and the Louisiana Association of Broadcasters.

In 1963 the Manships purchased KRGV-TV and KRGV-AM in Weslaco, Texas. And in 1980, Louisiana Television Broadcasting Corporation purchased two other broadcast properties—WXCL-AM and WZRO-FM in Peoria, Illinois.

Manda Brothers Provision Company

In 1947, the three Manda Brothers—Vince, John, and Bennie—realized their lifelong dream of owning their own business. Vince was a salesman for another packing company, John was employed by Standard Oil Company, and Bennie was a retail merchant. When World War II ended, they decided that the time had come to combine their skills and take their place in the Baton Rouge business community. In that brief time, Manda's has grown along with the city and today is recognized as a dominant force in the wholesale food industry as a manufacturer and distributor.

The Manda brothers learned to appreciate the importance of service while working in their previous vocations, and their philosophy of combining a good product with fair prices and excellent service remains evident in all aspects of company operations.

John Manda, Sr., died in 1958 and his position as vice-president and general manager is now filled by his son John Manda, Jr. Bennie Manda died in 1965 and his wife Isaure now serves in his stead as secretary-treasurer. V.J. Manda is the firm's current president and still works five days a week although he is semiretired.

By 1959, demand for Manda products had increased due to the rapid growth of the city, and expansion be-

came necessary. It was at that time that Manda Brothers began manufacturing their own sausage and headcheese on a large scale. The old icehouse in Zachary was purchased and converted into smokehouses and Manda Packing Company, Inc., was born. The immediate, overwhelming response from the Baton Rouge community and outlying areas has led to expansion of all phases of the operation. Manda's now has stainless steel smokehouses, automated packing equipment, and the most technologically advanced processing equipment available to the industry.

In 1968, The D.S. Packing Company was formed as a third component of Manda Enterprises, Inc. This packing plant operates at 2442 Sorrel Avenue, on the same premises as Manda Brothers Provision Company. The company was established to process cured meats, such as smoked hams and salted meats; however, the facility has now expanded to include a red-meat department. Not only does the firm process ham products second to none, it also cuts steaks to specifications for the fine restaurants in the area.

Since its founding, the company has remained abreast of current trends and processing techniques while carefully ensuring that quality is never sacrificed to quantity. Today, Manda Brothers Provision Company consists of three corporations which employ over 200 people. The firm now has statewide distribution, and supplies high-quality products to wholesalers, retailers, restaurants, and grocery warehouses, while maintaining a solid commitment to the growth of the Baton Rouge community and the state of Louisiana.

Benny, Vince, and John Manda, Sr., stand proudly in front of the newly completed Manda Brothers plant in this 1948 photograph.

NADCO Inc.

NADCO Inc. was founded by Nelson Dupuy in May 1978, in response to growing demands made by Baton Rouge's rapidly developing industrial community. Handling a diversity of industrial projects and maintenance contracts, NADCO Inc. specializes in the fabrication and erection of pipe, and also undertakes rigging, steel erection, and concrete installation projects.

An 8-foot by 16-foot portable building located behind Dupuy's home served as the firm's original headquarters. President Nelson Dupuy and vice-president Andy Dupuy worked long hours without compensation, subsisting on accumulated vacation pay while trying to establish the infant company. Further exemplifying this determined sense of dedication and self-sacrifice on behalf of the still-new concern, the NADCO staff, comprised of Dupuy and sons Andy and Steven, Phil Berthelot, and Lodis Duplechain, worked many evenings and weekends to construct the firm's new location on Perkins Road. The new facility not only serves the company's present needs but offers great potential for expansion and will successfully accommodate NADCO's continuing growth.

Industrial progress in southern Louisiana has been dramatic; the area has become one of the most strategic industrial locations in the nation in a relatively brief period of time. This phenomenal growth and the introduction of major industries to the area have created an increasing demand for the services provided by NADCO.

The unlimited opportunities resulting from this industrial expansion enable NADCO Inc. to provide its services as a contractor not only in Baton Rouge, but in neighboring areas such as Geismar and Donaldsonville.

Nelson Dupuy, the firm's founder and president, brings to NADCO nearly three decades of experience in the field. Beginning as a pipe-fitter apprentice in the early 1950s, Dupuy worked his way through the ranks of the construction industry, becoming part owner of a major industrial construction firm in 1974. In 1977, the decision to go into business for himself was made and, along with sons Andy and Steve, Phil Berthelot, and Lodis Duplechain, he formed NADCO Inc. A former candidate for mayor in the town of Brusly, Dupuy has been active in the Boy Scouts of America program for many years and was co-chairman of the West Baton Rouge Biracial Committee. His role in the

Left
NADCO specializes in pipe fabrication and erection, rigging, steel erection, and concrete installation, but the company's capabilities reach far beyond.
Right
Modern headquarters of NADCO Inc. are located just south of Baton Rouge on a 5.5-acre tract on Perkins Road, which is easily accessible to the nearby Interstate 10.

campaign to pass an important bond issue for schools in West Baton Rouge contributed to the successful passage of that measure.

NADCO Inc. is located just south of Baton Rouge on a 55-acre tract on Perkins Road, which is easily accessible to the nearby Interstate 10. The firm maintains a healthy professional relationship with skilled area craftsmen, thereby assuring the highest quality workmanship available. This insistence on quality reflects the pride and professional standards the young company has determined to maintain for itself.

Naylor's, Inc.

The three Naylor brothers, John, Duncan, and James, bought Quality Feed and Seed in October 1953 from C.C. Couvillion and began what is today Baton Rouge's oldest hardware store. When the brothers acquired the business it was basically a feed store, but under the Naylor management, it was soon expanded to include garden and hardware as well as houseware items.

Duncan left the company after a year, but John and James continued to see that the business flourished at its Government Street location across from Baton Rouge High School. There, the company, now known as Naylor Brothers Feed, Seed and Hardware, has remained a familiar part of the local business community.

In July 1958, a second location was added on Florida Boulevard at Monterrey. Four years later, the two stores were incorporated under the name of Naylor Brothers, Inc. At that time, the Government Street location was remodeled. The lot behind the store was acquired and the space for gardening supplies greatly enlarged. By 1969, when James sold his interest to John, the stores had been outfitted with air conditioning and spacious parking areas and had greatly increased the variety of merchandise available to their growing patronage.

Under the guidance of John Naylor and his wife Marguerite (who serves as bookkeeper), the two locations of Naylor Brothers have now distinguished themselves as being the old-

Top
The original Baton Rouge location of Naylor Brothers, Inc., was established at 2882 Government Street.
Bottom
The firm's second store was opened in 1958 at 9402 Florida Boulevard.

est hardware supplier still in operation in Baton Rouge.

The business joined the True Value line of Cotter, Inc., in 1970. Johnny Naylor, son of the present owner, joined the firm in 1975, working at the Government Street store. Two years later, his wife Gwynn joined the staff at Florida Boulevard, working with housewares and crafts. A daughter, Kathleen Naylor Savoie, serves as the corporation secretary.

John Naylor attributes his com-

pany's prosperity in large part to three important factors: the Lord's help; the substantial inventory which has been accumulated over the years, providing customers with a complete selection of items to meet their gardening and hardware needs; and the faithful service of the firm's knowledgeable employees. Many of these employees have worked for Naylor Brothers for over ten years; Beatrice and Albert Taylor have been actively contributing to the company's success for more than twenty years. All of Naylor's employees, many of whom are licensed horticulturists, have been instrumental in creating the reputation the business enjoys as *the* place to go for gardening information and supplies in Baton Rouge.

Ourso & Company, Inc.

Ourso & Company was established on March 23, 1923, by an enterprising young businessman, Dorastand R. Ourso. Leaving the little sawmill town of Sorrento in 1917, where his knowledge of lumber had brought him from Chamberlin, Louisiana, he settled with his wife and small children in Baton Rouge. The town was growing rapidly; Standard Oil facilities stretched for miles along the Mississippi. Envisioning the financial possibilities of a store in this industrial city, he borrowed $1,000 from an uncle of his wife, the former Bernadette Landry, and began his venture of forty-six energetic years.

Ships from around the world berthed at the refinery docks. Ourso's ability to speak French and Spanish, coupled with his genuine love of people and his fair business practices, made him a popular merchant. Customers were shown respect and consideration. Credit was extended and the hard-pressed treated with leniency. This wise and kindly man was known for his "good public relations." During the painful years of the Great Depression when families were hungry, Mr. Ourso fed them and sought to give spiritual aid by imparting faith in the country's future. His gentle wife had great strength of character and a strong belief in God's sustenance. Together they aided suffering humanity both materially and inspirationally.

A civic-minded person, Bill Ourso alerted himself to the needs of the community. In 1961, in recognition of his "constant interest and devotion to the future development of Louisiana," he was appointed honorary state comptroller. He was a supporter of the LSU Livestock Show sponsored by the Chamber of Commerce since its inception in 1935, serving as grand marshal of the parade in 1966. He participated in many drives, functions, and trips to further the interest of his beloved city. He was a devoted Lion and served as an usher in his parish church, St. Anthony, for forty-five years.

In 1946, Mr. Ourso was elected a director of the City National Bank, serving until his death in 1969. Upon his death, in a testimonial presented to his sons and daughters, the bank officers praised him for "his long tenure of service, his friendly approach, his infectious love of life, his devotion to the welfare of his fellow men and high sense of justice and understanding of human frailty, his impeccable honesty and the resultant esteem and respect which he deservedly created among those with whom he came in contact."

Mr. Ourso left to his children an invaluable heritage and five have continued the example of their father in serving the community in the family business. His daughters are Eloise Kirsch and Doris Bauch. Son Harold is a Rotarian and member of the First City Parish Council, the Chamber of Commerce, and the advisory board of Our Lady of Lake Hospital. Milton is currently serving his twenty-fifth year as advisory board member of City National Bank. A Lion, he has served on numerous boards and civic projects. Lynwood continues the work done by his father with the annual Chamber of Commerce Livestock Show and Rodeo and was the parade's grand marshal for 1980. Clifford is president and chairman of the board of the Great American Corporation and chairman of the board emeritus of the American Bank and Trust Company.

In 1923, Dorastand R. Ourso founded the company that bears his name.

Piccadilly Cafeterias, Inc.

Now represented by eighty cafeterias in thirteen southern and southwestern states, the dramatic success of Piccadilly began in downtown Baton Rouge, when the existing Piccadilly Cafeteria was purchased by company founder T.H. Hamilton in 1944. Blossoming from what was essentially a one-man show, today over 5,500 dedicated Piccadilly employees serve over 40 million meals annually, using only the highest quality ingredients to prepare the more than 1,000 time-tested recipes.

A visit to Piccadilly, located primarily in shopping centers, for Sunday lunch or special occasions has become a tradition in many families. For most people, though, the Piccadilly name simply represents a dependable place to take the family or friends anytime for a tastefully prepared, wholesome meal.

As an institution, Piccadilly has become a treasured asset in more than fifty communities. As a company, it represents a vital and growing part of the economy. With five new units opened in 1980 and five to seven scheduled for 1981, Piccadilly intends to grow and expand in the future.

In the last five years, twenty-nine new cafeterias have been opened. In a recent letter to shareholders, chairman of the board T.H. Hamilton and president O.Q. Quick confidently projected that the day will soon come when the company's present size will double.

The secret to 40 million satisfied

Top
Piccadilly cafeterias have enjoyed enormous success ever since the first one opened in 1944.
Bottom
This is one of five Piccadilly cafeterias in Baton Rouge. There are eighty such establishments throughout thirteen southern and southwestern states; continuing expansion is planned.

customers is 5,500 satisfied employees. The average time in service at Piccadilly for some key jobs clearly makes this point: district managers average twenty-five years with the company; managers, fifteen years; associate managers, nine years; chefs, eleven years; and head bakers, ten years. And this is in a company where the average cafeteria is less than nine years old.

From a modest beginning in downtown Baton Rouge, Piccadilly has become a major force in the food service industry. The spectacular success of Piccadilly has not diminished its commitment to the people of Baton Rouge or its economy. This is evidenced by the September opening of the fifth Baton Rouge Piccadilly next door to its 42,000-square-foot national headquarters building on Sherwood Forest Boulevard.

Port of Baton Rouge

The Indians knew it as a quiet wilderness. Early settlers knew it as a land of fields where the sugar cane grew. But today, the area along the Mississippi River at Baton Rouge is best known as the capital city's port, the farthest inland deep-water Gulf port of the Gulf of Mexico, and the fourth largest port in the United States. A $125-million complex now sprawls where the Indians once hunted and the sugar cane once grew.

Created by an act of the state legislature in 1952, the Greater Baton Rouge Port Commission was formed to ensure that Baton Rouge's natural port was properly utilized. An integrated, well-balanced waterways system and transportation plant were the port commission's main goals.

In the year of its creation, the port commission recorded in Baton Rouge the movement of 12 million tons of waterborne commerce. By 1968, that figure had increased to more than 34 million tons, elevating Baton Rouge to the position of the Gulf's third largest port, ranking seventh nationwide. Today's annual tonnage is in excess of 76 million, with the Port of Baton Rouge ranked fourth nationally.

Ships from more than thirty nations called at the port in 1980, utilizing its general cargo facilities; grain elevators; and the Burnside Bulk Handling Terminal, one of the largest and most modern facilities on the lower Mississippi River.

An integral part of the commission's overall plan to create a well-balanced water transportation plant, the bulk handling terminal is equipped to transfer heavy bulk cargo between ocean vessels, barges, and rail cars. The port's grain elevator, public commodity warehouse, tank terminal, and barge terminal all help to make the services offered by the port attractive to the wide variety of concerns that annually use its many facilities.

Providing jobs for hundreds of people and bringing millions of dollars into the local economy, the Port of Baton Rouge has been a significant part of the general development of the greater Baton Rouge area. The economic impact of the port on the state is estimated to be in excess of $160 million annually.

With the astounding growth that has come to the Mississippi River, the cane fields and cotton are giving way to tremendous industrial expansion, which brings a new dimension to the activity of the Port of Baton Rouge. The adjacent intracoastal canal provides access to the west, decreasing by 165 river miles the traveling distance to points west of Morgan City. Baton Rouge's deep-water capabilities at such a strategic point of river travel have been crucial in the port's development and ensure continued prosperity in the future. With continued area growth, the Port of Baton Rouge will realize expanded operations and capabilities, helping to bring prosperity to Baton Rouge and to the entire state of Louisiana.

Right
This traveling crane is one type of mobile equipment used to transfer heavy bulk cargo between ocean vessels and waiting barges or railway freight cars.
Below
Foreign ships such as this one daily weigh anchor at the Port of Baton Rouge, the fourth largest port in the United States. Here they deliver cargo for shipment around the country or are loaded with goods to be transported around the world.

Process Services, Inc.

With design offices located in Baton Rouge, Louisiana, and Houston, Texas, Process Services, Inc. (PSI), offers a wide variety of services in the engineering field, including project feasibility studies, budget estimates, process design, mechanical design and specifications, electrical and instrumentation design, scheduling and cost control, and field engineering and management.

PSI, founded in November 1973, was originally located in the Wooddale Boulevard business district on Dallas Drive. There, under the leadership of president Earl H. Carpenter, the fledgling concern set out to establish a reputation for quality and efficiency on all projects.

Those goals were quickly realized, and PSI's success and resultant growth caused the firm to expand into the buildings adjoining its original location. In 1977, a new facility was completed at Coursey Boulevard; major operations of PSI continue to be handled there today.

A professional organization providing total engineering project design and management capability, PSI is comprised of professional engineers and designers who possess the comprehensive backgrounds necessary for all phases of engineering and construction. The majority of the company's employees have more than ten years' experience in their respective fields. With this caliber of personnel, PSI is able to offer the highest quality engineering and construction

The new headquarters of Process Services, Inc., are located at 12158 Coursey Boulevard in Baton Rouge.

services with two principal considerations always kept in mind: budget and schedule.

The continuing industrial growth throughout the Baton Rouge area established a need for the creation of PSI. The company has continued to play a significant role in this exciting environment of expansion and development. With this ongoing atmosphere of healthy industrial activity, PSI can look forward to a productive future, as the firm continues its efforts to develop and expand through carefully monitored progress.

Rabenhorst Funeral Home

In 1866, on Main Street opposite St. Joseph Cathedral's modern location, one of the city's oldest and most recognizable enterprises was established.

Rabenhorst Funeral Home was founded by Charles F. Ranbenhorst, a native of Prussia who had immigrated to New Orleans in the 1850s. With the advent of the Civil War, Rabenhorst formed his own military company, which was attached to the Twenty-first Louisiana Regiment. Following his discharge at war's end, Captain Rabenhorst moved to Baton Rouge and established a funeral home.

The firm was moved in the years following from its original location to 115-117 Third Street and then to the corner of America and St. Louis streets. In 1932 it was moved once again to its present-day location at 825 Government Street. In 1978, a Florida Boulevard location, Rabenhorst East, was dedicated, adding the fifth location to the history of Rabenhorst in Baton Rouge.

Rabenhorst has always been, and remains today, a family-held corporation. Ownership and management of the firm has passed from its founder, Charles F. Rabenhorst, to his sons, O.F. and A.E. Rabenhorst, and subsequently to their sons, Allie, Alvin P., and Harry A. Rabenhorst. The general operations of the firm have been managed for many years by president and general manager C.B. Knight.

Rabenhorst Life Insurance Company

Rabenhorst Life Insurance Company, located at 833 Government Street, was founded by Oscar F. and Alvin E. Rabenhorst in the depression year of 1932. Originally named The Mortuary Benefit Association, the firm began by offering funeral benefit policies in the form of membership certificates. With a charter awarded in 1939, the name was changed to Rabenhorst Industrial Life Insurance Company. The year 1943 saw the authorization to issue cash policies, and four years later whole life funeral policies were approved for issuance. These two policies became the nucleus of the present policy portfolio, which has been expanded to meet changing policyholder needs. In 1964, to reflect increased capitalization, the name was changed to Rabenhorst Life Insurance Company.

An early commitment to provide home service has been strengthened by each succeeding generation of management and continues to play a large role in the present success and growth of the company. A.P. Rabenhorst, chairman of the board of Rabenhorst Funeral Home and Rabenhorst Life Insurance Company, has been joined in the businesses by his sons, A.P. Rabenhorst, Jr., David L. Rabenhorst, and George Scott Rabenhorst, who represent the fourth generation of active family management and ownership.

Right
Alvin E. Rabenhorst, seen here as a young man, would later found The Mortuary Benefit Association, now called Rabenhorst Life Insurance Company, with his brother, Oscar F. Rabenhorst, in 1932.

Saia Electric, Inc.

Saia Electric, Inc., which celebrated its twentieth anniversary in 1980, has become a leader in the Baton Rouge area and has established a nationwide reputation in the process. The firm, with this reputation of stability and competence, continues to maintain a well-controlled plan of conservative quality with initiative, integrity, and imagination as its core.

The industrial electrical construction field is a highly demanding one, requiring innovative ideas and well-designed projects. Saia Electric maintains an ongoing working relationship with general contractors, which enables maximum job completion success with minimum interference to plant operation. This valuable experience, accrued while working in all the major industrial plants in the Baton Rouge area, is the key to the remarkable growth of Saia Electric.

It is the company's main objective to provide fair bidding, complete delineation of the work to be performed, planning and scheduling to accommodate the client's requirements, and proper accounting. Completion of each project within time and budget limits is an important consideration of every Saia undertaking.

Carefully coordinated personnel ensure the prosperity enjoyed by the firm. Professionals in all phases of electrical construction, ranging from management to field installations and supervision, respond to each job with a thorough knowledge of their integrated part. This teamwork and fi-

The newly completed Governmental Complex in Baton Rouge's beautiful Riverside Centroplex is just one of the many notable projects on which Saia Electric has played an important part.

nancial reliability enables Saia Electric, Inc., to compete for all projects regardless of size or complexity.

Throughout the Baton Rouge and surrounding area, the Saia name is equated with quality electrical work. Recent commercial projects have included electrical construction on the Louisiana State University Assembly Center; the Louisiana Department of Education Building; the Louisiana Natural Resources Building, Zachary and Central high schools; the Baton Rouge Hilton Hotel; the Louisiana State School for the Deaf; the Baton Rouge Centroplex; and the Woman's

Hospital.

Frank Tickie Saia founded the company that bears his name in March 1960. Before establishing his own business he had been general manager of Sachse Electric. An active participant in community affairs, Saia has served on the Recreation and Parks Commission for the parish of East Baton Rouge, and on the Planning and Zoning Commission for the city of Baton Rouge and the parish of East Baton Rouge. Saia was named Louisiana's outstanding Small Businessman of the Year in 1969 by the Small Businessmen's Association. He is also a member of Baton Rouge High School's Hall of Fame, and has served as chairman of the Louisiana State Licensing Board for Contractors.

State National Life

One of the first legal reserves in Louisiana, the company that would become State National Life was organized on March 13, 1933, by Doyle Woodruff of Baton Rouge. Named Reliance Industrial Life Insurance, the new concern's primary function was to provide funeral service insurance.

Prior to that time, Woodruff had operated the Capital City Interment Association for several years. The nonprofit funeral association was maintained in conjunction with the Woodruff Funeral Home. With the formation of Reliance Industrial Life, the coverage was converted to legal reserve policies. Changed to Woodruff's Insurance Company in 1939, the business experienced substantial growth during the ensuing years, changing names again in 1942 to Woodruff's Life Insurance Company.

In 1945, three law partners, Warren O. Watson, Fred A. Blanche, and Charles W. Wilson, along with funeral home owner Merle Welsh, negotiated with Woodruff for the purchase of his life insurance company and funeral home. Upon completion of the sale, the new owners renamed the firm State National Life Insurance Company, setting a course in July of that year for modernization and expansion.

The ambitions of the four partners were realized as State National became one of the leading funeral and industrial life insurance companies in the state. Watson, Blanche, and Wil-

son subsequently sold to Welsh their interest in the funeral home, which continues in operation under different ownership today. Welsh later sold his interest in the insurance company.

In 1959, funeral policy coverage was offered, with the issuance of 100 percent funeral service policies in lieu of the usual discontinued-type funeral policy. Greatly enhancing the opportunity for operation expansion, State National was able to spread into areas where no official funeral homes existed.

A milestone in the growth of the firm occurred in 1964 with the creation of the Ordinary Department, placing State National in a competitive position with other combination and ordinary companies. This impor-

Left
Charles W. Wilson, Jr., has been chairman of the board and president of State National Life since 1977.

Right
The renovated Reymond Building in the downtown Baton Rouge business district has been adapted to meet the corporate needs of State National Life Insurance Company.

tant development was the work of the late Thomas P. Landry, who was agency director at the time. Landry served as president of the company from 1976 until his untimely death in 1977.

When the Woodruff purchase was transacted in 1945, the new State National Life opened with assets totaling $162,038. Today, assets exceed $29 million. Total insurance in force at the time of State National's founding was approximately $10 million. That figure now amounts to nearly $300 million.

The firm's four original purchasers served State National as its guiding officers. Warren O. Watson was chairman of the board from 1945 until 1973; he was succeeded by Fred A. Blanche, who served until 1977. Merle M. Welsh held the office of president from 1945 through 1976, when he was succeeded by Thomas P. Landry. Charles W. Wilson, Jr., has been chairman of the board and president since 1977. Under Wilson's capable and dynamic leadership, State National has doubled its capital and surplus.

State National Life became involved in an effort to preserve and revive the downtown business district when the company secured the Reymond Building at Florida Boulevard and Riverside Mall. The building was renovated and adapted to suit the company's needs in 1976. Today, the structure stands as one of the key factors in the continued prosperity of the downtown business district and the city in general. State National is proud of that accomplishment and of its many years of active participation in the history of the Baton Rouge community.

Shell Oil Company / Shell Chemical Company

Since 1916, when 366 acres of the former Good Hope plantation land above New Orleans became its first refinery site, Shell Oil Company has been a major force in all phases of Louisiana's petroleum industry. Construction was begun that summer, twenty-four miles upriver from New Orleans, under the supervision of the New Orleans Refining Company (NORCO).

By the end of that year, a wharf and storage tank had been constructed, and pumps and boilerhouses were nearing completion. With the beginning of World War I, the NORCO project was to gain significant importance as the site became a major supplier of petroleum products to the Allied forces. Known as the Sellars Plant in honor of an adjoining plantation, the original facility was capable of producing 5,000 barrels a day. Its present capacity is now estimated to be about 240,000 barrels.

An addition to the Norco facility, costing in excess of $700 million and able to yield 1.5 billion pounds of ethylene and 500 million pounds of butadiene a year, began operations in 1981. Providing 250 permanent jobs, the new facility also produces 28,000 barrels of gasoline, 10,000 barrels of low-sulfur fuel oil, and 6,000 barrels of ethane daily.

Shell Chemical Company's introduction to Louisiana occurred in 1955, when the Norco Chemical Plant was built one mile upriver from the established and growing oil refinery. A variety of industrial chemicals used in manufacturing everyday products are produced at the plant. In 1976, administration of the oil and chemical plants at Norco was combined under the Shell Norco Manufacturing Complex, which today is one of the company's largest facilities. This facility alone provides jobs for more than 2,000 Shell employees in Louisiana.

Farther up the river at Geismar, about twenty miles south of Baton Rouge, a new chemical plant was built in 1965 for the production of ethylene-based products and primary alcohols used in the manufacture of biodegradable detergents. Over 600 Shell people now work at the Geismar Plant.

Shell also operates a small chemical plant purchased in 1977 at Taft for the manufacturing of polybutylene. About 75 people are employed here. Shell has acquired a 2,400-acre tract near Edgard and tentative plans are set to begin construction there on the new Willow Bend Chemical Plant in 1983.

New Orleans is headquarters for Shell's Eastern Exploration and Production Operations, which cover the states and offshore areas along the Gulf of Mexico and Atlantic coasts from the Mexican border eastward to Maine. Over 4,000 Shell employees work in this region, and almost 300 work in Louisiana.

Exploration in Louisiana began in 1919, when several thousand acres were leased near Haynesville and an office was establshed in nearby Shreveport. It was ten long years, however, before any significant results were seen in Louisiana. The first well was established in 1929 at Black Bayou in Cameron Parish; it was followed during the next two years by discoveries at the White Castle and Iowa fields. All three of these initial fields are still producing today.

World War II brought accelerated exploration and production; another major discovery occurred in 1945 at Weeks Island, where Shell's first deep well was successfully drilled. Along with four offshore sites, the Weeks Island field has exceeded its millionth barrel of oil produced for Shell. To-

Opposite Left
Shell's Cognac platform, standing in 1,025 feet of water in the Gulf of Mexico, is the world's tallest offshore platform.
Opposite Right
These are biotreaters used to treat wastewaters at Shell's Geismar Plant, near Baton Rouge.
Top
With the combining of the original Shell Oil Company refinery (at right) and the Shell Chemical Company plant (to the left), the Norco facilities for the corporation are now known as the Shell Norco Manufacturing Complex.
Bottom
These are some of Shell's Norco chemical operations.

its pioneering efforts in offshore production. With Lockheed Petroleum Services, Shell in 1976 announced initial construction of a unique ocean-floor production system that gathers, measures, and controls activities at surrounding wells completed on the ocean floor. The system, devised for use in depths of up to 3,000 feet, will allow workmen to perform their duties in a normal atmosphere in an underwater chamber, reached from the surface by a diving capsule. In the summer of 1978, the company completed work on the tallest oil platform in the world. Located in the Gulf of Mexico, the structure with derricks atop is as tall as the Empire State Building, its base larger than a city block.

The Shell Pipe Line Corporation has its Gulf Coast Division headquartered in New Orleans. This office supervises operations of the company's more than 170 pipeline employees and about 1,000 miles of pipelines in Louisiana. The lines carry much of Shell's raw and finished products to market throughout the southern and eastern United States. New Orleans is also the headquarters of Shell's Marketing District, responsible for the sale of company products in Louisiana. Operating since 1929, the district now handles an annual sales volume of 300 million gallons.

Throughout Louisiana and in nearby offshore operations, Shell now employs more than 6,000 people in a wide variety of jobs. The company has progressed dramatically from its early years to be recognized today as both an important member of the Louisiana industrial community and as a vigorous force in national and international energy production.

day, Shell is the top oil producer in the Gulf of Mexico.

The emergence of offshore exploration and production found Shell a leader among companies reaching into this new frontier. The first hole in the Gulf of Mexico was drilled by Shell in 1949; the following year Shell discovered the South Pass Block 24 Field, which later distinguished itself as one of the petroleum industry's most vital finds.

In recent years, Shell has continued

Stauffer Chemical

Marking the beginning of sulfuric acid operations in Baton Rouge, the Louisiana Chemical Company, a subsidiary of Pacific Bone, Coal and Fertilizing Company, opened operations here in 1925. Initially, the sulfur-burning unit went on-line to produce at the rate of forty-five tons of acid per day. By 1929, the daily production rate had more than doubled. Encouraged by the increase in production at its Baton Rouge facilities, Pacific expanded its operations that same year, changing its name to Consolidated Chemicals Industries, Inc.

World War II and the Korean conflict found sulfur in short supply, but in each instance, Consolidated innovated to maintain operations. During World War II, the company pioneered the conversion of spent sulfuric acid from aviation fuel manufacturing into fresh acid. In 1944, a 200-ton per day sulfur-burning unit was added to the Baton Rouge facility. During the Korean War, with sulfur supplies again critical, Consolidated, in cooperation with a neighboring refinery, built a recovery plant to produce sulfur from waste oil refinery gases. The year 1954 saw the completion of a large sulfuric acid regeneration unit capable of processing sludges from a variety of operations. One year later, 77-year-old Consolidated Chemicals was merged into the Stauffer Chemical Company.

In 1967, negotiations began for the purchase of 570 acres of the Margaret Plantation tract at St. Gabriel, Louisiana, to construct a chlor-alkali plant. Construction began in November 1968

on forty acres of the tract. Completed in twenty-seven months, the plant was designed to produce 520 tons of liquid chlorine and 570 tons of liquid caustic each day. The St. Gabriel facility is the largest of the corporation's three chlor-alkali plants. When the St. Gabriel plant went on-line in December 1970, the operation employed approximately 100 people. Today, the facility's payroll is approximately 200.

Stauffer's Agricultural Chemical Division at St. Gabriel started construction in 1974, with the first product being realized in November of the following year. By early 1976, second, third, and fourth units of the facility were on-line, manufacturing crop protection chemicals primarily for corn. With the help of these products, farmers have realized significantly higher crop yields.

This photograph of Stauffer Chemical Company's North Baton Rouge facility shows the processing portion of the #2 unit sulfuric acid plant.

One of Stauffer's most modern agricultural chemical manufacturing plants, the St. Gabriel facility was designed and constructed using the most sophisticated technological advances available to ensure safe, efficient, and environmentally sound operations. Meeting challenges has been a fundamental objective throughout the many years Stauffer and the companies preceding it have operated in Louisiana. Continued success and growth can best be assured by the company's policy of carefully monitored, safe, and efficient operations. With this in mind, Stauffer looks ahead to a progressive and significant future.

Union National Life

Julius C. Greer, Fred J. Greer, and H.P. Huff were intent in 1926 on establishing an insurance company in the small but rapidly growing community of Baton Rouge. On October 4, 1926, the three started their own company.

It was a struggle at first to keep the business solvent. In 1927, the Mississippi River spilled over southern Louisiana in one of its most devastating floods. The stock market crashed in 1929, and the Great Depression followed immediately.

Early records reveal the problems the depression caused. Joined by J.L. Klein in 1927, the firm collected a total of $15,616. Two years later, collections had increased to $23,885, but by 1933, collections dropped to $15,905. In contrast, the average income of Union National Life agents in 1975 was more than $16,000. In 1980, the average income exceeded $27,000.

The company's original president, Fred Greer, turned the administration of the business over to Julius in 1931. In 1935, J.P. Craig joined the group as a special agent, and two years later Ira Greer and Ted McCullough were added to the force. Fred Greer, Jr., and Robert Greer both joined the company in the ensuing years.

Union National had operated exclusively in Baton Rouge until 1939, when expansion into other areas was initiated. By 1946, Monroe, Shreveport, Alexandria, and New Orleans were being served. Today, the firm is authorized to do business in Ar-

kansas, Tennessee, Florida, Louisiana, Mississippi, Georgia, Texas, Alabama, and Oklahoma.

The company now has a total work force of more than 750 employees. The total income for 1980 was $48,910,758; and assets amounted to $86,152,840. Receiving the highest possible rating from "Best Insurance Reports," Union National today continues in its efforts to see that those initial visions of the founders are fulfilled.

Top Left and Right
Fred Greer (left), the company's original president, turned the administration of the business over to Julius Greer (right) in 1931.
Left
Union National Life headquarters are located at 8282 Goodwood.
Right
H.P. Huff is one of the firm's founders.

United Fiberglass Company, Inc.

Established in May 1979, United Fiberglass Company, Inc., was the culmination of a dream for Baton Rougeans Joe Northern, Artis Talton, Sterling Wright, and Willie Shavers. The firm's creation was for these four men the opportunity to own and operate the first industrial and commercial minority-owned fiberglass company in the state of Louisiana.

Joe Northern was elected president and general manager, with Artis Talton serving as vice-president and superintendent of shop repairs. Sterling Wright became the firm's first secretary and manager of purchasing while Willie Shavers assumed the duties of treasurer and superintendent of fabrication and field repairs.

Northern and Wright had both been previously employed at Baton Rouge chemical plants, where they had gained valuable experience in the field of industrial fiberglass fabrication and repair. During that time, Talton and Shaver were also learning the skills of fiberglass work while working for one of the South's largest boat companies. Uniting forces in 1979, the four men brought to the Baton Rouge area their unique skills and determination, forming the first quick-service fiberglass company in the city.

Without the assistance of any financial institution, Northern, Talton, Wright, and Shavers founded United Fiberglass Company, Inc. Initially, they did all the work themselves, hoping that the income immediately generated by repairing fiberglass boats and other such items would sustain the business until an industrial market could be established.

After a brief period when work obtained consisted of boat and camper repairs, United Fiberglass secured its first industrial contract in October 1979 with the St. Gabriel plant of Stauffer Chemical. Other industrial projects followed immediately. As the talents and capabilities of United Fiberglass were acknowledged, the company was hired to do fiberglass work for several large Louisiana chemical corporations, among them BASF Wyandotte, Georgia-Pacific Corporation, Kaiser Aluminum and Chemical Corporation, ICI Americas, and Vulcan Materials Company.

To accommodate its expanding clientele, United Fiberglass found it necessary to augment its staff. Today, five experienced fabricators and a secretary share the work load with the four founders.

Years of specialized training have given the creators of United Fiberglass an expertise that has assured success for the young firm. A full range of manufactured and refabricated fiberglass products as well as emergency on-site repairs are offered by the business, located at the corner of North Foster Drive and Gus Young Avenue.

Left
Joe Northern is president and general manager of United Fiberglass Company, Inc.
Right
This ammonia nitrate solution tank was manufactured for Universal Oil Products of Shreveport. United Fiberglass tanks are impervious to most chemicals.
Lower Right
This fiberglass tank, manufactured by United Fiberglass for EPSCO, Inc., of Baton Rouge, meets all OSHA environmental requirements.

Ward Refrigeration

After several years' employment as service manager with a local Baton Rouge contracting firm, James L. (Red) Ward resolved to go into business for himself. He decided to enter the air conditioning industry, which at that time was beginning to undergo the tremendous surge of growth that the television industry had experienced five years earlier. With determination and ingenuity as his major assets, Ward established his own refrigeration company in March 1950. Initial operations were conducted from the trunk of Ward's car, a 1941 Ford, with his garage used as a shop.

Few houses had air conditioning in those days, but the demand for that luxury was rapidly growing. Residential contracts were not the only ones undertaken by the company, however. The Mississippi River brought to Baton Rouge numerous ships and harbor vessels that needed the services of a refrigeration maintenance company. Maintenance and mechanical contracting would eventually become the primary focus of Ward Refrigeration.

By the mid-1960s, after moving several times to increasingly larger facilities, Ward's business had expanded to the point that a permanent facility was needed to enable the busy operation to meet the demands for service that Baton Rouge's growth had created. Property acquired several years earlier on Old Hammond Highway became the chosen site as Ward moved into modern facilities in 1976. The company's headquarters are still close enough to town to allow the firm to respond quickly to any refrigeration and air conditioning service or maintenance needs that might arise.

Today, Ward no longer works out of the trunk of his car, nor does he work alone. The enterprise now boasts a staff of more than twenty. Most of the employees are mechanics who stay in close contact with the base of operations in the nine mobile units that make Ward's on-call accessibility an important factor in the company's success.

It has been an arduous but successful journey from the trunk of Red Ward's car to one of Baton Rouge's most outstanding mechanical contractors. In addition to satisfying the needs of its residential, commercial, and industrial customers, Ward Refrigeration today encompasses a much broader scale of operations, handling jobs on large offshore platforms in the Gulf of Mexico, ships from the many nations that visit the Baton Rouge port, and even the *Mississippi Queen* and *Delta Queen* riverboats. Determination and diversification have been major factors in the success of Ward Refrigeration, and the firm continues to grow and prosper with the city of Baton Rouge.

Left
Employees of Ward Refrigeration stand in front of company headquarters at 16722 Old Hammond Highway in Baton Rouge.
Right
Dottye Ward, secretary-treasurer of Ward Refrigeration, has been with the firm for fifteen years. Her husband, James L. (Red) Ward, Sr., founded the company in 1950 and serves as president. His son, James L. Ward II (at right), has worked for Ward Refrigeration for seven years and today is vice-president.

H.J. Wilson Co., Inc.

Today, H.J. Wilson Co., Inc. (Wilson's), is a catalog showroom retail chain of fifty-one locations, offering its customers fine jewelry and nationally advertised name-brand merchandise at discount prices. The firm's origin can be traced back to 1949, when a young jeweler named Huey Wilson opened a wholesale jewelry and manufacturing business in Baton Rouge.

Wilson's Jewelry, located in a 3,300-square-foot building at 430 Main Street, offered quality jewelry for prices less than those charged by traditional jewelers. Gifts and housewares manufactured by nationally known companies were added to broaden the showroom's appeal, and all were sold at discount prices. Today, showrooms average 60,000 square feet in size and contain more than 40,000 items, including housewares, sporting goods, cameras, electronics equipment, luggage, baby goods, and, of course, jewelry.

In 1957, independent of each other, fewer than six retailers throughout the United States began to utilize a small catalog, composed primarily of sheets supplied by manufacturers, to inform customers as completely as possible about the selection and prices of products they carried in their stores. Wilson's first catalog of 64 pages was sent to 10,000 customers in the fall of 1957. This offered consumers the convenience of shopping in their homes, and ensured that a trip to the showroom would result in immediate purchase of the item at the catalog price. The success of this experimental project has resulted in the publication each subsequent fall of an up-to-date catalog, which today is 448 pages of vivid, four-color illustrations, and is sent to more than two million Wilson's customers.

During the 1960s, a new Baton Rouge showroom on Florida Boulevard was leased, and showrooms in Jackson, Gulfport, and Lafayette were opened. In 1970, H.J. Wilson Co., Inc., became a publicly owned corporation, with investors throughout the United States and Europe. This event provided the means to support the company's rapid growth and development through 1980, during which time sales grew from $20 million to $300 million; the number of employees increased from five to 5,000; and the showrooms expanded from four to fifty-one, spanning an area from the Atlantic Seaboard to Colorado.

Today, Mr. Wilson is active as chairman of the board, and Mrs. Wilson is corporate secretary. Other family members and employees of the original showrooms remain dedicated, loyal workers, committed to the Wilson precepts of wide selection, excellent service, and reasonably priced quality products.

Left
In 1980, one of H.J. Wilson's early showrooms was converted into corporate headquarters, which now house the management necessary to operate the rapidly growing company.
Right
The cover of Wilson's 1969 catalog lists only three showroom locations; eleven years later, in 1980, the firm opened its fifty-first location encompassing a 10-state region.

WJBO-WFMF Radio

Before coming to Baton Rouge, radio station WJBO operated as WAAB in New Orleans. Licensed in 1922 by Valdemar Jensen, the station was called WAAB until 1927, when, with the creation of the Federal Communications Commission, the call letters were changed to WJBO, standing for Jensen Broadcasting Organization. In 1934, Charles Manship, president of the Baton Rouge Broadcasting Company, purchased the station from Jensen and moved it to Baton Rouge. Today, WJBO and its FM sister station WFMF are the two most listened-to news/music stations in the Baton Rouge area.

The station's original facilities on Oklahoma Street included two studios, an equipment room, and a reception area for its three-employee staff, but listeners within a 60-mile radius of the capital city could pick up the station's broadcasts and the popularity of WJBO began to grow. With permission from the FCC in 1937 to increase its power, WJBO qualified

for affiliation with the NBC Blue Network that same year. Also in 1937, the station moved to new facilities on Roosevelt Road, a transition that necessitated the installation of a 485-foot Lehigh tower, one of the first of its type in the country.

The NBC affiliation provided local listeners with worldwide news and programming, but the station adhered to its original objective—to be a communications forum for the Baton Rouge community. Local-interest programming, drawing on the resources of Louisiana State University and Baton Rouge's daily newspapers,

Left
WJBO-WFMF Radio moved in 1941 to its present location at 444 Florida Boulevard. The building, designed especially for the station, contains three studios, offices, a reception area, and a new RCA control board modeled after the huge Radio City board at NBC's New York studios.
Right
The station's 485-foot Lehigh tower, installed in 1937, was one of the first of its type in the country.

was always top priority.

A petition to increase WJBO's power even more was filed in 1938 and granted in 1940, ushering in the station's "golden era"—by the end of the decade, WJBO's audience would grow from 35,000 to more than 125,000. An Associated Press hookup was added, expanding the news and communications services of the station. In 1941, with a total staff of forty, the station moved to its present location at 444 Florida Boulevard. The building was designed especially for the station and contained three studios, offices, a reception room, and a new RCA control board modeled after the huge Radio City board at NBC's New York studios. Although the NBC Blue Network became ABC in the late 1940s, WJBO decided to stay with NBC, an affiliation that continued through the late 1970s.

During this same period, the South's first frequency modulation (FM) station, W45BR, began operating in Baton Rouge. Two small towers were erected for the FM broadcasts alongside WJBO's AM tower. In 1846, W45BR became WBRL with increased frequency power; the call letters were later changed to WJBO-FM and then to WFMF.

The proliferation of television in the early 1950s made survival for radio stations very difficult, of course, but WJBO and its FM sister have continued to grow. New downstairs studios were constructed at the Florida Boulevard building in the 1960s, and the original art deco studio upstairs still flourishes. WJBO and WFMF will continue to be responsible, educational, entertaining leaders of the Baton Rouge broadcasting community.

PARTNERS IN PROGRESS INDEX

APPENDIX:
A SOCIAL HISTORY OF MAGNOLIA MOUND PLANTATION

The publishers wish to thank Carol Nelson, director of Magnolia Mound, for permission to publish this article, which originally appeared in *The Museum Interpreter of Magnolia Mound* (Vol. III, No. 1).

1786—The property on which Magnolia Mound house is located is part of a large Spanish grant to James Hillen in 1786. An inventory of the property at his wife's death points to its use as an indigo plantation. There is also a description of a small house. From the description and measurements, Mr. Heck and Mr. Leake think that this is not the first stage of the Magnolia Mound house that was restored.

December 1791—John Joyce of Mobile purchased the property from Hillen and planted cotton and perhaps indigo on the plantation. From the inventory at his death, the house that fits the description and measurements of the first stage of the present house appears. Joyce was a contractor and it is assumed he supervised the building of the house. The inventory states ". . . upon which land is built the principal house, raised about three feet high, mud walls between stakes, about forty-seven feet long by twenty feet wide, roofed with shingles, with a gallery ten and one-half feet long, the said house having a double brick chimney and divided into four rooms, two of them in good condition, together with its doors and windows." (The house has been raised higher since then.) Mr. Heck said the bousillage walls were probably covered with a plaster wash at this time so that the construction showed through. The smaller house built by Hillen, as well as other buildings and slave cabins and a kitchen "about 14 feet long and 10 feet wide, roofed with stakes" also appear in this inventory.

Records in Mobile indicate that Joyce, his wife, and children resided in Mobile, and he or they traveled to Baton Rouge from time to time to supervise the property. He had a partner in Mobile, John Turnbull, who had moved to the District of Baton Rouge. They had had a successful merchandising business in Mobile and had also owned land together. Sometime between 1791 and 1798 they purchased, as partners, the land adjoining Joyce's Baton Rouge property on the north.

February 24, 1798—Joyce and Turnbull placed all of their individual properties in a partnership.

May 1798—Joyce died by drowning near Mobile when, during the night, he fell from a ship on which he was returning from New Orleans.

September 1798—Turnbull died at his home in the District of Baton Rouge.

1799—Proceedings to settle estates of Joyce and Turnbull began.

1800—Felipe Guinaut is appointed *curator ad litem* of the minor children of the deceased Joyce, Josephine and William Joyce. Armand Duplantier is appointed *curator ad litem* of the minor children of the deceased John Turnbull.

Circa 1800—Armand Duplantier and Constance Joyce married and lived at Magnolia Mound which Constance Joyce and her children inherited with other properties after the Joyce and Turnbull holdings were divided.

Armand and Constance Joyce Duplantier made additions to the house and "modernized" it to the Federal style popular at that time. The elaborate cove ceiling, tooled wood rosette, hand carved molds, and Federal style mantles were made and installed at this time.

Circa 1827—What appears to be the southern portion of Magnolia Mound Plantation was acquired by Fergus Duplantier and his wife, Josephine Joyce Duplantier (also his step-sister). They sold this plantation, which possibly was also called Magnolia Mound, to Bernard and Dubreuil Villars who sold it in 1837 to Achille Murat, Crown Prince of Naples, known for his books published in France about American life. (His wife was related to Martha Washington.) Six months later the property reverted to the ownership of the Villars, who sold it again a year later. It eventually became part of the Williams (Gartness) plantation, and is now part of Louisiana State University. Murat is also said to have owned or leased a home on Esplanade Avenue in New Orleans where he was famous for his extravagant parties. Unfortunately he was a poor businessman and was in debt when he left Louisiana. He moved to St. Augustine, Florida, where he died. Although we have no records that Murat owned the property now referred to as Magnolia Mound, there is a possibility that he leased the house from Constance who was widowed by this time. It appears that she allowed Fergus (her step-son and son-in-law) to handle much of her affairs. Murat's name has been so intertwined with the history of Magnolia Mound that

for many years, especially in the 20th century, the house has become known as "The Prince Murat House."

1827—Armand Duplantier died in 1827 at the age of 74. He was born in 1753 in Voiron, Department of Isere, France. He was a Cavalry officer in the French Army, and joined the French contingent that came to assist the Continental Army. During the Revolutionary War he served as aide-de-camp to his friend the Marquis de Lafayette, whose highest esteem he enjoyed. After the war Duplantier responded to the solicitations of an uncle who resided in Louisiana and came to the territory in 1781. When Lafayette visited Baton Rouge, his secretary reported that Lafayette's good friend Armand Duplantier and his son had accompanied them from New Orleans to Baton Rouge and that after his day's visit in Baton Rouge he was saddened to have to depart from Duplantier.

When Duplantier came to Louisiana he settled in Pointe Coupee and married Augustine Gerard by whom he had four children; three sons (Fergus, Armand, and Guy) and one daughter (Augustine). After his first wife's death he married Constance Joyce and they had four sons (Augustine, Didier, Alberic, and Alfred) and one daughter (Euphemic). Euphemic, who married Dr. Peniston from Virginia, died when her second son, Fergus, was born. Fergus Peniston and his brother were adopted by Fergus and Josephine Joyce Duplantier and took the name of Duplantier. Fergus and Josephine were quite wealthy and Fergus (Peniston) Duplantier inherited their estate. This is the Fergus Duplantier who built Chatsworth and should not be confused with his uncle Fergus Duplantier, who was also his father by adoption.

1841—Constance Rochon Joyce Duplantier died. Her three living sons by Armand Duplantier and her two children by John Joyce inherited Magnolia Mound plantation. Fergus Duplantier (husband of one of the heirs, Josephine Duplantier) was executor of the estate.

1846—The heirs of Constance Duplantier sold the property to Alverez Fisk and David Chambers who were not from the Baton Rouge area. Apparently they purchased the property as a plantation or real-estate investment or both.

1849—Fisk and Chambers sold Magnolia Mound Plantation to George Hall who had married Emma LeDoux of Pointe Coupee parish. Six of their 12 children were born at Magnolia Mound. Hall and his wife had many relatives in England and France. On a visit to the continent, Hall left his wife and children in France when the Civil War began. Hall returned to Louisiana and Magnolia Mound several times, but apparently lost much of his fortune during the war. Federal troops then occupied the plantation. Fortunately Hall's relatives in France furnished some of the letters he wrote before, during, and after the war.

1869—Hall sold the property to Mrs. Helen Walworth McCullen. Her husband, who had her power of attorney, sold one-third of the plantation to Charles Weick, and one-third to Mrs. Christine Redwitz. Mr. McCullen managed the plantation and carried out the cultivation. Mr. Weick kept the books of accounts on all plantation business, and Mrs. Redwitz advanced money for supplies for cultivation.

1885—Magnolia Mound plantation, listed as 800 acres, was sold to Louis Barrillier, August Strenzke, Edward Whitting, and Henry Schortin (each owned one quarter). By 1890 all had been sold to Louis Barrillier who raised cotton and sugar there. An 1880 map of the plantation shows all of the outbuildings, slave quarters, sugar house, and fields in cultivation. It is an important document and since it is transparent it can be overlaid on a present map of the city, enabling one to see what part of the city now was once part of the plantation.

1904—The heirs of Louis Barrillier sold the property to Robert Andrew Hart, a land developer and one of Baton Rouge's earliest mayors. The plantation consisted of approximately 800 acres and included the plantation house, the sugar house, and an overseer's house. Mr. Hart was a bachelor and never occupied the old home himself. He chose instead to have a house built close by, within a few yards of the old home. The original plantation home was at one time occupied by a niece, Mrs. Gertrude Hart Aldrich, and her sons, after her husband's death. At another time, Mrs. Belle Hart Bynum, another niece, and her sons lived there.

Mr. Hart subdivided and sold most of the 800 acres, but maintained the two houses and surrounding grounds, amounting to about 75 acres.

1929—Mr. Hart sold the 75 acres now comprising Magnolia Mound to his niece, Miss Marie Blanche Duncan. Miss Duncan subdivided part of the property into Magnolia Terrace subdivision. She retained the houses and 12 acres. In 1951 Miss Duncan commissioned the architectural firm of Goodman and Miller of Baton Rouge to do alterations and additions on the old plantation house.

1958—Miss Duncan died and her cousin Anna Belle Hart (the present Mrs. John Anderson) became the owner of the 12 acres which included the two houses.

1965—Mrs. Anderson offered the house for sale and after some time she sold the house and about five acres to Al German, a developer from Texas.

1966—The house, which had fallen into disrepair in the late 1960s, was to be destroyed in order to make way for the construction of an apartment complex. The Foundation for Historical Louisiana, supported by The National Trust for Historical Preservation, Louisiana Landmarks, Architects, Architectural Historians, Historians, and others, prevailed upon Baton Rouge Recreation and Parks Commission (under the authority of East Baton Rouge City Parish Government) to purchase the property from Mr. German but he refused to sell. The property was subsequently expropriated because of its architectural and historical value to the East Baton Rouge Parish.

Baton Rouge Recreation and Parks paid for the house and about five acres. The Foundation for Historical Louisiana contracted to restore and maintain the house and appointed a Board of Trustees to supervise the restoration.

1972—Magnolia Mound house was added to the National Register of Historic Places and restoration was begun. Baton Rouge City-Parish government contributed to B.R.E.C. a generous amount of money to aid the Foundation in the restoration of the house. George Leake, a restoration architect from New Orleans, was engaged to design and supervise the restoration. Al Drumwright won the construction contract.

1981—The fully restored Magnolia Mound house, furnished in the Federal style with pieces that have been brought from the Eastern United States (as they were, no doubt, by the original owners), is open and gives guided tours to the public every day except Monday. Special programs are also held for school groups and members of the public.

BIBLIOGRAPHY

Primary Sources

Although this book was designed to be written, and was written, from a base of secondary materials, several available primary sources too valuable to be ignored had to be consulted:

"Baton Rouge, La., A City of Factories, Banks, Fine Hotels, Newspapers, Mercantile Establishments, Schools . . .," *The Southern Manufacturer* (New Orleans, 1908).

Baton Rouge *Chronicle* (Magazine Edition), September, 1915.

Margaret Dixon and K. H. Knox (eds.), Baton Rouge *Home News*, 1942-1945.

Charles East Collection (restricted access), Department of Archives and Manuscripts, Troy H. Middleton Library, Louisiana State University, Baton Rouge.

Pictorial Review of Baton Rouge, Baton Rouge *Sunday News*, 1921.

Vertical File (newspaper accounts, features and stories), Louisiana Room, Troy H. Middleton Library, Louisiana State University, Baton Rouge.

Secondary Sources

Books

Mark T. Carleton, *Politics and Punishment: The History of the Louisiana State Penal System* (Baton Rouge, 1971).

Edward Cunningham, *Battle of Baton Rouge* (Baton Rouge, 1962).

Margaret Fisher Dalrymple (ed.), *The Merchant of Manchac: The Letterbooks of John Fitzpatrick, 1768-1790* (Baton Rouge, 1978).

Edwin A. Davis, *Louisiana: A Narrative History* (Baton Rouge, 1965).

Charles East, *Baton Rouge: A Civil War Album* (Baton Rouge, 1977).

J. St. Clair Favrot, *Tales of Our Town: The First 100 Years* (Baton Rouge, 1972).

Peter Finney, *The Fighting Tigers II: LSU Football, 1893-1980* (Baton Rouge, 1980).

William I. Hair, *Bourbonism and Agrarian Protest: Louisiana Politics, 1877-1900* (Baton Rouge, 1969).

Florence B. Huguet, *Zachary Taylor: A Baton Rougean* (Baton Rouge Bicentennial Commission, 1976).

—————————— , *The Dutch Highlanders* (Baton Rouge Bicentennial Commission, 1976).

John L. Loos, *Oil on Stream: A History of the Interstate Oil Pipe Line Company* (Baton Rouge, 1959).

Rose Meyers, *A History of Baton Rouge: 1699-1812* (Baton Rouge, 1976).

Thomas Parrish (ed.), *The Simon and Schuster Encyclopedia of World War II* (New York, 1978).

Frank James Price, *Troy H. Middleton: A Biography* (Baton Rouge, 1974).

Evelyn M. Thom, *Lafayette Honors Baton Rouge with a Visit on the Fiftieth Anniversary of American Independence* (Baton Rouge Bicentennial Commission, 1975).

Robert I. Vexler (ed.), *Chronology and Documentary Handbook of the State of Louisiana* (Dobbs Ferry, 1978).

John D. Winters, *The Civil War in Louisiana* (Baton Rouge, 1963).

C. Vann Woodward, *Origins of the New South: 1877-1913* (Baton Rouge, 1951).

Articles

Robert W. Heck, "Historic Baton Rouge: An Urban Planning Perspective for the Preservation of Its Heritage . . ." (Baton Rouge, 1970).

William L. Richter, "Slavery in Baton Rouge," *Louisiana History*, Vol. X, No. 2, 1969, pp. 124-145.

Terry L. Seip, "Municipal Politics and the Negro: Baton Rouge, 1865-1880," Mark T. Carleton, Perry Howard and Joseph Parker (eds.), *Readings in Louisiana Politics* (Baton Rouge, 1975), pp. 242-266.

Evelyn M. Thom, "Baton Rouge Story: An Historical Sketch of Louisiana's Capital City" (Foundation for Historical Louisiana, Baton Rouge, 1967).

Sidney Tobin, "The Early New Deal in Baton Rouge as Viewed by the Daily Press," *Louisiana History*, Vol. X, No. 4, 1969, pp. 307-337.

Unpublished Theses (All at Louisiana State University, Baton Rouge).

Robert J. Aertker, "A Social History of Baton Rouge during the Civil War and Early Reconstruction," M.A., 1947.

Frederick Stuart Allen, "A Social and Economic History of Baton Rouge: 1850-1861," M.A., 1936.

Chester B. Beaty, "Baton Rouge, A Photogeographical Study," M.A., 1950.

G. J. Biedenstein, "The Cognitive Elements of Baton Rouge: How the Citizens Perceive Their City," M.A., 1978.

Fannie Day Booth, "Annals of the Parish of East Baton Rouge," M.A., 1933.

Andreas Brandt, "The Urban-Rural Interface: A Study of the Perception of the Southeastern Urban Area of Baton Rouge, Louisiana," M.A., 1978.

Meriel L. Douglas, "Some Aspects of the Social History of Baton Rouge from 1830 to 1850," M.A., 1955.

Wilbert J. Miller, "The Spanish Commandant of Baton Rouge, 1779-1795," M.A., 1965.

John Andrew Moore, "Growth and Cost Trends in Baton Rouge, Louisiana, From 1942 to 1976," M.A., 1977.

Donald G. Rhodes, "The Baton Rouge City-Parish Consolidation: A History and Evaluation," M.A., 1956.

Alban Fordesh Varnado, "A History of Theatrical Activity in Baton Rouge, Louisiana, 1819-1900," M.A., 1947.

ACKNOWLEDGMENTS

The author is indebted to many people for the help they have rendered in connection with this book, but wishes to give special thanks to the following: Evangeline Lynch and her always cheerful staff of the Louisiana Room, Troy H. Middleton Library, Louisiana State University; Charles East, a fine historian of Baton Rouge who generously gave me access to his collection of Baton Rouge materials and served as an editorial advisor; and to Carolyn G. Bennett of the Foundation for Historical Louisiana, who allowed me to explore the Foundation's extensive files.

Stone Miller energetically and enthusiastically located and put together the quite exceptional illustrations for this book, which makes him the co-author. He has done a splendid job and a great service to Baton Rouge.

My publishers have provided me with much encouragement and editorial help. Lissa Sanders has patiently endured some unavoidable delays and flaps, but was able to convince me that the impossible could be accomplished in spite of it all. Randall Smoot, whose careful attention to the details (large and small) of the text would be gratifying to any historian, and Phyllis Rifkin are also to be commended and thanked.

My good friend and colleague, Professor James D. Hardy, also a perceptive adopted Baton Rougean of 16 years' duration, read the entire manuscript and offered many valuable suggestions. The fact that he was positively impressed overall leads me to believe that the tale as I have told it possesses some merit.

Finally, I would like to dedicate my contribution to the book to Alice, Amy, Jean, Michelle, Al, Bill, Jim, Joe, Murray—especially Karol—and other alumni, past and future, and to thank the Power who arranged that I be born, raised, and live most of my life in Baton Rouge: not everyone gets the chance to compose his home town's history.

Mark T. Carleton

A number of universities, libraries, and museums provided courteous assistance while I assembled copies and wrote descriptions of illustrations for this book. A special word of gratitude is due to Michele L. Fagan, Gisela J. Lozada and Merna W. Whitley of the LSU Department of Archives and Manuscripts, Baton Rouge; to Evangeline M. Lynch, Librarian and Head, Louisiana Room, LSU Library, and to Donna N. Boé and Ruth C. Murray, her assistants; and to Harriet H. Callahan, Head, Louisiana Section, Louisiana State Library.

I am likewise indebted to various administrators and staff members of the following depositories for both their help and permission to publish prints from their respective collections. These include H. Parrot Bacot, Curator of the Anglo-American Art Museum, LSU, Baton Rouge; John B. Richard, Director of the East Baton Rouge Parish Library and Rose Meyers, Head of the Centroplex Branch; Lou Thomas, Librarian, Capital City Press; Nora Lee Pollard, Archivist, Diocese of Baton Rouge, Catholic Life Center; Dorothy Jones, Public Relations Department, Exxon Company-USA, Baton Rouge; Carolyn G. Bennett, Executive Director, Foundation for Historical Louisiana; Director Stanton Frazer and Curator John H. Lawrence, The Historic New Orleans Collection; Director Carol S. Gikas and Curator Kathleen Orillion, Louisiana Arts and Science Center; Louisiana Department of Transportation and Development; Superintendent Richard N. Day, Louisiana School for the Visually Impaired; Director Robert R. Macdonald and Curator J. B. Harter, Louisiana State Museum; LSU Museum of Anthropology; Steele Burden and Curator John E. Dutton, LSU Rural Life Museum; LSU Office of Public Relations; LSU Office of Sports Information; Mississippi Department of Archives and History; Curator Martha Wright of the Old Arsenal Museum and James D. Morgan, Historic Sites Administrator, Office of State Parks; Sisters Judith Brun and Carolyn Brady of St. Joseph's Academy; Southern University Department of Archives; Southern University Office of Public Relations; Director George J. Guidry, Jr., of the Troy H. Middleton Library; and Ann S. Gwyn, Bill Meneray and William Cullison of the Tulane University Special Collections Division.

Numerous individuals also loaned me cherished photographs, family manuscripts and rare printed items in addition to giving generously of their time and helping in other ways. Among those were: Miss Debora Abramson; Mrs. John T. Anderson; Miss May Lynn Amiss; Dr. Russell Ampey; Lloyd A. Babin; Dr. B. V. Baranco, Jr.; Alton Barillier; Fred G. Benton, Jr., Fred G. Benton III; Murphy W.

Bell; the Robert A. Bogan, Sr., family; Jared W. Bradley; Mrs. H. Payne Breazeale, Sr.; Mrs. Betty Brown; Miss Ione Burden; Richard C. Cadwallader; Sergeant M. B. Cantu; Powell Casey; the Eugene R. Cazedessus, Sr., family; Mrs. Herbert Courtney; Mrs. Peggy L. Davis; Joseph A. Delpit; Mrs. Donald A. Draughon; Major-General and Mrs. Charles F. Duchein; W. W. "Woody" Dumas; Charles East; Lee Faucette; the J. St. Clair Favrot family; Alfred Gensler; Gilbert Funeral Home; Councilwoman Pearl George; Dr. William G. Haag; W. Benton Harelson; Mrs. Shirley J. Hawkins; Frank Hayden; Don B. Hearin III; Mr. and Mrs. A. M. Hochenedel; Mrs. Catherine Herget Huckabay; Mrs. Orene Muse Huckabay; Mr. and Mrs. James H. Huguet; Mrs. Virginia Lobdell Jennings; William L. Jenson; Miss Ellen Roy Jolly; Dr. and Mrs. Henry W. Jolly, Jr.; Mrs. Lucy Prescott King; Mr. and Mrs. Samuel J. Lambert, Jr.; Colonel and Mrs. Rollo C. Lawrence; Ms. Gayle LeBlanc; Bentley B. Mackay III; Dr. Charles McVea; Dr. Lawrence Mann, Jr.; the Matrons Club; Ray Maurer; Mrs. James E. Moise; Lovell Muse; Mrs. Gwendolyn Neitzel; A. P. Rabenhorst; Philip Rabenhorst; Mr. and Mrs. Claude F. Reynaud, Jr.; Mrs. Claude F. Reynaud, Sr.; Mr. and Mrs. Parry N. Richardson; Mrs. Theodore Rosenberg; Mrs. V. L. Roy, Jr.; Mrs. Jean Harwell Smith; Dr. Valerian Smith; Mr. and Mrs. J. E. Snee; Mrs. Joan S. Shoptaugh; B. B. Taylor, Jr.; Bill Vega; and Fonville Winans.

Meriting special mention are Dave Gleason and Don Nugent for the color photography in the book, and Don P. Morrison, who produced most of the black-and-white prints from the Baton Rouge area. My cordial thanks also to Charles Vincent for helping me to secure photographs from the black community and to Teri Davis Greenberg at Windsor Publications, who skillfully kept hundreds of pictures organized throughout the many steps involved in putting together a book of this scope.

Last, but in no means least, is my indebtedness to my family. Without the exemplary patience and encouragement of my wife, Georgia Anne, and my two children, Marshall and Leigh Anne, my part in this project would have been exceedingly more difficult.

M. Stone Miller, Jr.

INDEX

THIS BOOK WAS SET IN
PALATINO AND CASLON TYPES,
PRINTED ON
70 LB. WARRENFLO
AND BOUND BY
WALSWORTH PUBLISHING
COMPANY.
COVER AND TEXT DESIGNED BY
ALEXANDER D'ANCA
LAYOUT BY
DON GOULD AND LISA SHERER